WHOLLY HUMAN

WHOLLY HUMAN
Western and Eastern Visions of the Self and its Perfection

Guy Claxton
Swami Anand Ageha

ROUTLEDGE & KEGAN PAUL
London, Boston and Henley

First published in 1981
by Routledge & Kegan Paul Ltd
39 Store Street,
London WC1E 7DD,
Broadway House,
Newtown Road,
Henley-on-Thames,
Oxon RG9 1EN and
9 Park Street,
Boston, Mass. 02108, USA
Printed in Great Britain by
St. Edmundsbury Press, Suffolk
© Guy Claxton 1981
Excerpts from -Burnt Norton- and -Journey
of the Magi- by T.S. Eliot are reprinted
from his volume 'Collected Poems 1909-1962'
by permission of Harcourt Brace Jovanovich,
Inc.: copyright 1936 by Harcourt Brace
Jovanovich, Inc; copyright © 1963, 1964 by
T.S. Eliot.

Library of Congress Cataloging in Publication Data

Claxton, Guy.
Wholly human.

Bibliography: p.
Includes index.
1. Self.   2. East and West.   I. Anand Ageha, Swami.
II. Title.
BF697.C55   158'.9   81-10620
ISBN 0-7100-9004-8   AACR2

This book is gratefully dedicated to those people who have, in very different ways, infected me with their clarity, integrity and love:

my mother and father
Jude Brown and Anita Semjén
Gabriella Szuchy and Gail Taylor
Ted Long
Lena Snow
Swamis Anand Rajen and Anand Veeresh
Douglas Harding
and my Master, Bhagwan Shree Rajneesh

Oh, that one might be able, at this point, to speak rightly!
For at this point what the talk is concerned with is the life that
most men lead: they desire the Good, and yet the world is still
so filled with double-mindedness. Here, too, the speaker has
his own life, his own frailties, his own share of doubleness of
mind. Oh, that the talk might not seem to wish to judge or
accuse others. For to wish to judge others instead of one's
self would also be double-mindedness. Oh, that the talk might
not seem to press demands that are binding upon others but
that exempt the speaker, as if he had only the task of talking.
. . . Oh, that one might wound no one except to his healing;
that the talk might embitter no one and yet be the truth, that
the talk along with the truth might be sufficiently penetrating
to reveal that which is hidden! Oh, that the talk might wipe
out double-mindedness and win hearts for the Good!

> Søren Kierkegaard: 'Purity of Heart is
> to Will One Thing'

Pooh got up slowly and began to look for himself.

> A.A. Milne: 'The House at Pooh Corner'

All this was a long time ago, I remember,
And I would do it again, but set down
This set down
This: were we led all that way for
Birth or Death? There was a Birth, certainly,
We had thought they were different: this Birth was
Hard and bitter agony for us, like Death, our death.
We returned to our places, these Kingdoms,
But no longer at ease here, in the old disposition,
With an alien people clutching their gods.
I should be glad of another death.

> T.S. Eliot: 'Journey of the Magi'

CONTENTS

PREAMBLE

In the summer of 1976 I visited Japan briefly and was fortunate
enough to have arranged for me an interview with a Zen Master,
Abbot Sōgen Asahina of Engakuji Temple in Kamakura. During
the hour we had together Asahina gave me a kōan. A kōan is an
insoluble problem which forms the heart of contemporary rinzai
Zen training, and is designed to confront the intellect forcibly
with its own limitations. My kōan was 'What am I?'. This book represents probably the longest and most absurd attempt to answer
a kōan there has ever been. It is clear that I am nowhere near its
real solution yet. Indeed, as that better-known of Japanese Zen
exponents, Daisetsu Suzuki, says: 'Those psychologists or theologians who talk about the bundle of successive perceptions or
impressions, or about the Idea, or about the principle of unity,
or the dynamic totality of subjective experience, or about the
non-existential axis of the curvilinear human abilities are those
who are running in the direction opposite to Zen. The harder
they run the further they go away from Zen.' My only hope, on
the principle that the fool who persists in his folly becomes wise,
is that writing this will contribute towards running myself into
the ground.

The question 'What am I?' - what am I really, below and beyond
what my common sense tells me I am - is one that brings together
the wisdom of the enlightened teachers and the theorizing of
modern psychology. Both are concerned with what man consists
of and how he works, with the origin of his sense of 'self', and
the control of his actions. Yet they speak in very different
tongues and address very different audiences. Having a foot in
each camp, it was natural for me to ransack both the scriptures
and the monographs for help in answering my kōan. What follows
is my attempt to put the two sets of findings together: to show
how and where they complement, inform and transcend each other.
It turns out that psychology contains many trails that lead in the
right direction - that start out towards the insights about human
nature that are the commonplaces of Buddhism or Taoism - but
they all peter out. Here and there one gets the scent of a model
of the Enlightened One, the Fully-Functioning Person, Integrated
Man, but it is as if the deep assumptions they hold about themselves prevent their perpetrators following their theoretical
notions to the end. On the other hand we shall find, when we
understand what the difference between me-as-I-am and me-as-
I-think-I-am really is, that psychology can help us put together
a working model of enlightenment. It clarifies the fact that we

1

work on two levels and that it is only through mistakenly identifying ourselves with just one of these that the two seem to be
thrown into opposition, and our sense of harmony, of being an
integrated whole, is lost.

A word about the business of psychology and psychologists.
Psychologists, like everything else, can be divided into two sorts.
There are those whose urge is to dismantle things, to make distinctions, to draw boxes with arrows between them, to analyse.
And there are the synthesizers, people who seek the similarities
in diversity, who focus on the unity of process with process,
organism with environment. There are dividers and encompassers.
The dividers are much more common, and I think it is time there
were more encompassers. This is a book by an encompasser,
about encompassers. It is an attempt to integrate many traditionally quite separate areas of psychology into an account of integrated people.

The dominance in psychology of the dividers, the reductionists,
has rendered it almost impossible for anyone to express a concern for the big issues, and be taken seriously. We are not ready,
they say. One day, when we have thoroughly understood the
processes involved in students' short-term memory for long, unfamiliar numbers, and the function of the ventromedial nucleus
of the hypothalamus in the control of eating in the white rat, and
the origin of certain visual illusions, then we shall be ready for
the big chaps. But unfortunately this has not turned out to be a
very good strategy, and it is not hard to see why. For 'theories'
are not distilled out of 'facts', like brandy from wine; they are
the languages which give birth to the facts. Facts are descriptions, and descriptions are collections of concepts and concepts
are tacit agreements between people to chop the world up in a
certain way. Facts are the world construed, and construing is
something done by people.

It is very important to see that theories are languages, for
then one can also see that they do not determine reality, they
simply describe it as if it were divisible into certain convenient
chunks. The world is not perforated, like a toilet roll, so that
all you have to do is tug gently and it will fall apart into ready-
made 'concepts'. The divisions are attributed to it, for the purposes of talking about it and predicting it.

What the reductionistic mainstream of psychology has done is to
create many different races of psychologist all inhabiting different islands of specialization, some of which are within sight of
each other, but none within hailing distance. So all these different tribes have developed, quite naturally, entirely different
languages with which to describe their separate concerns. As
Kelly points out, every theory has a focus of convenience. That
is to say there are certain specific things it is designed to do,
or explain, or account for, or describe. And the focus of convenience determines the range of convenience, which is the wider
circle of phenomena to which the theory can apply conveniently.
As you stretch any theory further and further from its original

focus, so its language becomes inadequate, and its explanations
clumsy and cumbersome. You cannot explain how Concorde works
with the ideas contained in a push-bike manual. You cannot
explain the behaviour of subatomic particles with the ideas contained in everyday English. Operant psychology is pretty good
for rats in boxes, not so good for the linguistic intuitions of a
fluent adult. Psychoanalysis is applicable to the relationship between a patient and therapist, not applicable to the learning of
motor skills. And so on. What is needed is a kind of high-level
conceptual Esperanto in which these curious specialists could
converse, and from which their own technical languages could
be derived. Without such a common core, the biggest things in
psychology - which are also the biggest things in the whole of
human understanding - will never be touched.

So the book turns out to have two complementary purposes.
One is to use psychological ideas in a fairly non-technical way to
help people understand who they really are and how they really
work. The other is to make a contribution to academic psychology
itself by shaking together areas as disparate as client-centred
therapy and neurophysiology, behaviourism and simulations of
human reasoning, and seeing what drops out. Specialists in different fields will, I hope, recognize the signposts to their own
province that I have left in the text.

Part of the reason that psychologists tend to stay on their
separate islands lies in their failure to see that their theoretical
languages are not 'the truth' in any absolute sense; nor are they
'the whole truth', in the sense of being applicable to all the
phenomena of human experience and performance. Theorists are
motivated not to explore the boundaries of their theory - i.e. to
expand gradually its range of convenience - but to assert and
defend its 'truth' in areas that may be very different from its
original focus. Instead of extending the territory by little raids,
in which the nature of the grounds to be captured can be assessed
as you go, whole continents are annexed, and their possibilities
cannot be explored because all able-bodied thoughts are occupied
full-time defending the borders. No wonder this attitude of intellectual imperialism leads to the fragmentation of psychology into fractious factions. So Skinner talks about 'behaviour', Rogers
about 'feelings', Bruner about 'intellect', Chomsky and Miller
about 'language', Piaget about 'development', Bower about 'memory', and so on and so on, and their only collaboration is a mutual
conniving at the indivisibility of the in-dividual that is their
object.

It is rather surprising that Integrated Man, and the links with
Eastern thought and practice that must accompany him, has not
surfaced yet within academic psychology, for the wisdom of the
East is becoming increasingly familiar in other areas of science
and in mathematics. In physics we have Oppenheimer saying,
'What we shall find [in physics] is an exemplification, an encour-
agement, and a refinement of . . . Buddhist and Hindu thought';
Neils Bohr, on being knighted by the King of Denmark, choosing

as his coat-of-arms the old Chinese symbol of *yin* and *yang*, and
the legend 'Contraria sunt complementa'; Heisenberg acknowledging that the great post-war contributions of the Japanese to theoretical physics 'may be an indication of a certain relationship between philosophical ideas in the tradition of the Far East and the
philosophical substance of quantum theory'. Supposedly sensible
and rational men such as Heisenberg come out with mystical pro-
nouncements like, 'The reason why our sentient, percipient and
thinking ego is met nowhere within our scientific world picture
is . . . because it is itself that world picture . . . Mind is a
singulare tantum . . . The overall number of minds is just one.'
A widely-used text-book of cell biology by Loewy and Siekevitz
begins with a quotation from the third century B.C. taoist sage,
Chuang Tsu. The biophysicist L.L. Whyte asserts, 'the individual
only becomes mature through his recognition of himself as a component in the unitary system of nature' and 'Unitary man must
find eternity in the passing moment, for it can be found nowhere
else.' Sir Charles Sherrington, most distinguished of British
physiologists, in his Giffard lectures of 1937, concurs, 'The sail-
ing cloud, the bird below it, the setting sun, the coast and sea,
the ship and harbour, the lighted window, the flock and the
grass down, the voice of the shepherd; [energy] unites these all
into one consistent existence whose identical underlying nature
becomes through it insofar intelligible to us.' And George Spencer
Brown's 'The Laws of Form' is a mathematics of Buddhism, showing how what we take to be the laws of everyday experience follow not from the nature of the world, but from the act of con-
ceptualizing.

Any 'behavioural scientist' who wrote such things would be
signing himself a ticket to the Arctic circles of humanistic or
dynamic or para-psychology by so doing. Yet, as we shall see,
Integrated Man haunts the whole of psychology. It is only when
the torch is turned full on him that he seems to slip away.

The rock on which my tower of speculation is built is that what
people really are is integrated. The truth is that people are indivisible; reason and emotion are not antagonists but allies, just
as heart and liver are. And people are integrated and harmonious
fragments of a greater system that ultimately constitutes the entire
universe. Often at the beginning of the spiritual search, an
ordinary person surveys his disintegrated and discordant sense
of self and concludes that his integrity has been lost, and his
work is to re-establish it. Later he realizes the irony that nothing has been lost at all, that even the discords are necessary
parts of the music, and that all he has to do is be at home. His
only sin has been to spend too much time 'out to lunch'. The
Integrated Man of whom we shall speak does not know or possess
anything that the rest of us do not. He just sees more clearly
what's so. He knows his own integrity, not just in the sense of
understanding that it is so, but of feeling it in his bones, of
living the realization in every moment. In the Hindu myth, we are
all God playing hide-and-seek with Himself, pretending that we are

separate, long-lasting, autonomous selves so well that we actually
forget our true nature.

Integrated Man has seen through the game. It is necessary to
say something about the spirit in which to approach Integrated
Man, for although he is our true selves, he is a stranger to us.
As his main characteristic is his integrity, he is difficult to get
hold of, for our normal way of apprehending things, ourselves
included, is by division and contrast. Like Buddhism's 'awakened
man', who 'leaves no trace, like a goose flying over a still pond',
or St John's comment that 'the wind blows where it will, and you
hear the sound of it, but you do not know whence it comes or
whither it goes: so it is with every one who is born of the Spirit'
(John 3: 8), he is mysterious, hard to perceive in his unity,
mystical. It requires, as I have found, much patience, in the face
of literature that seems often obscure, waffly, incoherent or contradictory, to get a sense of what Integrated Man is about. And
it is very much a matter of 'getting a sense' rather than an
intellectual understanding, for Integrated Man, by definition,
transcends the dualistic categories of intellectual thought.

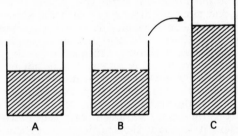

Figure 1
A   B   C

Perhaps an analogy will help in seeing how we can grow to
appreciate a unity that underlies apparent diversity. (I am grate-
ful to Skip Alexander of Harvard University for this 'parable'.)
Imagine a five-year-old confronted with the three beakers A, B
and C, as in Figure 1. A and B contain what he has already
agreed is the same amount of water, and C is empty. B is now
tipped into C and he is asked whether C now contains the same
amount of water as A. The standard conservation-of-volume task.
He will look at you as if you are mad, and say 'Of course not'.
To him there is obviously more in C than A. It doesn't matter why
he thinks so; whether he doesn't understand what 'more', 'less'
or 'amount' mean. It's self-evident. Now you introduce his eight-
year-old brother to the situation, perform the same manoeuvres
and ask the same question. He fixes you with an equally pitying
stare and tells you that of course they are the same. Depending
on the brothers' relationship either the younger will climb down,
for the sake of peace, or a fight will ensue. But the thing that
we can see is that they are both 'right' from within their own
world views. The understanding of the older has deepened to
allow him to recognize an essential sameness despite perceptual
change. The younger simply cannot see it. To him his older

brother is either an idiot or a mystic seeing unity where he cannot. And we can react to the baffling words and deeds of Integrated Men in just the same way. If we are hostile, they are
crackpots. But if we can allow that they, like an elder brother,
might be able to see things that we cannot, then there may be
something to learn, even if it means putting up with things that
are 'obviously' rubbish, or a con-trick, for a while. It is to my
mind not a matter of humility, but of making a good bet, to assume
that some of the authors of this apparent nonsense - like Buddha,
Jesus, Lao-Tsu, Heraclitus, Goethe or Bhagwan Shree Rajneesh -
actually know something that I don't, and that I may be able to
get an inkling of what it's all about if I give them (at least for a
while) the benefit of the doubt.

So if Integrated Man is unfamiliar to you, I would urge you to
approach him with what my father used to call 'a modicum of
respect'. He is very easy to make fun of, but you miss him if you
do. For, as author, his linguistic contortions result from his
efforts to intimate to us things that language cannot really tell.
His impossible task, as Alan Watts has said, is to speak the unspeakable, eff the ineffable and scrut the inscrutable. He speaks
from the heart, and must be listened to with the same organ.

One thing that may need stressing is that Integrated Man is in
most respects very ordinary. He does not go through life with a
dove on each shoulder in a shining white robe turning water into
wine and quelling the waves. His experience is not psychedelic,
his life is not ecstatic. The Gospels do a disservice in painting
him more like Bionic Man than Integrated Man. All that is different
is, in a difficult-to-understand way, that Integrated Man has
shed some falsity rather than acquired some truth. This book is
not about miracles: it is about the subtle magic of the everyday,
mundane, unexceptional things that our lives are made of. Much
of it - the book - is about a different way of viewing things like
perception, motivation, memory, decision-making, talking, that
seem miles away from the esoteric world of Zen masters and
strange, orange-clad folk squirrelled away in the Himalayas. But
these ordinary things are exactly what these extra-ordinary quests
are about.

There are several accounts of Integrated Man, his philosophy
and his relationship to Nature, that are much fuller than the one
I shall have space to give here, and which have been seminal in
developing my own understanding. One is Alan Watts's 'The Book
on the Taboo Against Knowing Who You are', which is probably
the best introduction. Any book by Watts is worth reading, though
as well as 'The Book', I would recommend 'The Wisdom of Insecurity', 'Psychotherapy East and West' and 'Nature, Man and Woman'.
The other easy introduction from a philosophical perspective is
Robert Pirsig's overnight classic 'Zen and the Art of Motorcycle
Maintenance'. Three other key books come at Integrated Man
from different perspectives. Fritjof Capra's 'The Tao of Physics'
shows how an integrated view of nature and human nature is
demanded by the twentieth-century advances in sub-atomic and

astro-physics. Lancelot Whyte, a biologist writing as long ago as 1944 ('The Next Development in Man') anticipates in a scholarly and literary way the recent integrated biology of von Bertallanfy, Paul Weiss and the popularizations of their views by Arthur Koestler. Finally, the best psychological introduction to Integrated Man I know is Erich Fromm's essay Zen Buddhism and Psycho-analysis, in the book of the same name by Suzuki, Fromm and de Martino.

The book goes like this. In Part I we will establish some of the ideas on which the notion of integrity is founded, some of the considerations, philosophical and scientific, that make us see man as a harmonious part of a harmonious world (Chapter 1). Then we get inside Integrated Man (Chapter 2) and look at how his experience differs from ours. We shall identify what disinte-gration feels like, where it comes from and how it is transmitted (Chapter 3). Then we see what happens in the West when a man's fight with himself becomes hopeless enough to force him to seek help: we explore (in Chapter 4) how integrity is tackled in therapy. When the therapeutic quest becomes a spiritual one, we follow the seeker into the deeper waters of meditation, prayer and disciplehood (Chapter 5).

Once we know what the relationship is between the first person and his original face, we go on in Part II to show how human experience actually comes about. This is where we begin to use psychological theories to help us out. First we take four parti-cular theories - those of Rogers, Kelly, Fromm and Skinner - and hold them up to the light of integrity (Chapter 6). Then (Chapter 7) we will cobble together a model that shows how thought and action can arise simultaneously, and yet the thought is a pack of lies while the action is true. The story ends by showing how particular domains of our life, such as perception (Chapter 8), thought (Chapter 9) and action (Chapter 10), can carry on quite happily even when the self we thought we were has packed its bags and slunk off.

This preamble needs concluding with some thanks. First to the people who housed me when I needed to get away from the phone and work on the book in peace. They include Tomoko and Masaki Soma of Tokyo; the monks of a small temple in Kōya-san, the name of which I forget; Laci Várádi and Anita Semjén, my Hungar-ian friends; Professor Stuart Sutherland, whose basement I in-habited for a month without his knowledge, having swapped flats with Paulette Goudge; Sam Westmacott; and Val Curran and Howard Reid, who not only gave me space to work in their cot-tage in Cambridge but buoyed me up with their confidence in the book at the times when I needed it. I would also like to express my gratitude to the Central Research Fund of the University of London for giving me the money to fly to India for a term's study leave, where this book was completed. I must thank three critics who were kind and subtle enough to open me up with their enthus-iasm so that I could take in what they thought was wrong - Don Bannister, David Godwin (my editor at Routledge) and my typist,

Judy Keep. Finally two intellectual debts will be obvious: to Bhagwan and Alan Watts. If I have managed to transpose into psychological terms just some of their insight, and to present it with some of their eloquence, I shall be happy.

Guy Claxton was initiated as a disciple of Bhagwan Shree Rajneesh in 1977 and given the name Swami Anand Ageha. In retrospect this book seems like a dialogue between the two sides of me that the two names represent, so I have chosen to give them both credit for its authorship. It is probable, however, that left-hemisphere Guy wrote the words and right-hemisphere Ageha the music.

Part I

1 THE PHILOSOPHY OF INTEGRITY

Tunes or pebbles, processes or substantial things? 'Tunes'
answers Buddhism and modern science. 'Pebbles' say the classical philosophers of the West. Buddhism and modern science
think of the world in terms of music. The image that comes to
mind when one reads the philosophers of the West is a figure
in a Byzantine mosaic, rigid, symmetrical, made up of millions
of little squares of some stony material and firmly cemented to
the walls of a windowless basilica.

Aldous Huxley

The model of man one produces depends very much on one's
philosophy about him and about his relationship to his environment. The purpose of this chapter is to set the stage for what
follows by considering two diametrically opposed philosophies.
One of these represents the way things actually are, while the
other describes the way we think they are. We see the world, and
ourselves in it, as pebbles - but in truth, we are tunes.
    The first thing to realize about the way things are, is that they
are changing. The whole of nature is dynamic: everything is
growing, developing, declining; everything is in flux, in process.
Certainly things differ in their rate of change, and in their
regularity. But change is the norm, and what we see as stasis,
as permanence, represents only aspects of nature that are temporarily quiescent, or whose rates of change are considerably
slower than our own. At one end of the spectrum we have the
flow of music, in which individual sounds are born and die quite
quickly, yet which comprise a harmonious whole that may linger
in the mind like footprints. There is the rhythm of the sea, of
the wind rising and falling; clouds pile up and disperse, tides
ebb and flow. And there are other processes of change and
development that take much longer. The alternation of the seasons,
the melting of ice-caps, the erosion of pebbles, the construction
and demolition of buildings.
    Solid objects - 'things' - exist in the same way that a flame
or a whirlpool exists: as a relatively stable set of processes that
create an illusion of substance by existing together in a pattern.
We can talk about a whirlpool as a 'thing', but in fact there is no
stable 'stuff' that it is made of. Its 'boundary' is not something
that isolates it from its surroundings, but is actually vital in ensuring its existence. And exactly the same is true of any outline,
however definite: whatever 'outforms' an object also 'informs' it.
Its skin is not a barrier but the site of interaction, and active

interaction is essential for the persistence of its identity.

The second fundamental aspect of nature is its indivisibility: nothing exists on its own. Everything acquires its identity by virtue of the relationships into which it enters with other things. If you isolate something, some one small portion of the world, from its environment, and try to describe its features and behaviour, you soon find yourself having to pay attention to precisely that context that you had hoped to ignore. You cannot say when a cloud will rain just by inspecting the cloud: you must also know about the atmospheric pressure, the temperature and the nature and contours of the land over which it is passing. You cannot describe how someone is sitting in a chair without also describing the chair, nor the path of a stone rolling down a hillside without describing the hill. The motion of one planet occurs only within the context of all the planets. The action of an enzyme like adenosine triphosphatase, which is concerned with the utilization of energy-storing molecules within the mitochondria of a living cell, depends on what is happening to the body of which that cell is a minute part. And not only can things not be described or predicted out of context; they depend for their very existence on that context. The flame dies in a vacuum; the whirlpool dies if you try to take it home in a bucket; the mitochondrion dies when its host breathes too much water. This picture of nature as the continual interaction of processes is now a commonplace in physics. Capra in 'The Tao of Physics' summarizes it thus:

> The exploration of the subatomic world in the twentieth century has revealed the intrinsically dynamic nature of matter. It has shown that the constituents of atoms, the subatomic particles, are dynamic patterns which do not exist as isolated entities, but as integral parts of an inseparable network of interactions. These interactions involve a ceaseless flow of energy manifesting itself as the exchange of particles; a dynamic interplay in which particles are created and destroyed without end in a continual variation of energy patterns. The particle interactions give rise to the stable structures which build up the material word, which again do not remain static, but oscillate in rhythmic movements. The whole universe is thus engaged in endless motion and activity; in a continual cosmic dance of energy.

The two aspects of this world view, those of change on the one hand and unity on the other, are represented in the two major innovations in physical thought in the twentieth century - relativity theory and quantum theory. 'Relativity theory showed that mass has nothing to do with any substance, but is a form of energy . . . The fact that the mass of a particle is equivalent to a certain amount of energy means that the particle can no longer be seen as a static object, but has to be conceived as a dynamic process, a process involving energy which manifests itself as the particle's mass.' While 'quantum theory shows that we cannot decompose the world into independently existing smallest units.' And Teilhard de Chardin, in 'The Phenomenon of Man', makes the same point. 'The farther and more deeply we penetrate into matter by means of increasingly powerful methods, the more we are confounded by the interdependence of its parts. . . . It is impossible to cut into this network, to isolate a portion, without it becoming frayed and unravelled at all its edges.'

So far we have been able to keep these ideas at a distance. But quantum theory begins to bring the matter closer to home. For we are ourselves included in the unity; we are part of the 'inseparable network of interactions'. Capra goes on:

These relations always include the observer in an essential way. The human observer constitutes the final link in the chain of observational processes, and the properties of any atomic object can only be understood in terms of the object's interaction with the observer. This means that the classical ideal of an objective description of nature is no longer valid. The Cartesian partition between the I and the world, between the observer and the observed, cannot be made when dealing with atomic matter.

As we shall see, this is not just an academic nuisance, but is central to the difference between the way the world is both understood and experienced by Integrated Man and Dissociated Man. These insights apply not only to sub-atomic particles and pebbles but to those larger, more intricate patterns of process that we call human beings. We exist in the world like whirlpools, sucking in a variety of different forms of energy like air, water vapour, egg and chips and vodka martinis, and pushing it out as carbon dioxide, sweat, urine, faeces and semen. We also take in energy in the form of light and sound and give it out as behaviour. The former set of inputs and outputs are transformed by, and help to sustain, what we think of as the physiological, autonomic, processes of the body such as heartbeat, breathing, eating, ejaculating, excreting and sweating. The latter set relate to the psychological processes of thinking, feeling, experiencing and acting. In the Integrated Man there is no essential difference between the physiological and the psychological, the voluntary and the involuntary, the 'necessary' and the 'chosen', for he is integrated not only with his environment, but also within himself.

We are, while we are alive, in harmony with our environment. Like the whirlpool, the human body is sustained by, indeed it is, a symphony of processes, orchestrated to produce endless variations on the same underlying form or theme. And, like the whirlpool, when our relationship with our environment is considerably altered, or cut off – when we cease to be compatible – we alter our form or die. There is no necessary relationship between life and death, between us and our environment. There is no Divine Ordinance that says we must live or we must live for so long. It is simply 'in the nature of things', as it is for leaves to grow in the spring and wither in the autumn. We are implied by the world: we are the fruits of a world that 'peoples' in the same way as apples are the fruit of a plant that 'apples'. Sometimes an apple tree fails to bear fruit, sometimes a gale destroys the blossom, and sometimes an apple falls before it is ripe.

This idea of internal consistency, in which all the parts of a system imply each other without there being any underlying reason or motive for it, finds its place in modern nuclear physics too. Geoffrey Chew, expounding what he calls 'the bootstrap hypothesis', says:

The bootstrap hypothesis states explicitly that the world cannot be understood as an assemblage of entities which cannot be analysed further. In the new world view the universe is seen as a dynamic web of inter-related events. None of the properties of any part of this web is fundamental; they all follow from the properties of the other parts, and the overall consistency of their mutual interrelations determines the structure of the entire web . . . Carried to its logical extreme, the bootstrap conjecture implies that the existence of consciousness, along with all other aspects of nature, is necessary for self-consistency of the whole.

Every part of the system, every aspect of it and every event within it is implied by – more exactly, is entailed by – the whole system. There is no cause or governor outside the system to whom one needs to, or even can, appeal.

It is difficult to experience the integral nature of things, much more difficult than to understand it, because our limited awareness cannot comprehend the enormous subtlety of the circumstances, both current and historical, that have culminated in any particular moment. It is difficult for us to see, for example, that there are no such things as Causes and Effects, for to isolate such entities is to impute a divisibility to nature that it does not have, and to confer responsibility on one of these artefacts for the other. Ambrose Bierce in 'The Devil's Dictionary' pokes fun at this delusion. 'Effect, n. The second of two phenomena which always occur together in the same order. The first, called a Cause, is said to generate the other – which is no more sensible than it would be for one who has never seen a dog except in pursuit of a rabbit to declare the rabbit the cause of the dog.' Or for someone to declare wood the cause of ashes, summer the cause of autumn, or life the cause of death. Like the form that the human body takes, these conjunctions of events simply demonstrate that nature makes patterns, and contains consistencies. There are no necessities in nature, but lots of tendencies and trends. Things tend to occur in certain forms, sequences or patterns not because they must but because they do.

If this is true generally about nature, it must also be the case that human nature is not something separate from and alien to nature, but an integral part of it. We do not come into the world, we come out of it. Kahlil Gibran in 'The Prophet' says: 'Your children are not your children. They are the sons and daughters of Life's longing for itself. They come through you but not from you. And though they are with you yet they belong not to you.' It is necessary, therefore, to spell out some of the implications that the true nature of nature has for the true nature of man.

First, man is neither a free agent nor a puppet, for both views presuppose a real separation between ourselves and our environment, between subject and object. Only if A and B really exist separately can A 'determine' B, or B 'decide' what to do about A. But if A and B are two different aspects of the same unity, then questions of free will and determinism are inappropriate. The system's development is inevitable, and the direction of its development is a function of its nature. As Alan Watts puts it:

Our deeds, our feelings, our thoughts, our sensations just happen of themselves, as the rain falls and the water flows along the valley. I am neither a passive and helpless witness to whom they happen, nor an active doer and thinker who causes and controls them. 'I' is simply the idea of myself, a thought among thoughts. Taken seriously it gives the illusion of being something apart from nature, a subject reviewing objects. But if the subject is an illusion, the objects are no longer mere objects. Inside the skull and the skin as well as outside, there is simply the stream flowing along of itself. States of the central nervous system come and go, some of them resulting in overt action and some not, in the same way that eddies come and go in a river. Just as what a river does is a joint function of its own nature (the physical and chemical properties of water), of its history (what has been happening upstream), and of its environment (the shape and texture of the river banks and bed), so is what a person does. The river does not 'do' its actions, nor do they 'happen to it', the events arise mutually, effortlessly, 'of themselves'. And while the events of the stream will not always be placid, and will sometimes be blocked, both the blocks and the turbulence are always temporary and the stream will, in its own way, flow on.

This state of harmony, in which the organism and the environment are not so much acting on each other as actually indivisible is nicely described by Pirsig in 'Zen and the Art of Motorcycle Maintenance', in a very down-to-earth context - that of fixing a motorbike.

Sometime look at a novice workman or a bad workman and compare his expression with that of a craftsman whose work you know is excellent and you'll see the difference. The craftsman isn't ever following a single line of instruction. He's making decisions as he goes along. For that reason he'll be absorbed and attentive to what he's doing even though he doesn't deliberately contrive this. His motions and the machine are in a kind of harmony. He isn't following any set of written instructions because the nature of the material at hand determines his thoughts and motions, which simultaneously change the nature of the material at hand. The material and his thoughts are changing together in a progression of changes until his mind's at rest at the same time the material's right.

Looked at from the biological, organismic perspective, man is *in* nature, he is indissociable from it and necessarily in harmony with it. He is a complicated bundle of nervous and muscular tissue that reacts with its environment and is, in the process of reacting, continuously modified by it. He learns, but in the way that a stone rolling down a hillside learns. As it rolls it bumps into other stones, and these interactions leave their mark. Usually the stone will be smoothed by its friction with other stones so that its subsequent passage down the hill will be made easier. The learning that the stone does, and the 'memories' it carries with it, are represented directly in terms of functionally relevant changes of structure. Its nature is changed by contact with an environment so as to make it more compatible with that, and similar, environments. There is no intention, motive or effort behind this: it is the basic process of development in all forms of matter, both living and non-living.

To say that development is a downhill process is another way of saying that change is basic, stasis secondary. Growth does not have to be produced any more than a car on a downhill gradient has to be pushed. Development is the biological analogue of gravity; as gravity is the name we give to the universal tendency to move physically, so development refers to the natural tendency towards internal, organic movement. It follows, as we shall see later in the book, that if development has stopped, we do not need to push the car but simply to unjam the brakes, for change can only be permitted, not manufactured. L.L. Whyte, in 'The Next Development of Man', summarizes this view by saying that all structures (e.g. the shape of the stone) tend to facilitate the processes that develop them (e.g. rolling down the hill). But he is also at pains to stress that the distinction between structures (objects, things, organisms) and processes (events and actions) is a relative, not an absolute one, as I have been arguing earlier. 'A structure is a system which is internally developed, is stable, and tends to develop externally. But separation is never complete, structure is never static, and the concept of structure is valid only where the process of the whole (i.e. the whole object-environment field) can be neglected. There is no sharp division between structure and process, because structure is a limiting case of process.'

One way in which to conceptualize how 'things' fit together is in hierarchical terms. A molecule of ATPase is a system within a mitochondrion, which is a system within a cell, which is a system within an organ, which is a system within a body, which is a system within an environment. Each system has certain internal tendencies, but the actualization of those tendencies depends on the tendencies of the higher-order systems of which it is a part. If the hierarchy of control between systems is interrupted at any level, and the lower ones isolated from the higher, their internal tendencies will assert themselves, and those, previously rather stable, systems will break down into simpler, more 'inorganic' forms. Thus Whyte says:

'Organism' . . . means a self-regulating system of processes tending to maintain themselves, i.e. to maintain the life of the individual or species. But the processes of the organism do not

of themselves maintain life; without the continuous influence of
the environment the internal organic processes cannot sustain
life for more than a moment, their tendency being to break
down organic material towards more stable states.
Any organism deprived of such fundamental parts of its usual
environment as air and water becomes incompatible with the new
environment, its own internal processes cease to be governed (in
the sense of regulated and harmonized) by the environment, and
the organism as a system ceases to be, as its components pursue
their anarchic development. The organism ceases to be because
the organism-environment system has ceased to be. Life inheres
in the harmonious development of an organism-environment field.
Death reflects a critical lack of harmony in which the total system
breaks down. The internal tendencies of the organism are towards
a breakdown into simpler forms - death. The continuous development of the organism in interaction with its surroundings we call
life. Thus we have biological equivalents of Freud's Thanatos and
Eros which provide natural, non-mystical explanations of the idea
of a 'death-wish' and a 'life-wish'. Thanatos is not some kind of
ultimate masochism, but the inevitable tendency of our organisms
to assert their intrinsic natures.

Whyte contrasts this view of man's relationship to his world,
with the 'common-sense' view of it.

While life is maintained, the component processes in man never
attain the relative isolation and static perfection of inorganic
processes; the human process consists in the continual development of process forms. The individual may seek, or believe that
he seeks independence, permanence or perfection, but that is
only through his failure to recognize and accept his actual situation. As an organic system man can never achieve more than a
continuing development in response to his environment.

And the final chord of that development heralds its resolution and
dissolution.

Once one sees the unity of organism and environment, one sees
the fact that life and death imply each other. Living results in a
continuously developing compatibility between man and his world.
Yet because the world is itself a process of change and development, perfect compatibility can never be achieved, and it must
ultimately frustrate itself. For as one adapts more and more to one
small range of circumstances, so one becomes more and more
specialized, and more and more at the mercy of changes in the
environment which take it, even transiently, outside that range.
No human organism is capable of adapting to an environment of
200°C, nor one in which air is replaced, even for ten minutes, by
water. A young, relatively unspecialized person, however, can
accommodate to changes such as flying in Concorde, or having
flu, or being cold, which an older person might not be able to.
Living is a process that frustrates itself, for it is a process of
becoming compatible with a small range of environments which will
eventually not be present. The fact of death follows inevitably
from the fact of life.

It is also clear that the increasingly routine, stable, stereotyped way of life that people adopt as they get older could be a reflection of two things. The first is a restriction of activity and exploration to familiar - that is, known-to-be-compatible - environments, which follows quite naturally from what I have said about the tendency of organism-environment fields to maintain themselves. The world has a tendency to produce live organisms, and they tend to live for about sixty or seventy years. That is the usual length of time it takes for the organism to become too specialized to cope with common fluctuations in its environment. Seventy-year-old ladies do not tend to go in for sky-diving or assaults on Everest, however much they may have come to terms with the inevitability of their own death.

On the other hand it is also true that much of the search for security and stasis derives not from natural tendencies but from the inability to face, or face up to, the prospect of one's own death. Cats and dogs naturally get more sluggish as they get old, but they do not seem to display the disquiet that is reflected in the crown toppers, supported breasts, insurance policies and bed-time rituals of their owners. There is a general fallacy, it seems to me, in thinking that because life tends to go on, it must go on - and that if it doesn't, there must be some good reason why, with which one can console oneself.

A falling tree kills one's child. A meaningless event, but of such terrible consequence that one can't bear to leave it empty of meaning. One goes over its blankness again and again in one's mind, until one begins to see in it the hand of some occult power punishing one's spiritual pride, or one's shortcomings as a parent. A terrible conclusion to reach about oneself, but at least mere conjunction can now be read as tragedy. (Michael Frayn, 'Constructions')

The distinction between the natural and neurotic approaches to death is important, for it symbolizes the difference between Integrated and Dissociated Man. Everyone has a natural reaction, quite spontaneously, to danger. The other day my motorbike skidded unexpectedly, and in that split second I performed the most sophisticated sequence of manoeuvres to stay on. There was no necessity to think, or plan, or worry about what to do: indeed, there wasn't time to do so. My body had saved itself before my mind had even grasped the situation. That is the natural reaction, and it can be trusted. But the neurotic attitude does not have this trust: it neither accepts the inevitability of death, nor the whole organism's ability to go on living if it can.

It is a commonplace that if an enlightened master is asked whether he is afraid of death, he will say 'No'. But I was told by a student of Asahina's that if you ask him that question, he will say 'Of course!' - not because he is unenlightened, but because he is answering in terms of his natural, not his neurotic, fear. One way of characterizing Integrated Man is as one who has realized - in the dual sense of 'become aware of' and 'made real' - his true nature, and has seen through the illusions that give rise to his neurotic search for security and permanence.

It is time to say something more about these illusions. The world is a dynamic web of interrelated processes. Man is part of this web, and therefore cannot but act in accord with it, and be changed by it. His nervous system quite automatically comes to incorporate those consistencies and trends to which it is sensitive, and the behaviour of that nervous system comes to act or react in terms of those consistencies. One may say it develops 'expectations', or the ability to 'predict', or 'anticipate'; yet these are not rational acts, any more than the smoothing of the pebble in its down-hill journey is a rational or conscious decision as to how to ease its travel. So far we do not have to speak of reason or intention or consciousness.

But people indisputably are both conscious and rational. Not only do the nervous system and the world interact with and modify each other, we also conceptualize these changes and chop up reality into categories. For descriptive purposes these categories are very useful, for they pick out recurrent features and sets of features and enable them to be communicated as a single composite abstraction. But - and this is really the nub of the matter - those abstractions are neither the reality that exists 'out there' (which we can never know directly) nor the effective reality to which we respond, represented as a certain fleeting, complicated pattern of activation within our nervous system.

We may postulate an external reality that exists independently of an observer, but in a sense this famous philosophical issue is quite trivial, for we can never experience this observer-free reality directly. All we experience is the transient pattern of activity which results from the impinging of certain types of energy on a particular nervous system. Indeed 'we' do not even experience those patterns: the state of the nervous system is the experience itself. To postulate an 'I' that experiences is to perpetuate the ridiculous illusion that there is a screen inside my head being watched by a little man - presumably with a screen inside his head, too.

When we see a rainbow, three things are necessary to 'make' the rainbow that 'we' see: some rain, the sun and us. All three must bear a certain spatiotemporal relationship to each other and then the experience called 'seeing a rainbow' happens. If any of the three components changes, the rainbow changes. If I point a hamster at the sky he will not see the same rainbow that I see. Do I see the 'real' rainbow? Does the hamster? Is it 'really' there at all? From the point of view of Integrated Man these are silly questions, for they presuppose a distinction between experiencer and experience that exists only in words.

The difference between our conceptualization of reality and reality itself is sometimes likened to that between a map and the territory it represents. The map is useful for getting about and predicting features of the landscape, but it is not itself the landscape. It can represent the landscape only by ignoring most of the fine detail, and by creating artificial conventions that do not

correspond to anything 'out there'. There is much in the world
that isn't on the map and much on the map that isn't in the world.
To confuse the two would lead one to look out for contour lines
while climbing a mountain, or, to change the analogy, to expect
to get a sun-tan from reading holiday brochures. Yet these are
precisely the kinds of activities which we are forever getting ourselves in a stew about. Our map tells us that something ought to
be so - a man with a dog-collar ought to be trustworthy, for
example - and when we find out that he has absconded with the
Tower Restoration Fund, we berate ourselves for having been so
stupid. The map ought to be infallible, we think, so that when we
find it wrong, or inadequate, we cannot simply update the map,
but must conduct an internal enquiry to see whether the cartographer should be indicted for negligence.

The easiest, but wrong, way of thinking about the psychological
map and territory is to assume that the map is 'inside' and the
territory the 'outside world'. This is wrong because we have already seen that the organism and environment are indissociable.
The map must not be taken for the territory, but it is itself part
of the territory. The organism and environment create the territory jointly. So the map that we make is not just of the world, but
it is of 'ourselves-in-the-world'. It is as useless to have a map of
the world without you in it as it is to be confronted with a street-
map of Tokyo from which someone has removed the 'You are Here'
arrow. You must know where you are - what the current situation
is, and how you fit into it - before you can do anything about it.
We can get nearer the truth (though all distinctions are ultimately
inadequate) by looking at two aspects of man. One is that of the
organism-environment unity - the bit that we often call 'myself' -
and the other is the 'map', which describes, simplifies and concep-
tualizes myself-in-the-world in order to predict it, and talk about
it. Myself is the sum total of my experience, feelings, and actions.
The map is the way I conceive of those experiences, feelings and
actions and of what caused them, how my needs relate to them,
and what I can do about them. The map does not decide on courses
of action. What one does is one aspect of the dynamic and harmonious set of processes that constitute the organism-environment
field. The map, being derived from that unity, and dependent on
it, can only reflect and predict; it cannot control.

So far, although we have postulated a split in man between him-
self-in-the-world, and his map, there is no necessity for conflict
between those two parts. (They are not, of course, two separate
parts at all, for the map, as I have already said is itself a part,
or aspect, of the territory it represents. To be completely accurate the map in the hands of a mountaineer on the top of a mountain
should contain a little picture of him on summit.) As one acquires
language as a baby, one is beginning to conceptualize the world
in terms of those conventional divisions that are accepted by the
society into which one is born. One cannot help developing a map,
and a map of a certain kind.

Nor is conflict inherent in the fact that the map as it develops is a mixture of things that are learned - from the inside out, as it were - and things that are taught, from the outside in. Aspects of the map that develop from the inside out are grounded in the reality of myself-in-the-world. They describe and predict consistencies that emerge from the interaction of the person that one is, with the world as it is. And if one remains open to changes and developments in those consistencies, then the map will continually develop in its accuracy, sophistication and utility. But conflict does arise from the fact that some aspects of the map that are taught, that are received from an external authority, do not stem from the unique territory that the recipient is, and may well not correspond to his natural reality. It is in this case, where there is a disparity between myself-in-the-world and the way I have been taught to conceptualize myself-in-the-world, that Dissociated Man is born.

Unfortunately we all become dissociated, for there is a tacit, but very powerful, social conspiracy about how we shall view ourselves that none of us escapes in childhood, and few manage to see through later on. Trigant Burrow, in his profoundly interesting 'Science and Man's Behaviour' discusses how the perfectly integrated young child succumbs to this illusion.

The healthy infant represents the acme of what is biologically fitting. It sleeps seasonably: its food intake and elimination are properly regulated. The infant's muscular coordination, its space sense, and the gradually increasing excursions of its interests and activities - all this is right, all this is fitting, all this is biologically sound and healthy. Such a biological right admits of no dichotomy, no alternatives. It is the total organism of man in balanced function. It is the constant and harmonious principle of homeostasis in man's relation to man . . .

But the sense of right imparted by the adult generation definitely distorts the child's innate capacity for organismic coordination with his fellows. It is not continuous with the common rights of his kind. It is organically irreconcilable with his inherent, biological mode of feeling and thinking. For the sense of right that is drilled into the child is based upon a divisive mood of private advantage, of socially sanctioned personal gain in respect to one's interrelations with the community. Owing to the development of this type of personal, moralistic rightness and the divisive mood which accompanies it, man has departed from the fitting behaviour that is the law of his nature . . .

The sense of right inculcated by the parent is arbitrarily induced through moralistic precepts *and cannot be supported by the child's objectively verifiable experience.* It is seldom conformable with the coordinating principle of organism-environment rapport inherent in the behaviour of the healthy organism. [My emphasis]

Man, in Burrow's view, is naturally social, but is socialized into seeing himself as an individual - separate, egotistical and competitive. He is not propounding the naive and sentimental view of children as innocent and altruistic angels: his point is deeper than that. It is that a child grows up in an environment which contains other beings, whose deeds and personalities must be reckoned with and accommodated to, in just the way he discovers and adapts to the physical world. It is not a moral, but a biological requirement that he be an integral part of a social world. In this he is no different from a shoal of fish or a litter of tiger cubs. His social learning is grounded in the reality of his own experience of the internal and external world. The guiding principle of his development is adaptation: that is, the result of every experience is to make his dealings with subsequent, similar experiences easier and more successful. And this applies as much to his interactions with other people as to those with toys or food.

But on top of this continual adaptation to what's what, the child also, through instruction, adapts to what isn't. Language confers on one person the ability to tell another about the way things are, and thus to save him a considerable amount of effort in finding out for himself. But it also gives the former the power to lie, either intentionally, or, as in the case of the socially transmitted delusions, unwittingly. The fact that the child is dependent on others for support and approval, and that his obtaining these is contingent on his accepting their beliefs, means that he has no chance to resist. In any conflict between his sense of what is right and what he is told is right (or, more usually, wrong) he simply cannot afford to press his case, for at that stage the love of others is more valuable to him than his authenticity. And thus he is divided, and set at odds with himself.

So one misconception which a person buys is the confusion of the map with the territory. Another crucial error is the independence of contrasts. The assumption of the independence of contrasts leads us to believe in the possibility of good without bad, beauty without ugliness, happiness without sadness, or life without death. We create a contrast, a division in the map, ally ourselves with one side of it, and strive for total goodness, beauty and happiness, or everlasting life, without realizing that it is we ourselves who have created the pole that we are trying to deny. With the same breath that we announce 'this is good', we are also declaring 'that is bad'. Goodness does not inhere in things or events; it is imposed on them by a particular way of construing we have chosen to adopt. I cannot create an 'inside', by drawing a circle on a blank piece of paper, without also bringing to life an 'outside'. As the 'Tao Te Ching' says:

When everyone recognizes beauty as beautiful,
There is already ugliness.
When everyone recognizes goodness as good,
There is already evil.

The mutuality of oppositions is not only a logical necessity, it is a psychological fact of life. For in order to be able to experience intense pleasure, or happiness, or beauty, we must also be open to the experience of their contrasts. 'As high as we have mounted in delight, in our dejection so we sink as low.'

And things are actually even worse than this. Not only can we not hang onto the nice bits and exclude the nasty; the niceness itself depends on its transience. Much human activity seems to be designed to make permanent those experiences and joys that are pleasurable precisely because they are fleeting. The attraction of music rests in its rhythm and flow. The delight and excitement of a love affair rely on its spontaneity and unpredictability. If it does not flow it is literally and affectively stagnant. The moment you stop the clock and prolong the note or the kiss too long, its charm is lost. Life is only lively because it is already dying. And while we may mourn the passing of what we cherish, a healthy, 'non-neurotic' mourning is grounded in an acceptance of its own inevitability (see, for example, Lily Pincus's 'Death and the Family').

2 THE EXPERIENCE OF INTEGRITY

The other day upon the stair,
I met a man who wasn't there.
He wasn't there again today –
Oh! How I wish he'd go away.
(Silly poem my father told
me when I was small)

So far we have talked mainly in terms of the fluid, connected nature of Integrated Man – that is, our own true nature – from the outside, as it were. I have tried to demonstrate, by argument and by example, that this is how we really are, if we did but know it. But what is Integrated Man like from the inside? How do his experience and his actions seem to him? When he is 'at large' in the world, at home with his transient and integral belongingness, clear about what is map and what is territory, what is his immediate experience of himself and his world? Alan Watts, writing about it in terms of the Zen state of enlightenment, captures the flavour well.

> The adept in Zen is one who manages to be human with the same artless grace and absence of inner conflict with which a tree is a tree. Such a man is likened to a ball in a mountain stream, which is to say that he cannot be blocked, stopped or embarrassed in any situation. He never wobbles or dithers in his mind, for though he may pause in overt action to think a problem out, the stream of his consciousness always moves straight ahead without being caught in the vicious circles of anxiety or indecisive doubt, wherein thought whirls wildly around without issue. He is not precipitate or hurried in action, but simply continuous. That is what Zen means by being detached – not being without emotion or feeling, but being one in whom feeling is not sticky or blocked, and through whom the experiences of the world pass like the reflections of birds flying over water. Although possessed of complete inner freedom, he is not, like the libertine, in revolt against social standards, nor, like the self-righteous, trying to justify himself. He is all of a piece with himself, and with the natural world, and in his presence you feel that without strain or artifice he is complete 'all here' – sure of himself without the slightest trace of aggression.
> ('This Is It')

This last phrase is amplified in a delightful story of Chuang Tzu.

Chi Hsing Tzu was a trainer of fighting cocks for King Hsuan.

He was training a fine bird. The King kept asking if the bird
were ready for combat. 'Not yet', said the trainer, 'he is full
of fire. He is ready to pick a fight with every other bird. He
is vain and confident of his own strength.' After ten days he
answered again: 'Not yet. He flares up when he hears another
bird crow.' After ten more days: 'Not yet. He still gets that
angry look and ruffles his feathers.' Again ten days. The
trainer said: 'Now he is nearly ready. When another bird crows,
his eye does not even flicker. He stands immobile like a cock of
wood. He is a mature fighter. Other birds will take one look
at him and run.'
The cock has such a fearless presence, he is so completely un-
concerned with victory, or even with fighting, that he is invinc-
ible.
Yet in this story, something of the feel of Watts's 'adept in
Zen' is missing - for in his fearlessness the cock provokes fear
in others. His model is the strong, silent samurai of a Kurosawa
film, powerful and awesome. And this is why the story says that
the cock, in his invincibility, is only nearly ready. He has yet to
go beyond the power and recapture the lightness of touch, even
ordinariness, of the man of Tao or the adept in Zen. There is
another story in which a samurai (more mature than Kurosawa's)
is pestered and challenged by a fiery young man to fight. Eventually the samurai agrees, but stipulates that the fight must take
place on an island in the centre of the lake by which they are
standing. They climb into a boat and the samurai rows them to
the island. 'After you,' he says to the young man, who jumps out
and rushes on to the island with sword already drawn. The
samurai, with a little smile, rows away, back to the shore. For us,
such an act would have been borne of cowardice. For the samurai
the joke reflects his compassion - he does not need or want to
kill the boy - and his wry concern to teach him a lesson.
Most people, I suspect, can identify one or two experiences
in their history that possess, even partially, these characteristics
of artless grace. They may come after a period of intense effort,
when the way seemed blocked and sticky, and one's thought
'whirled wildly around without issue', when one felt acutely self-
conscious, striving vainly for a decision or an exit that would
not come. In the moment of complete despair, and complete acceptance of despair - what alcoholics call 'bottoming out' - in which
all the striving is abandoned, one may experience a sudden,
spontaneous shift from desperation to omnipotence, as if instead
of nothing being possible, everything were possible, and one
experiences a contained, calm, powerful and sensitive peace of
mind. You are no longer at the mercy of your own or other
people's judgments. The split between 'I' and 'myself' is healed,
because the illusion of 'I' is at last revealed as an impotent
megalomaniac, and the stream, of which one is part, is felt to
flow again, in directions that are absolutely fitting. Such glimpses
- for unfortunately they do not last more than a few minutes or
hours - are called in Japanese *satori*. The nearest Western psy-

chology has got to an acknowledgement of their existence, and importance, is Maslow's studies of 'peak experiences', which seem to possess many similar characteristics. They occur most typically when listening to music, or in places of great natural beauty, rather than following a period of great effort and great doubt, and seem to focus more on an indefinable feeling of being part of something greater than oneself, than on the experience of invulnerability and power. Yet I am sure that they both represent peeks behind the same veil: the veil of the separate and wilful 'I'.

Two other types of experience are characterized by this same overwhelming experience of unity or belongingness with nature, the mystical and the psychedelic. The former are typically produced by prolonged periods of fasting, meditation or prayer; the latter by the ingestion of certain psychoactive drugs like LSD or mescalin. There is much debate about whether these are 'really' the same state, that seems to me rather beside the point. It is not surprising that people from different cultures and different times find very different forms of words to attempt the communication of experiences that are beyond the normal scope of language. The word 'water' is a useful noise for one person to utter in the presence of another if both of them know what water is, if they have had experience of it, and can cash the word in terms of what they know. The word 'God' may be the same. But more often such a word arouses in the minds of speaker and hearer not an experience but another string of words. They may if they wish exchange these strings, like making transactions with Monopoly money, and the exchanges may prove entertaining. But at the end of the game neither is richer or poorer, for the words, like the money, have no purchasing power in the 'real world'. Or to take a different game, to try to come to God through processes of reason and definition is like trying to create a picture of a new animal by shuffling together jigsaw puzzles of a dog, a rabbit and an elephant. You're unlikely to do it, and even if you do, you will not know if your creation is real unless you search for its referent in the real world - and that is the world of experience.

It is only such mythical creatures that we have to believe in, and in expressing the belief we tend to close ourselves to the experience that could make the belief redundant. We may believe in unicorns, the Loch Ness monster, God, justice or breast-feeding, but we only have to because we don't know. I do not have to believe in my feet or Beethoven or carrots: if my knowledge is based in my experience, beliefs are simply unnecessary.

Perhaps some hedging is needed here. A belief is something, at least partly based on hearsay, by which I live, and to which is usually attached a value-judgment ('Breast-feeding is better than bottle-feeding', 'God is good'). It is something in which I have an ego-investment: it is more important for me to maintain my belief than to find out the truth. They are to be distinguished from inductive, organismically-based expectancies, which represent one's intuitive understanding of the way the world works, and me in it. These expectancies will be dealt with in Chapter 6.

Let me give just two examples - one of each - to demonstrate the nature of drug-induced and mystical states. Here is Aldous Huxley in 'The Doors of Perception' seeing the world unwrapped by mescalin. He is gazing at a bunch of flowers -

[but] a bunch of flowers shining with their own inner light . . . what rose and iris and carnation so intensely signified was nothing more, and nothing less, than what they were - a transience that was yet eternal life, a perpetual perishing that was at the same time pure Being, a bundle of minute, unique particulars in which, by some unspeakable and yet self-evident paradox, was to be seen the divine source of all existence.

While from the domain of the mystical, we have William James, quoting in 'The Varieties of Religious Experience': 'I was alone upon the seashore as all these thoughts flowed over me . . . to return from the solitude of individuation into the consciousness of unity with all that is, to kneel down as one that passes away, and to rise up as one imperishable Earth, heaven and sea resounded as in one vast world-encircling harmony.'

The experience of Dissociated Man needs little introduction, for we are all too familiar with it. We plan for the future, trying to insure and ensure our security in a world that remains obstinately whimsical and slippery, 'where moth and rust doth corrupt, and where thieves break through and steal'. And where stock markets, drunken drivers, earthquakes, flight cancellations, broken watches, faulty memories and the weather conspire to wreck the best-laid plans of mice and men. Where our books are ignored and the marriages of children for whom we have done our best suddenly fail and seem to make a mockery of all our care and effort. We pin our hopes on a future we cannot know and flee in resentment and disappointment from the malformed present to which it gives birth. We have the same ambivalence about the past, peppered with missed opportunities and failures, secret guilts and shames, and yet, we kid ourselves, despite it all, 'the good old days'. From the rear we are haunted by the bogies of our childhood, moulded by experience we did not choose and can't undo: and in the distant future the final fall of death to trivialize our aspirations and achievements.

Preoccupied with hopes and regrets, and squeezed in between the past and future, is our absent-minded present, never free of the yamayamayama of the internal dialogue, and requiring us to take decisions on insufficient data, whose outcomes are always uncertain. The scent of the past is regret, of the future is hope, of the present is doubt, and over all hangs the acrid smell of fear: fear that we may fail, fear that we may lose control, fear that we may be exposed as fakes, fear that we may not be the person that we think or hope we are. And all unnecessary; all an artefact of our mistaken assumptions and beliefs.

The body stores regularities: it detects and incorporates consistent patterns in its own transactions with the world, derived from experience and always tentative, always open to the possibility that things might be different this time. The mind takes these and with its own logic and its own language turns them into beliefs that are no longer labile. The conflicts between these two levels generate the feeling that we can separate ourselves from the flow of events and control them. We can fashion our world to our own liking. The conflict between this and the reality that, even in our own terms, there is much we cannot do (make the rain stop, the bus leave on time, the love-making ecstatic), generates anxiety and worry about our image and our competence. And this in turn is escaped from through the many devices of defence. The belief that we should be competent - no mistakes, no breakages, no faux pas - leads to a fear of failure that leads, as John Holt has documented in his 'How Children Fail', to all sorts of clever strategies for avoiding the experience of failure. One may play the rebel, another the dunce, another the sloth, another the clown and another the accident-prone. All are ways of denying that we have failed to be something that there is no reason to be, or possibility of being.

The subtle lengths to which we will go to disguise these fears from ourselves are extraordinary. De Tocqueville wrote: 'I have always thought it rather interesting to follow the involuntary movements of fear in clever people. Fools coarsely display their cowardice in all its nakedness, but the others are able to cover it with a veil so delicate, so daintily woven with small plausible lies, that there is some pleasure to be found in contemplating this ingenious work of the human intelligence.'

The many forms of lie are well-documented and need little intro- duction. In *repression* we forbid a conflict or one of its compon- ents to conscious awareness. In *projection* we attribute a disowned portion of ourselves to another person, scapegoating them for our own inadequacies. By *rationalizing* the mind spins itself a yarn that it can accept in mitigation ('Everybody does it', 'She kicked me first', etc. etc.). *Reaction formation* helps us to bury something of which we have been taught to be ashamed - sexuality and anger are the two most obvious candidates - by an exagger- ated espousal of a contrary personality trait. By *regression* to behaviour of a younger age a person can hope to persuade others (and himself) to lower their expectations about his degree of responsibility and maturity. *Displacement* enables us to direct our feelings - an angry outburst, let's say - not at the real object, who may react in a threatening way (boss), but at another (spouse, children, cat) with whose reaction we can cope more easily. At a more pathological level *obsessions, compulsions* and *phobias* may be crippling, but may also have some avoidance value.

And finally, if none of these partial attempts to deny the sense of responsibility that 'I' has for 'me' is successful, that is if the bad feelings persist in breaking through into consciousness, one can always flip one's lid and embrace psychosis, in which the res- ponsibility and guilt are avoided totally, but only at the cost of avoidance too of the experiential reality of the organism. The

enlightened man resolves the conflict by rediscovering his
identity with the organism-environment field; the madman finds
his integrity in a total identification with a fantasy whose bizarre
premises prevent any break-through from the 'real world'; and
the rest of us, neither fish nor fowl, are left to sweat it out in
the middle. If the whole cycle were not so tragic a despoilation
of humanity, it would be very funny. (It is said in Buddhism
that the smile that statues of the Buddha usually wear represents
this dual recognition of the pathetic and the farcical in human
life - being half-way between a cry and a laugh.)

To the extent that one's web of defences is comprehensive and
effective one will not recognize oneself as Dissociated Man. Only
when the dyke is breached, and one's thumb proves inadequate
to staunch the flood of fear does the picture come into focus. For
many people it is the imminence of death alone that has the
strength to overcome their defences and, at last, shows them to
themselves. For others it may be a broken relationship, the death
of a parent or friend, or the sudden loss of an inanimate exten-
sion of oneself such as one's job (as in retirement) or one's
house or savings.

Reaction to the 'tragedy', and to the feelings of anxiety, helplessness or purposelessness that follow, may be despair or liberation. Usually the former, though if one's surrender to it is deep
enough, the latter. But the process takes time, and people who
do not meet themselves till very late in their lives may never
transcend the feeling of futility and waste. So there is something
to be said for encountering one's sadness and disappointment
sooner rather than later. Bhagwan Shree Rajneesh has written:

If you are happy because you are young you will not be happy
for long, soon your happiness will be shattered. And if you
can become aware before it is shattered, it is good. This is the
beauty: if you can become sad while you are young, you will
be happy when you become old. Otherwise you will become
sad . . . Soon that which is given to you will be taken, and if
you can be happy when everything is taken, only then is your
happiness unshakeable (from 'When the Shoe Fits').

It is interesting how we insulate ourselves not only from growth,
but from awareness of our limitation too. There is a boundary between ME and ME-AS-I-THINK-I-AM, but within that boundary
there is a no-go area. When we happen to stray into it, bells go
off almost imperceptibly and we withdraw without ever realizing
what has happened. Thus (a) awareness of the cage is avoided;
and (b) we never know whether any particular bit of the cage is
still there - whether the pain that we once avoided still exists -
because we never get near enough to the bars to be able to
rattle them. Some friends and I recently gave another friend -
an attractive but slightly 'straight' young married woman - a pair
of metallic silver mesh 'punk' tights for her birthday: she was
unimpressed, did not even see it as a joke, and will never wear
them. 'They're not me', she said, and that was that; the possibility of a little experiment was pre-empted by her beliefs. And

we all react in the same way, having a ridiculous investment in the clothes we wear, the food we eat, the car we drive, the company we keep. Little children have no such qualms about experiment: they fail, they make fools of themselves and yet they don't seem to mind, and their failures often turn up surprising successes. It is sad that this innocence has to be lost.

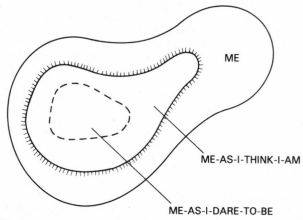

Figure 2

The story of Ronnie and the Tights illustrates the usual nature of our perception: it is about 10 per cent information and 90 per cent projection. Some experience begins in the organism, but before a full picture of 'what's out there', or 'what I'm feeling' is allowed to form, recognition takes place. That is, the sample of experience triggers off a conceptualization – often in the form of a verbal label – which triggers in turn beliefs about what's going on and value-judgments about it which take over and prevent a fuller pick-up of information about the object or event in question. On the basis of minimal data we jump from the level of experience into the (often verbal) level of belief, and then operate in terms of the caricature of reality. Perception is largely false, embroidered with our own fancies and phobias (continually seeing 'a man who wasn't there'), and action cannot be maximally effective because it is based on a narrow and selective picture of the context in which it is occurring.

There was a gourmet who heard on the gourmet grape-vine that one special dish that he had always wanted to try was available in a small, difficult-to-find restaurant in the backstreets of New York. All the flights from Paris, where he lived, were booked up that day; but he had to go immediately, so sparing no expense he hired a private plane, and had a car waiting at the airport in New York. It was getting late and the traffic was heavy, and his excitement and anxiety lest the restaurant be closed when he arrived, increased as they drove. Eventually they arrived. He dashed out of the car, across the street, and tugged at the door.

It didn't move. Yet the restaurant was still open because he could see people eating inside. He pulled and pulled at the door with mounting frustration, and after ten minutes with no success staggered off along the pavement, tears of rage and disappointment in his eyes . . . not noticing the little sign on the door saying PLEASE PUSH. Dissociated Man with his I-know-best, let-the-dog-see-the-rabbit attitude, is always missing little clues like that and ends up doing the wrong thing. And by 'wrong' I don't mean morally wrong, bad, but simply inappropriate and therefore ineffective.

So-called Staircase Wit is another example, where we key ourselves up for an important event - an interview, say, or a date - rehearsing how we are going to present ourselves and what we are going to say. Then afterwards we lie awake thinking of all the witty, intelligent, charming things we should have done and said, and didn't because we were so busy trying to remember and revise the plan, instead of being there, and trusting ourselves to be whatever was necessary. As Bhagwan has put it: 'Before you are wise; after you are wise. In between you are otherwise.'

Integrated Man, not needing to defend or project, does not slam down the lid on his experience so fast. He is not prejudiced, in the literal sense of pre-judging, as Dissociated Man is. His perceptions he can allow to come to term: they are not premature, and never stillborn, as Dissociated Man's often are. He can allow his awareness to flow with no reservations into his organismic experience, so that he becomes that experience in an aware and total way. This is the meaning of acceptance: it is not resignation or fatalism but totality. When Jesus said, 'Except ye become as little children ye shall not see the Kingdom of God', he was not urging a regression to blissful ignorance, but a rediscovery, through further growth, of that quality of totality and commitment, presence and whole-heartedness that little kids possess before disintegration starts.

People fear the idea of acceptance because it seems to be dangerous and irresponsible. Consider this speech by Kirillov from Dostoyevsky's 'The Possessed', for example.

'Man is unhappy because he doesn't know he's happy. It's only that. That's all! That's all! If anyone finds out he'll become happy at once, that minute . . . It's all good.'

'And if anyone dies of hunger,' asks Stavrogin, 'and if anyone insults and outrages the little girl, is that good?'

'Yes! And if anyone blows his brains out for the baby, that's good too. And if anyone doesn't, that's good too. It's all good, all. It's good for all those who know that it's all good. If they knew that it was good for them, it would be good for them, but as long as they don't know it's good for them, it will be bad for them. That's the whole idea, the whole of it! . . . They're bad because they don't know they're good. When they find out they won't outrage a little girl. They'll find out that they're good and they'll all become good, every one of them.'

As expressed these sentiments are both repugnant and non-

sensical. They are repugnant because the suggestion that a
sexual assault on a young girl is good raises an involuntary cry
of horror and disgust in our throats. If that is good, what on
earth can possibly be bad? But that is precisely the nonsense,
for Kirillov doesn't mean good as opposed to bad. He explicitly
says 'It's *all* good, all', which excludes the possibility of anything
bad. And if there is nothing bad, then the very idea of good
loses all meaning. He is constrained by language to speak in terms
of distinctions, and the value-judgments that necessarily accompany
them. But what he wants to do is point beyond the partial and
prejudiced map to the territory that simply exists in its 'suchness'.
This is the world in which the best you can say is 'A rose is a
rose is a rose', or 'We're 'ere because we're 'ere because we're
'ere'; and in which things themselves are not nice or nasty,
beautiful or ugly, sacred or profane - they are just 'thus'. Words
like 'fitting' or 'natural' capture the spirit of this world-and-me-
in-it better than 'good', yet they too do violence to it in attributing to it properties and values that it does not itself contain. We
think of the world as perforated, and it is difficult to see that it
is we, as individuals and societies, that choose where to site the
dotted lines. Why is 'nose' part of 'head', but 'neck' isn't? Why
does my 'hand' become a 'fist' when I fold it up, but a 'letter'
remains a 'letter' when I fold it up? Because that's the way we
have decided it shall be.

All of this is not to say that concepts, values, likes and dislikes are 'wrong': as we have said, the map is part of the territory, it is just as 'natural', or as valid, as other aspects of the
territory like a cup of tea, or a sneeze, or a distant bird call.
But it creates problems for us, what Buddhism calls 'suffering',
or 'dis-ease', when we attribute to it the special status of determining or controlling other parts of the territory; when the desires it incorporates generate a picture of what ought to be that
blinds us to what is.

Hand in hand with the picture of what ought to be, as we have
seen, goes the idea that 'I' ought to be able to do something
about it. I am worried. I ought not to be worried. I ought to be
able to stop myself. I feel angry at an old woman who is taking
ages at the supermarket check-out. I ought to feel sympathetic.
I ought to be able to make myself tolerant. And so on. All such
examples end up in this fruitless spiral of 'ought' and 'can't',
which leaves me feeling powerless and frustrated. And all arise
from an unwillingness or inability to accept that the reality of me
is at odds with the picture of me as I ought to be. Conversely a
complete acceptance of and absorption in the present felt reality
of myself-in-the-world leads to that wonderfully easy feeling of
potency in which I know I can do anything that I can conceive of,
because the only things I can conceive of are things that I can do.
Actions appear with the same ease and naturalness with which, at
exactly the right moment a leaf dips to shed a load of snow, or a
chick breaks its way through the shell of its egg. As Watts says,
these acts are not necessarily immediate, in the sense of following

a preceding act instantaneously. There is a span of time between
the start of the snow-storm and the dipping of this leaf, or between the laying and the hatching of the egg. But they are immediate in being free from the conscious and rational mediation
which attends our 'voluntary' actions, and which can on occasion
envelop even a simple sneeze in an agony of self-consciousness
and indecision: the sort of state that such writers as Sartre or
Dostoyevsky have analysed in claustrophobic detail.

Although for Integrated Man im-mediate actions are not necessarily instantaneous, for Dissociated Man it is virtually impossible
for a response to be delayed without some mediation leaping in to
fill the gap. Thus, as we shall see, many of the traditional forms
of training in ego-less action use tasks where lightning reflexes
are required, and where he who hesitates is lost. Such actions,
evident for example in many sports and in martial arts like swords-
manship or karate, must arise as does the spark when the flint
hits the steel, with 'no thought, no reflection, no analysis, no
cultivation, no intention, settling itself' (The Six Precepts of
Tilopa). Herrigel, in 'Zen in the Art of Archery' says that the
expert swordsman 'sees and feels what is going to happen, and at
that same moment he has already avoided its effect without there
being "a hair's breadth" between perceiving and avoiding.
This . . . is what counts: a lightning reaction which has no further need of conscious observation.' Training in these arts and
sports can lead to experiences of integration that may inform all
areas of one's life.

Integrated Man is a strange character, and hard to get a feel
for. Our everyday consciousness of ourselves as separate, skin-
encapsulated centres of consciousness that perceive an outside
world about which we make decisions and on which we choose
how to act in a more or less rational way, is so firmly convinced
of its own rightness that it is reluctant to admit of any alternative.
Its fighting weapons are reason, logic and language, and any
suggestion that these are limited or limiting are easy to challenge.
Any statement that tries to point beyond the map can be shown,
in terms of the conventions of the map, either not to do so, or
to be nonsense, or both. Unless you know that mountains do not
naturally have contour lines marked on them, there is nothing on
the map to tell you. The conventions of a map 'work' only because
one already has experience of the territory.

It follows that the best one can do, in trying to point beyond
our common-sense views of ourselves, is to allude to the reality
of a territory that, at some level, one already knows. Descriptions
of Integrated Man can only be personally meaningful to the extent
that something in oneself recognizes itself in the description. If
it does not - if one's conviction that one is an independent, autonomous 'I' is complete - that recognition is impossible. That is why
this chapter has been discursive and illustrative, rather than
straightforwardly argumentative.

Out of all the levels of understanding it is possible to have
about Integrated Man, perhaps three are worth identifying. At

the most superficial, which we might call understanding with the head, it is possible to appreciate the facts of change, of inter-connectedness and of the conventional nature of knowledge in a way that avoids any personal commitment to the implications that these facts have for one's view of oneself. John Barth in his novel 'The Floating Opera' says: 'The truth is of course that it is one thing - an easy thing - to give what Cardinal Newman calls "notional" assent to a proposition such as "There is no justice"; quite another, and more difficult matter to give it "real" assent, to learn it stingingly, to the heart, through involvement.' It is easy to give notional assent to 'Everything is interrelated'; hard to recognize that this means you, too.

The second level of understanding, then, is understanding with the heart, in which one not only assents to a proposition, one feels an involvement with it. One's emotions are engaged as well as one's intellect. Unless you have been stung or challenged by the picture of Integrated Man I have sketched, unless he, in you, has recognized himself just a little, I fear that the rest of this book will appear much ado about nothing, being as fanciful as a psychology of Piltdown Man, or Gnomes. But if this chapter *has* made some sense to you, it may be of more than academic interest to see whether it is possible to give a coherent psychology of Integrated Man, which accounts for the way his perceptions, thoughts, feelings and actions 'really' arise, and also for the status of our disintegrated common sense with respect to them. If thought does not influence action, for example: (a) how do we act, and (b) how come we think that it does? That is what Part II of this book is about. It is a kind of feasibility study. If we can show that contemporary psychology already contains the bits and pieces out of which a model of Integrated Man can be built, it may make him a little less strange, and less threatening, to us.

Chapters 7 and 8 review and plunder some of the existing theories in psychology for traces of Integrated Man, and ideas that may point the way towards a psychology of integrity.

The third level of understanding, by the way, is that which transcends understanding. It is achieved when Integrated Man is a fully realized, moment to moment reality. You do not understand him, you are him. Whether or not you understand the nature of gravity, its existence is incorporated in and manifested through your every action: so it is for Integrated Man with respect to the truths that we have been discussing in this chapter. He does not just understand with his head or his heart. The understanding is in his bones.

3   THE ADULT-ERATION OF THE CHILD

For the newly born child nothing in the world has significance, because everything has equal significance. It is only through his experience that he comes to differentiate between things that matter to him and things that do not. His nervous system gradually becomes tuned by, and therefore attuned to, aspects of the world that interact differentially with his own nature. This, as we have seen, is not something he has to learn to do: it is part of what being alive means. His potential begins to be selectively developed through interaction with that subset of the world of sensation to which he happens to find himself exposed. And all this development is, to start with, grounded in its personal impact. Other people, parents, may have a hand in determining what situations he is to meet - as a lioness has, for example, with her cubs - but how he reacts, and what he learns, depends upon the infant himself, and his own pattern of long-term and transient needs and desires.

But as the child comes to learn language, the picture complicates; for now adults have a way of pointing to divisions and events in the world that have no acquired significance to the child. He is asked to take on trust a judgment that has no counterpart in his existing experience. What is more, he has no choice whether to accept this imposition or not, for his tutors have the use of powerful sanctions, like the withdrawal of their love, that he cannot risk. Language functions as a parasite, like a virus. It depends for its initial sustenance on a partially developed, immature map of reality; but once established it very rapidly subverts and distorts the development of its host, calling the tune not only for how we describe things, but how we see them and react to them as well. It is nonsense to talk about a blue tree, and it is literally nonsense to see one. Only someone with a very clear and anti-social eye - like the Impressionist painter in Zola's novel 'L'Oeuvre' - can see that a tree, this tree, in this light, despite what people say, actually is blue.

Parents, however well-intentioned, are somewhat at odds with their own habits and desires. Their intuitions have been muddled, their actions doubted, so that they cannot trust themselves to behave in the ways they believe to be right. How, then, can they trust their children? It seems only proper that they should help their sons and daughters not to make the same mistakes, and to acquire the understandings that they have hewn so painstakingly from their own experience, or bought unquestioningly from their own upbringings. I do not see that it could, or should, be other-

35

wise. Yet the canker of dissociation is unavoidably latent within
the core of this caring logic. As we will see when discussing
morality, a code of conduct can be helpful if it leads, sooner or
later, to the experience that can put it to the test. 'Do it this
way, and eventually you will find out why.' But a morality that
is based on fear and distrust must manifest itself not as exhorta-
tions but as prohibitions. And to say 'Do *not* do this. Never let me
catch you doing this. No person worthy of my esteem could ever
want to do this' is to create a tension in the child, to sell him
the idea that morality is not to be understood but obeyed, and to
prevent him from ever gaining the experience that could validate
or falsify the admonition. Instead of leading to a more sophisticated unity, it engenders a stultifying division.

If the child were not in such a weak position he could refuse to
play. Parents, though, are able to make their child an offer he
cannot refuse. One of the earliest learnings he records is the
correlation between the presence of other people and the satisfaction of his needs. Left alone he will die, and it cannot take long
before this dependency is borne in upon him. Situation: hunger
plus people; consequence: decreased hunger. Situation: hunger
plus no people; consequence: still hungry. When very small, this
contingency is (if he is lucky) unconditional. All he has to do is
get noticed, and the need will be attended to regardless of what
else he is doing. But as soon as he is ready for it, his parents
succumb to the temptation to use their power to introduce the
codes of behaviour in whose absolute value or practical sense
they believe. Consequence does not follow situation automatically
any more: the child has to interpose an acceptable behaviour –
or, more usually, eliminate certain unacceptable behaviours. Of
course he isn't starved if he gets it wrong: the clues are subtle,
more a matter of the warmth, enthusiasm and concern with which
needs are met than of actually withholding something important.
But even very young children are quite capable of registering
such consistencies.

Such training is not in essence pathogenic: the child's ability
to learn is helping him to notice and register ways of being that
work. Unfortunately though it is inevitably overlaid with a message that begins to inhibit learning itself – a message that relates
not to the efficacy of an act, but to the worth of the actor. In
est (Erhard Seminar Training) they tell a story about a hungry
rat in a box with four tunnels leading out. The experimenter –
to the rat 'the great God in the white coat' – puts a lump of cheese
at the end of the fourth tunnel and the rat, after a few false
starts, learns to run down the fourth tunnel to get the cheese.
Put the rat in the box, down the fourth tunnel he goes, gets the
cheese. Now when God moves the cheese, the rat continues to
run down the fourth tunnel for a while, maybe for a long while,
but eventually he starts exploring again to find out where the
cheese has gone to, and if there's any about, he'll get to it. The
trouble with the human being, who in this notional experiment
compares very unfavourably with the rat, is that he comes to

have a BELIEF about the fourth tunnel. And he would rather be right than get the cheese. So he keeps on running down the fourth tunnel for ever, repressing ('Cheese . . . what cheese?'), projecting ('That guy really wants me to keep on going down here, I know it'), rationalizing ('Who cares about cheese? It's really pretty down this tunnel, the view is so much nicer than those other tunnels . . .') and so on and so on. And still not getting any cheese.

The great God in the white coat, existence, is unfortunately always moving the cheese, and some of the best kinds of cheese (like being in love) only exist because they are moving and changing. Any belief about where the cheese is going to pop up guarantees that it won't pop up there. You have to keep experimenting, exploring, trusting, risking and experiencing failure just for the hell of it, and sometimes, surprise, surprise, it's Camembert and champagne. And the really strange thing is that the less bothered about cheese you are, the fewer beliefs you have about what constitutes cheese, and where it's to be got, the more you are on the qui vive, the more open to all possibilities, and the more cheese turns up. Even ordinary habits and unexceptional skies get a cheesy tinge to them when one is purposelessly alert.

This is the central Catch-22 of Dissociated Man, and there are a number of ways of expressing it. You can find cheese everywhere, but you cannot look for it. Or 'you become what you resist: and you transcend what you accept.' Or, as Alan Watts again says in the preface to 'The Wisdom of Insecurity': 'Insecurity is the result of trying to be secure, and, contrari-wise, salvation and sanity consist in the most radical recognition that we have no way of saving ourselves.'

There is a danger here to be noted: it is easy to assume that somehow it is social conditioning itself that is to blame for man's internal conflict between his need for cheese and his desire to be right, as if the social world were 'artificial', and therefore less legitimate, less natural, than the physical world. But this is not so. If you receive a smack for putting your elbows on the table, this is, from your point of view, as much a contingency to be aware of as getting burned if you put your elbows on the stove, or losing your orange juice if you throw the cup off your highchair. It is easy to forget that, in a very important sense, man is part of nature, part of the balance of nature, and his behaviour, both individual and social, is as valid a part of the mystery the child has to unravel as any other. No, the problem revolves particularly around language, for, as we saw in Chapter 2, in conferring the power to represent the world, language also confers the power to misrepresent it, and to hand on, for the most part unknowingly, lies and delusions about the way things are. What the child is told may have no basis in his own sense of reality; it may even contradict it. And whenever it does, a blow is dealt to his faith in his own organism to behave, and to learn to behave, in an appropriate and satisfactory way. His body says that playing with his willie is nice; his Mummy says it's bad.

If he follows his organism he gets a wallop, so what is he to do?
He toes the line, tries not to get caught, and begins to feel those
symptoms of internal division that we call guilt or shame.

It may be worth labouring the point that it is not the cuff, but
the judgment that accompanies it, that is the source of dissociation. The lioness will belt a cub if it nips her tail, and he will feel
hurt for a while and go off and nip somebody else's. He does not
go off with the suspicion that he is a bad, dirty little cub, not
fit to be seen in the company of nice cubs like Jeremy, and just
you wait till your father gets home! He is not made to feel worthless and unloved. He has not suffered a blow to his self-esteem
that will flower, in his adolescence, into schizophrenia. He has
just learned that you don't bite your Mum's tail if you know
what's good for you.

Now the cub certainly has a reason to go around biting things -
it's in his nature, as it is in the nature of children to explore,
practice with, try out anything that comes to hand. That is what
play in a young animal is about: it is experimenting with the
world, and with his behaviour, to find out what the contingencies
are, so that he can have a fair idea what the best way of satisfying this need is in this kind of situation. Like new dancing partners, he and the environment are working out ways of getting
along without treading on each other's toes too much. He can
tolerate a painful outcome of an experiment because there are
lots of other experiments yet to be made; lots of alternative ways
of satisfying each need to be explored.

The outcomes that cannot be absorbed so smoothly are those
where it is not just one way of getting satisfaction that is punished but any way; where the need, or pleasure or whatever word
you care to apply to the 'organic urge' is itself punished in words.
'Bad boy' often means not 'I don't like you doing that', but 'You
are wicked for even wanting to'. And this kind of admonition is
one you can only give through language. The lioness could not
convey this even if she felt inclined to.

In addition to the effect of language in denying specific areas
of experience into conscious awareness, we might remind ourselves
here that there are more general properties of language that
further limit the accuracy of consciousness. The grid that
language imposes on the territory of experience is relatively
coarse and static. It creates apparent divisions where there are
none and creates things out of processes. When I sit down I
mysteriously acquire an object called a 'lap' that just as mysteriously vanishes again when I stand up. Language, by its words,
its grammar, its syntax, by the whole spirit which is frozen in
it, determines how we experience, and which experiences penetrate to our awareness. While I would not go as far as Erich
Fromm in saying that 'Generally speaking it may be said that an
experience rarely comes into (conscious) awareness for which the
language has no word', it is impossible to deny that when linguistic information becomes incorporated into the map it dramatically
influences behaviour and distorts perception, and if it cannot be

incorporated then it may serve to prevent access of certain areas of experience to conscious awareness totally or in part. One might add that from the point of view of society it is better for incorporation and distortion to occur, for then people will perceive themselves as wanting to do and see things in the way that society wants them done and seen.

To summarize, those learnings that are divisive and pathogenic are those where a child is told that any behaviour or behavioural features directed towards the achievement or expression of an organismic need is unacceptable, and that, by implication, he is unacceptable for having such a need. All significant learning must involve the risk of an unsuccessful and/or painful outcome. You cannot explore the limits of harmony with your environment without, sometimes, transgressing them. To pretend otherwise is unrealistic and dangerous. But to be punished for exploring is to be punished for being alive.

Let us consider a case in point: the way a child learns to inhibit the force or energy of his actions. Anger, fear, frustration and hurt show themselves not so much in what we do but in how we do it. We shout, scream, squirm and howl; we 'tremble' with fear and 'shake' with rage, and these intensities are characteristic of young children. They seem to be natural reactions to stress and threat, as passing water is a natural reaction to a full bladder. And they are reactions of the whole body. A baby does not just cry with his eyes and mouth but with his fists, torso and toes as well. Now it is quite true that as he grows up, he would have to learn to modify the production of this high energy behaviour, in terms of when it turned out to be appropriate and effective to 'have a turn', and when not. The logic I have been propounding is that there is a time, a place and a manner for everything, and the child's job is to find out, as accurately as he can, what they are. Unfortunately this is just what many children cannot do, however, because of the premature prohibitions that parents provide. Rage and terror are not seen as inappropriate here and now, but undesirable ever. Society, school and parents tend to collude in making sure the child understands this: it is to the benefit of society to inhibit these extreme forms of saying 'No', and to the benefit of parents in that they are not disturbed by these distant echoes of their own dissociated demons.

The child finds himself in a bit of a fix, from which he may escape in either or both of two ways. He can avoid incurring the actual displeasure of his parents by preventing the exhibition of his feelings. He can have them, but not give vent to them. But this does not save him from internal conflict (guilt) that arises between the organismic expectation of satisfaction (through the forceful expression of his needs) and the acquired and now internalized expectation of punishment: the voice of his conscience, his super-ego. The only way he can avoid that is by learning to anticipate these conflicts and divert his attention from them. Detours are built in to the routes on his map that enable the flow of awareness to by-pass these danger zones. They do not

go away, they are not un-learnt, but they are effectively repressed - or, if elements of perception or action are avoided
rather than the whole package, distorted.

Take the first strategy first: how can the child learn to inhibit
the physical signs of his unacceptable reactions? By developing
competing physical reactions that will overpower and mask the
others. And here he can capitalize on two simple correlations that
he will probably have discovered through his motor play already.
A part of his body cannot move if it is tensed up. It becomes
seized. And vigorous action requires a lot of oxygen to sustain
it. Thus he can effectively inhibit the force of his actions in
general by constricting his breathing; and he can prevent specific
movements by tensing the relevant muscles. Through experimenting with ways of avoiding the unpleasant consequences of his
violent behaviour, he can learn the utility of these methods of
containing himself.

In the worst possible case these physical controls become generalized, through the acquired fears of failure and of rejection, to
learning situations per se, and thus develop into chronic and
ubiquitous features of bodily function. Breathing becomes permanently shallow and tight, the muscles of the face set (the upper
lip literally stiff), the neck, shoulders and lower back tense,
preventing free movement of the head, arms and pelvis; and so
on. The child grows into an adult who is, again literally, 'tense',
'wound up', 'uptight'. Not surprisingly the body rebels against
these unnatural and unrelenting distortions with the full range
of 'psychosomatic' disorders with which Dissociated Man is only
too familiar; eyestrain, headaches and migraine, backaches, res-
piratory and coronary troubles, ulcers, constipation and the rest.
How ironic that our frequent response to these desperate cries
for attention is to jam the transmitter with biochemical static, in
the form of pain-killers and other awareness-limiting drugs. It
is like fixing up a loud-speaker from the baby's room, and then
responding to his nightmares by turning down the volume. Some
of us are lucky to avoid the full retribution of this physical
strategy, which came like Dr Jekyll in response to an urgent call,
and took up residence as the tyrannical and secretive Mr Hyde.
But few escape his influence entirely. Yet he can, as we shall
see in the next chapter, be evicted, with relatively little trouble,
if we wish.

This physical way of coping allows the internal and external
concomitants of the problematic behaviour to be activated, while
suppressing the behaviour itself. But this is often not enough.
We have seen that through language the child gradually learns
the idea 'bad'; and he learns to apply it not only to the actions
he produces but to the needs and feelings that attend the actions.
Arousal of a need, or perception of an anger or anxiety-provoking
situation thus comes to prime the natural reaction and the learnt
verbal censure. One way to avoid this archetypal internal conflict
is to attach to the very preliminary signals of this discomfort
alternative behaviours that effectively by-pass both of the incom-

patible expectancies: to indulge in what psychologists call 'displacement activities'. The actual consequences of these may be of
little value in themselves, but they gate out the painful awareness
of being pulled in opposite directions. When caught between the
devil and the deep blue sea, one solution is to develop an overwhelming interest in the beautiful shells on the beach, the likelihood of rain or geological problems of erosion. The trouble is that
these short-term evasions only remove awareness of the conflict,
they do not resolve conflict itself. In fact the problem persists
precisely because it is ignored.

These strategies create diversions. They literally 'take one's
mind off' the trouble. Alternatively it seems as if we have the
ability to inhibit awareness of dissociation and its signals directly,
without putting anything specific in its place. This is the path
of repression, in which the thresholds for awareness of feelings
are set so high that they cannot, in the normal run of events,
break through. As control of behaviour may generalize into a
living rigor mortis, so may control of emotional awareness grow
into a widespread 'deadening of affect', and/or chronic depression.

We are now ready to see how the child's sense of himself as
being separate from the rest of existence, and possessing reason
through which he can make choices, and volition through which
he can implement his decisions, comes about. By the time he gets
to two years old or so, the child's organism is functioning pretty
well. He has detected and registered many of the significant
regularities in his world and can intervene in the flow of events
to his own advantage with considerable skill. His repertoire of
acts is constantly expanding, as is his sense of occasion. Of particular importance, he has discovered the power of language and
cracked the code. Now comes the cumulative process of developing
the range and delicacy of the messages he can express and understand.

In one corner of this clear sky the clouds of delusion begin to
gather. The first is the learnt inattention that we have just discussed. In specific domains the child is becoming not more but
less sensitive to his bodily reactions and the circumstances that
elicit them. He develops blind-spots to some of the events and
occurrences that are significant in shaping and calling forth his
thoughts and deeds. At the same time, especially if he is a Western child, he is deeply immersed in a language and a culture where
to know the causes of one's behaviour is seen as important. Children's fascination with the word 'why' demonstrates their sense of
its significance, and simultaneously their puzzlement about it.
So our child begins to have a problem. On the one hand he is
learning to express what controls or elicits his words and actions,
and to value that expression. On the other he is denying to his
conscious awareness some of the very triggers - feelings and
events - that he is looking for. The answer to what directs and
influences me is always some facet of the interaction between
organism and environment: the territory of me-in-the-world. Yet
often, like a man searching for his hat everywhere but on his head,

this is the one place where the child is increasingly inhibited
from looking.

At the same time as this is becoming an issue the child is grap-
pling with a particular linguistic problem: to what do the words
'you' and 'I' refer? These common little symbols do not seem very
special to begin with: the first sensible hypothesis is that they
are addresses, the names of the locations of bodies, rather like
'here' and 'there' but somewhat more restricted. But this turns
out not to be good enough. What is the young learner to make of
'I didn't mean to do that', 'You shouldn't have done that', 'I will
try to be home early'; of the fact that he is allowed to say 'I am
drinking my milk' but not 'I am gurgling my tummy'? 'I' seems to
refer to an internal cause of things, or a control that may try or
mean to cause things without being successful; but what does the
child have inside him with which this strange idea can be identified? Answer: the vacuum, created by his learnt ignorance of
the full complexity of events that trigger actions. On the one
hand he has, in language, an agent looking for something to do:
on the other a gap in his conscious awareness of the antecedents
of some of his actions. Clearly the peg without a function and
the hole without a peg were made for each other, and the peg
happily slips into the hole with very little prompting. The social
fiction of the ego engages with the gap in the child's awareness
of himself and the illusion clicks into place.

Now he falls prey to the confusion between prediction and
control. Up to this point the child has, quite rightly, been
developing and using his ability to predict changes in the world
and his effect on them. His actions are called forth by fluctuations in the organism-environment field - they are 'caused' we
might say, by these fluctuations - and the child has no reason to
think otherwise. Until, that is, he is introduced to the game of
'I Did It'. He is like a man, sitting by a stream, idly watching
things float past him. After a while he notices a regularity: whenever a cork goes by, a bottle follows. In order to amuse himself
the man invents a game in which he pretends not to notice the
corks, and every so often calls out 'Let there be a bottle!' Sure
enough, whenever he does this, a bottle heaves into view. By
ignoring consciously the cue that enables him to predict bottles,
he is able to sustain the illusion that he can control or produce
the appearance of bottles. Unfortunately the man falls prey to
his own magic and, enthralled by his new-found 'power', wanders
back into town, where he discovers that the game is all the rage.
'Who did it?' 'I did', the child learns to say, and I, that label for
a vacuum in his own perception, is bestowed in the child's developing fiction about himself, with the captaincy of the ship. The
ship ploughs on, its course set out by the responses of wind and
sea, metal and sail to each other, while the captain, through his
experience, manages to issue orders that precisely anticipate
what was about to happen anyway.

The generalization of 'I' to cover the prediction of perceptions,
thoughts, feelings, and, most importantly, the so-called voluntary

actions, occurs easily through the child's continuing attempts to understand his parents' language. Not so slowly but very surely the ideas of his own responsibility, control and agency seep into the core of his understanding of himself. Someone says 'You are a clever boy' when he has produced an action without effort or intent, and again he is led to believe that 'I' must have had a hand in it somewhere. People furrow their brows, look concerned and say 'I tried' when they didn't manage it, and he dutifully learns to do the same, attaching the muscular sense of strain that accompanies physical exertion to quite inappropriate mental activities. And so it goes. His awareness of what is going to happen next becomes more automatic and more immediate until the swiftness of the 'I' deceives the hand completely.

At the same time another aspect of the sense of self develops and becomes attached to the chimerical agent, buttressing it still further: his 'personality'. He learns to define who he is in terms of the actions, and their attendant percepts and feelings, that are acceptable to those around him. As well as learning that he is, he is taught what he is. Through his parents' comments on his behaviour he begins to construct an image of himself, his character. You are clever, or naughty, or clumsy, or pretty, or helpful, or dirty, or brave, they say, with obvious approval or disapproval, and the twin pictures of 'me as I am' and 'me as I ought to be' emerge. These are not expectancies about himself in the organismic sense, for they are not related to the world outside. They make no reference to when it is or is not appropriate to be that way: they are aspects of his interaction with his surroundings that are dissected out of their contexts and confined within the skin.

Again there is a danger of this being taken too simply. All children grow up in worlds that have recurrent features and make recurrent demands; and all possess certain physical and biological characteristics. Naturally, therefore, their actions and perceptions become tuned to what is usual. Cats, dogs and monkeys develop 'personalities' in this sense. But they do not become attached to these consistencies in the way that people do. When the environment changes, and makes a new demand, an animal can shed his normal habit, and the organism rises to meet the challenge. Not so the person, who would rather 'be himself' than allow his natural intelligence to find a solution. When put to the test, personality turns out to be not a flexible do-it-yourself manual but a prison. For personality reflects the way a child has been taught to limit himself: it is characterized more by holes, by the no-go areas of action and feeling, than by the habits it permits. Luke Rinehart in 'The Dice Man' muses:

> What if - at the time it seemed like an original thought - what if the development of a sense of self is normal . . . but is neither inevitable nor *desirable*? . . . What if the sense of being some*one* represents an evolutionary error as disastrous to the further development of a more complex creature as was the shell for snails or turtles?

And he goes on to explain where this error comes from:
Like the turtle's shell, the sense of self serves as a shield
against stimulation and as a burden which limits mobility into
possibly dangerous areas. The turtle rarely has to think about
what's on the other side of his shell: whatever it is it can't
hurt him, can't even touch him. So too adults insist on the shell
of a consistent self for themselves and their children and appreciate turtles for friends; they wish to be protected from being
hurt or touched or confused or having to think. If a man can
rely on consistency he can afford not to notice people after the
first few times. The sense of a permanent self: ah, how psychologists and parents lust to lock their kids into some defin-
able cage. Consistency, patterns, something we can label -
that's what we want in our boy.
The formation of these patterns was a good idea at the time: it
enabled us to get the very important cheese of our parents' love.
But they have become beliefs and thus untestable. We do not dare
to put to the test alternative ways of being that others - our
grown-up friends now - might not like, but equally well might
react to positively. When we were small, we learnt to play to an
audience - usually a small one, consisting only of our parents to
start with, it's true, but one whose approval of the performance
mattered terribly. Gradually the audience widened to include
other adults, brothers and sisters, and later friends and peers,
but still somehow what Carl Rogers calls the 'locus of evaluation'
remained outside, and we, our 'personality' becomes defined by
the crowd to whom we choose to play. Our limits are set not by
ourselves, by the nature of the organism that we are, but by the
fear of disapproval or rejection if we do not provide the show that
other people, our 'esteem-arena' I have heard it called, want.
Thus from the very early fear of rejection proliferate many other
fears that become manifest in the ways we must and must not behave. The child learns to fear failure - failure to achieve his tar-
gets, and failure to live up to the standards that he has internalized and those that others around him set. A particularly potent
form of this, that children tend to meet first when they go to
school, is ridicule. His inadequacies are not pointed out subtly
by the ebb and flow of parental enthusiasm, but generate tidal
waves of derision. Here is an evocative example from V.S.
Naipaul's 'The Mimic Men':
'Today' the teacher says, 'while I full (sic) up this roll-book, I
want you boys to sit down quiet and write a letter to a prospec-
tive employer asking for a job after you leave school.' He gives
us details of the job and on the blackboard writes out the opening sentence and one or two others for us to copy. I know I am
too young for employment and I am bewildered. But no other
boy is. I write: 'Dear Sir, I humbly beg to apply for the vacant
post of shipping clerk as advertised in this morning's edition of
the *Isabella Inquirer*. I am in the fourth standard of the Isabella Boys' School and I study English, Arithmetic, Reading,
Spelling and Geography. I trust that my qualifications will be

found suitable. School overs at three and I have to be home by
half past four. I think I can get to work at half past three but
I will have to leave at four. I am nine years and seven months
old. Trusting this application will receive your favourable attention, and assuring you at all times of my devoted service, I
remain, my dear Sir, your very humble and devoted servant,
R.R.K. Singh.' The letter is read out to the class by the
teacher, who has fulled-up his roll-book. The class dissolves
in laughter. It is an absurd letter. I know; but I was asked
for it. Then the letters of other boys are read out, and I see.
Absolute models. But how did they know? Who informs them
about the ways of the world and of school?

I suspect most of us could recall such terrible occasions, and the
earnest promise that we made ourselves: I'm not going to let that
happen again. If my well-intentioned best is so very poor, I shall
keep my poverty a secret. Other layers of evasion and defence
have had their foundations laid.

Interestingly enough, these tricky machinations may produce
out of fear of failure a fear of success. The more I succeed, the
higher I must set my standards, and the more the world will
expect of me. 'From them to whom much is given, from them shall
much be required.' A child may learn early on not to be too smart,
to hide his light under a bushel, for the heights from which he
can fall will then not be too great. And the same machinery manu-
factures out of a need for other peoples' love defences that will
prevent our ever getting it. Once a child has developed guilty
knowledge about himself, about the murky disparity between what
he thinks he is, and what he thinks he ought to be, he fears the
intimacy he craves. He dare not open himself to another lest they
find him out. As one experience of ridicule may be enough, so may
one misplaced confidence, one cruel abuse of trust, work the
vicious trick. 'Here you guys - you know what Jim just told me?
He WET HIS BED last night! Can you believe that?' Later, in his
adolescent explorations with the other sex, such breaches of
promise, real or assumed, may be especially traumatic. For a lover
to abscond with all the self you have invested may teach you, for
good and all, that the game is just not worth the candle. When
you stick your head cautiously out of your shell, you may meet
thieves, monsters and judges. It can be very hard to keep one's
faith in the existence of nice snails.

The fear of inconsistency, of being not oneself, also breeds
further bogeys. One, stronger in some than others, is the fear
of 'losing control'. While it may be very real to its owner (or it
may be quite unconscious), the fact that people have very different ideas about when and how control might be lost confirms
its acquired, rather than biological, nature. I know of a woman
who dare not let herself cry because 'I'm afraid that once I start
I'll never stop', and because of this absurd idea she thinks she
is 'going crazy'. I know a man who has never been overtly angry
in his life because be believes he has inherited a violent temper
from his father, and that if he opens the door on this temper an

uncontrollable hurricane of rage will come pouring out. He may
be right, of course. But he has condemned himself to a life-time
of dead feelings (he could not, in the end, trust any emotional
energy at all, 'good' or 'bad') on the basis of a belief, a hypothesis, that has never been put to the test. The sad thing is that
this untested belief is compounded by another that we know to be
false: namely that 'I am capable of violence' means 'I am a violent
person' - which means 'I always will be a violent person and I'm
stuck that way'. The truth is: everybody is capable of violence
and nobody is a violent person. 'Being violent' is not a character
trait: it is a transient, self-eliminating need in people at odds
with themselves or threatened by others. The more you resist
and suppress it, the more divided your house, and the greater
the need: self-perpetuating. Conversely the more you accept it,
the more united you become, and the less the need: self-
eliminating. And there is another level too: very few people know
this to be true, because most of us, holding the contrary belief
(that change happens through our own efforts, not through
acceptance), dare not go through the experiences that would enable us to find out that it is true. All these beliefs and meta-
beliefs pack together like Russian dolls, one inside the other. As
de Tocqueville might have noted, it is really amazing the intricacy
of the cage that man has devised to contain himself.

I have heard it said that there are three fears that are often
associated: of heights, of sleep and of being in love: all of them
connected by the image of 'falling', and all to do with being 'out
of control' and relinquishing any pretence at conscious guidance
and supervision of events. When we say 'I fell in love', that is
literally true, for 'I' - the sense of 'I'-the-controller, the ego -
does fall (i.e. collapse, disappear) in love. Being in love is being
out of your mind, and can provide some experience of what it is
like to trust, and to give up all the planning, projection and pre-
varication that our normal lack of trust requires of us. Love is
not blind. On the contrary it gives an insight into the effortless
omnipotence of surrender that we met in the adept of Zen.

Why does falling in love last such a short time, as a rule?
Because the good old ego snaps back into action and starts generating lots of stultifying beliefs about how to hang onto this rare
and beautiful gift blah . . . blah . . . blah. It tries to catch the
whirlpool in a bucket, and in interfering, starves it of the one
essential nutrient - trust, surrender, abandonment - that it
needs.

The fear of being out of control applies especially to feelings,
but also to thoughts and behaviour too. Sometimes one's body
develops tics or habits, sometimes one's mind entertains thoughts
and fantasies, that are unwilled - that is to say, unanticipated,
unbargained for. Instead of learning from these signals of one's
wider self, though, people may fear and fight them simply because
they are unbidden. Their very existence threatens the thin illusion of control. For such people even a second sherry may seem
like slipping the catch on a cage of wild beasts. And the LSD

taker's 'bad trip' usually reflects not an encounter with demons,
but a terror-stricken attempt to regain control of one's thought
and perception when they become strange and plastic. He died not
bitten by a snake, but of a heart attack brought on by misper-
ceiving the coil of rope. Even real insanity is sustained by a desperate resistance to experience that may be weird, but cannot
possibly be wrong.

And underlying all these derived fears is the original one: the
natural seed from which the poisonous fruit have sprung, the
resistance to the fact of death. Camouflaged so well it may be
difficult to see, it is the refusal to be mortal that energizes the
neurotic fight against one's own vitality.

The central fact of my own life is my death. After a while it will
all come to nothing. Whenever I have the courage to face this,
my priorities become clear. At such times nothing is done *in
order to* achieve something else. No energy is wasted on main-
taining the illusions. My image does not matter. I do not worry
about how I am doing. I do what I do, am what I am. That's
it. The imminence of my own death is the pivot around which
things turn (Sheldon Kopp: 'If You Meet the Buddha on the
Road, Kill Him').

The next two chapters explore ways and means for dismantling,
undermining, or blowing up the complex scaffolding of illusions
to which Kopp refers, and thus releasing the energy, that has
been taken up in holding that precarious structure together, for
doing what one does and being what one is, with unprecedented
perspicacity and zest. Chapter 4 looks at the distress that is
caused by a perceived disparity between me-as-I-am and me-as-I-
ought-to-be, between those aspects of territory and map that
define the reality of me and the distorted, idealized character that
I think or want myself to be. And it looks in some detail at the
therapeutic methods that have evolved this century for helping
people to react to this disparity by improving the map rather than
denying the terrain. Chapter 5 follows the process of questioning
and testing one's beliefs to the point where the notion of 'me'
itself becomes problematic, and the quest is transformed from a
therapeutic into a spiritual one.

4 LIBERATION FROM DE-LIBERATION: The West and psychotherapy

> And a woman spoke, saying, Tell us of Pain.
> And he said: Your pain is the breaking of
> the shell that encloses your understanding.
> Even as the stone of the fruit must break,
> that its heart may stand in the sun, so must
> you know pain. And could you keep your heart
> in wonder at the daily miracles of your life,
> your pain would not seem less wondrous than
> your joy.
>
> Kahlil Gibran: 'The Prophet'

All psychological disorders are caused not by the painfulness of living but by the misguided and unfounded belief that pain is always avoidable. Dissociated Man has lost what Ivan Illich called the 'art of suffering'. The very idea sounds distasteful and alien to Western ears: it smacks of masochism, because we have forgotten how to lump things that we cannot like. It is contrary to our second nature to suppose that tolerance is an essential ingredient of a healthy reaction to stress. This chapter traces out the assumptions behind a person's cry for help in the face of his intolerance, and the methods that modern Western therapy has evolved for responding to that cry.

COMING TO THERAPY

What brings a person to therapy in the first place? Although a great number of people are seeking psychological help these days, the majority of the world's population lead dissociated lives without being incapacitated. What makes the difference between a coper and a seeker, and what turns the former into the latter?

Mark Twain said that a cat that had once sat on a hot stove would never sit on one again - but he wouldn't sit on a cold one either. Having paid attention to an area of experience, and investigated it, only to receive a painful consequence, he becomes, naturally enough, disinclined to sample it again, for fear the same thing will happen. But this in itself will not make the cat unhappy: the loss of the ability to sit on the stove will not lead to a feline neurosis. The person who has successfully and completely withdrawn attention from an area of experience will not miss it. He might seem to others limited or bigoted in his construing and reacting, but he will not feel in need of help. No, the voluntary

client must be one who cannot entirely ignore the danger zones
of experience. There must be a chink in his armour of withdrawal
that lets a little of the anxiety-provoking feelings through into
consciousness.

Thus the person in trouble is one for whom the need to attend
to an experience, or his belief in the value of doing so, outweighs,
however slightly, his learnt tendency to ignore it. The cat is in
a much trickier position if, having had his bottom burnt, he discovers that the only food available is on a shelf above the stove.
Or if he has been trained by an eccentric owner to hump onto the
stove whenever he hears the jingle of the ice-cream van. Now he
is caught between approaching and avoiding, and it is this, in
animals and man alike, that is the breeding ground of distress.

But conflict is still not sufficient to cause neurosis: it is the unsuccessful attempt to deny conscious awareness of the conflict –
those states of awareness we call anxiety, confusion or blocking –
that cause the evasion piled on distortion piled on defence of the
overt sufferer.

We saw in the last chapter that children learn to defend in two
ways: by inhibiting their behaviour and by constricting their
conscious awareness. Correspondingly the symptoms with which
the client presents himself may be either 'objective' – to do with
a perceived strangeness in his overt actions – or 'subjective' –
arising from the breakthrough of forbidden feelings into consciousness and the conscious effort to prevent them – or both. The
typical neurotic client who seeks help voluntarily will certainly be
troubled by his experience. He may in addition show compulsive,
obsessional or phobic habits that he can neither comprehend nor
change. In contrast people who are committed to psychiatric care
by others, without their own consent or co-operation – the insane
as opposed to the merely distraught – usually show bursts of behaviour that are seen as cause for concern to others but not to
themselves. In such people especially the tacit workings of their
dissociated mind give rise to actions whose significance, strangeness, or even occurrence is not registered consciously. It is very
important to remember in this context that we can learn ways of
denying to conscious awareness the products of a bodily process
without inhibiting the process itself. It is very difficult to prevent
the publication of the way we feel, through gesture, posture,
intonation, particularly to an alert and sensitive audience: much
easier to fool ourselves. Part of the art of therapy, as we will
see, is in showing to the client aspects of the dislocation between
the self he experiences and the self he publishes (or leaks), but
without censure. The client has to allow his awareness to comprehend his dissociation, and embrace it.

How does a person come to be hoist with the petard of his own
defences? It seems to happen either through crises, or through a
slower, cumulative realization of the ways in which he traps himself. Defences were originally constructed against experiences of
a certain kind and a certain intensity. In times of crises such as
the death of a spouse or child, the loss of job or savings, divorce,

or other large and sudden change in the circumstances with which
a life-style has been designed to cope, and within which it has
been effective, the natural organismic reactions may flood consciousness with strange feelings, and one may find oneself acting
in ways that are 'out of character'. And while these primary reactions are healthy manifestations of the adjusting organism, the
secondary reactions of the 'character' to defend itself are pathological. If 'I' does not see itself as capable of weeping or raging
uncontrollably, it must try to batten down the hatches. In so
doing it prevents the system cleansing itself, and, like a wound
deprived of air, the grief festers and persists, unseen but un-
healed.

It is true that Dissociated Man's reactions to loss or change are
infantile: because he was not able to experiment with such feelings
when little, they have not had the chance of being developed and
incorporated into his repertoire of adapted acts, and remain raw,
extreme, incoherent and overwhelming. They frighten himself
and they frighten others. Strong feelings are the Third World of
experience, seeming impoverished, primitive and wild to the urbane
eyes of reason and perception. Yet their underdevelopment is
dependent on the repressive imperialism of the intellect. As with
other prejudices, if one treats one's own feelings, pre-emptively,
as savages, that is indeed how they will behave.

Everything depends, therefore, on how a man reacts to his own
crisis. He can defend, and lose. Or he can seize the opportunity
to grow nearer to himself: not to oppress his darkness and chaos,
but to live with it, learn its ways, allow it light, and watch it
grow. As a little seed can miraculously transform mud into a white
lily, so can the seed of awareness transform our hidden selves.
As Mahayana Buddhism says, 'The passions *are* the Buddha
Nature; the Buddha Nature *is* the passions.'

Alternatively people come to therapy as a result of creeping,
cumulative dissatisfaction with their ordinary life. They feel
lonely, out of touch with their family, unfulfilled at work, unable
to let go and have fun any more, and envious of those who can,
feeling old and tired, asking more and more urgently 'Is this all
there is?' There is no catharsis; just a gradual build-up of quiet
desperation, which, because it is resisted, intensifies into an
alternation between mild depression and the mild sexual and
alcoholic excesses of the suburban party or the residential con-
ference. If a person begins to be sensitive to the vacuum that
lies behind his shifts of mood, he may seek help before they
spawn their own explosion.

The potential psychotic, in contrast, defends all too well. Not
only is the lid on the pressure cooker, the steam vent is bunged
up as well. If the body cannot rebel against its increasing restriction, he may achieve the total cramp of catatonia. If the experience of the organism cannot break through at all into conscious
awareness he may reap empty wastes of complete depression, the
whirlwind of mania, or the psychedelic landscape of schizophrenic
fantasy. If the threads that tie him to a terrifying and meaningless

reality are severed, he can replace it at last with a cosmos of his
own invention that may not be always welcoming, but is at least
ordered.

    I once had a patient who used to practise the most horrible
tortures on himself, and when I asked him why he did such
things, he said, 'Why, before the world does them.' I asked
him then, 'Why not wait and see what the world will do,' and
he said, 'Don't you see? It always comes at last, but this way
at least I am master of my own distruction.'

(This and the following quotations are taken from Hannah Green's
autobiographical novel 'I Never Promised You a Rose Garden'.)

    There comes a point where so much data about the real world is
missing that it becomes subjectively chaotic. If I can only register
5 per cent of what is happening, of course events will seem
bizarre and inconsistent. Whereas the hallucinations of John Lilly,
suspended for hours in a tank of lukewarm water, are the organism's reaction to a real sensory deprivation, the hallucinations of
the madman arise from a deprivation for which he is himself responsible.

    All behaviour, weird or not, is an attempt by the organism to
get what it needs from the world it is in. Psychotic behaviour represents a more and more frantic search for satisfaction, acceptance, connectedness or understanding in a social world that has
consistently denied more 'normal' solutions. For example an
adolescent's circumstances are rapidly changing ones. His body is
changing shape, and a new area of feeling - sexuality - is emerging. From this arises the urgent mystery of what to do about the
opposite sex, as well as the demands that are being made on him
by peers and school to shed the familiar but constricting chrysalis
of his childhood and try out ways of being adult - life-style,
clothes-style, moral-style, ideas about career, and all the rest.
It is a time of transition and experimentation, as the pupa finds
out the kind of butterfly it can comfortably become. This in turn
demands that his parents accept the need to renegotiate their
relationship with him: the adolescent son or daughter, in changing, forms a changing part of their life that they have to learn to
handle.

    If parents refuse to enter into this negotiation, there will be
trouble. Their child has not suddenly become free of the need
for their love: this need remains a variable in what is now a more
complicated equation. He is not rejecting them lock, stock and
barrel (though they may construe his gambits and excesses as
such). Other goals have become desirable whose attainment seems
to demand behaviours that conflict with those his parents approve
of. And if both sides are prepared to make concessions, to try
out as yet unpredictable ways of being a family, the problem can
be resolved. But if Mum and Dad are too committed to their own
morality, to the exclusion of all others, or if they react to the
apparent rejection of themselves and their values by being puni-
tive, then no resolution is possible and the child cannot win. He
then has two choices. Either to suppress his own need for his

parents, and leave home, physically, psychologically or both. Or
he must conduct ever more speculative experiments with them. If
these mild changes do not work, perhaps more extreme ones will.
The stage is then set for a vicious circle of increasingly wild bids
from the adolescent and increasing fright, incomprehension and
rejection from the parents, who may eventually allow themselves
to voice the hidden fear: 'He's sick.'

> He laughed, and catching himself in the real
> enjoyment, said, 'My god - I laughed so
> much tonight. When before did I have so
> much fun!' And then: 'Has it really been
> that long? Years?'
>   'Yes, she said, 'it has been that long.'
>   'Then maybe it's true that she was . . .
> unhappy,' he said, thinking of Deborah.
>   'Sick,' Esther said.
>   'Unhappy!' Jacob shouted and left the
> room. He came back a few minutes later.
>   'Just unhappy!' he said.

This in turn produces a quantum jump for the worse, for the
parents now have a rationale for preserving their values by denying their child the right or ability to decide on his own. Disen-
franchised and depersonalized, the adolescent's model of himself
is shaken to the core. 'Are they right? Am I wicked and ungrate-
ful? Am I ill? *What* am I, that they talk about me in vacant voices
and avoid my gaze? That my sisters are kept from me, and the
bathroom cabinet suddenly locked? Is this what they mean by
mad?'

> Who had not heard all the old-style high melodrama of insanity;
> of the mad woman in *Jane Eyre,* of bedlam, of the hundreds
> of dark houses with high walls and little hope, of lesser dramas
> in lesser memories, and of maniacs who murdered and passed
> on the taints of their blood to menace the future? . . .
> People paid lip service to new theories and new proofs, but
> often their belief was no more than the merest veneer, yield-
> ing at a scratch to the bare and honest terror, the accretion
> of ten thousand years of fear and magic.

And fearful though this is, the adolescent, in urgent need of
an identity, an image of himself to replace the one he must relinquish, may accept it as being the only possible solution. 'If you
are ill, we can at last care for you, as we have wanted to, *because* you are ill.'

It is ironic that in the cleft between two falsehoods lies the
truth that the adolescent dare not embrace. If 'I' am not a 'child',
and yet not 'adult' either, if my actions and the reactions of
others are unpredictable, if people tell me 'I' am not responsible,
then what am I? As Laing says, in 'Self and Others':

> The schizophrenic does not take for granted his own person
> (and other persons) as being an adequately embodied, alive,
> real, substantial and continuous being who is at one place at
> one time and at a different place at a different time, remaining

the 'same' throughout. In the absence of this 'base' he lacks
the usual sense of personal unity, a sense of himself as the
agent of his own actions rather than a robot, a machine, a
thing, and of being the author of his own perceptions, but
rather feels that someone else is using his eyes, his ears, etc.
By not being able to defend himself he comes close to the truth
of his own integrity. Yet the last-ditch stand of his tuitions, and
of the universal conspiracy that he longs to rejoin, prevent him
from realizing it. Even now he must contrive an acceptable face,
albeit that of lunatic, and deny his accurate perception of the
lies that surround him.

Once again, suffering is caused not by the need for growth
but by the effort to resist it. In our example the description 'ill',
and its implied 'no one is responsible' is a cop-out for both parents
and child. Unfortunately it is one that is corroborated by the
psychiatric machinery. Only very rarely does a hospital refuse
to admit a person who is distressed and distressing to others. So
the professionals do not make the diagnosis of 'mentally disturbed';
they simply ratify one that has already been made within the
'patient's' lay community. However, through this tacit confirma-
tion, family and friends are vindicated. Their suspicions are con-
firmed, and they can shed, from their conscious minds at least,
the last doubts about their own role in the affair.

Jacob . . . whispered hard in his wife's ear, 'Why are we
sending her away?'

'The doctors say she has to go,' Esther whispered back,
lying rigid and looking towards the silent wall . . . 'It's a
good place,' she said, a little louder because she wanted to
make it so.

'They call it a mental hospital, but it's a place, Es, a place
where they put people away. How can it be a good place for a
girl - almost a child?'

'Oh, God, Jacob,' she said, 'how much did it take out of us
to make the decision? If we can't trust the doctors, who can
we ask or trust? Dr Lister says it's the only help she can get
now. We have to try it!'

It has been too easy to cast psychiatrists and especially parents
as the villains in a murder story, when they and the identified
patient are all victims in a much more moving tragedy. Many
parents sincerely believe they are doing their best: the tragedy
is that their best is pernicious because it grows out of their
sincere beliefs.

THE PROCESS OF THERAPY

Two premises underlie the rediscovery of integrity and its facilitation by psychotherapy. The first is that learning is an organismic process, not an ego process. It is not something 'I' do; it is
something that happens of itself. It happens in spite of I, not because of it. The second is that awareness is another name for the

subjective experience of learning. It is tempting to say that awareness produces, or causes, learning, but this is to separate the
two, and make one, awareness, responsible for the other, learning. In fact they are the phenomenal and the objective sides of a
single process. Whatever an organism is aware of, that is what its
learning is about. If it is not diverted, activity builds up in that
area of the central nervous system where learning is required:
modification or experimentation occur in that area in order to discover appropriate ways of construing and responding to the
world as it is found to be. We might imagine water flowing down a
hillside, and being temporarily blocked in its downward path by
falling into a depression in the ground. The flow is halted while
the water level rises, until eventually it overflows the depression
at the lowest point on its rim, and the stream then continues. We
do not have to describe the behaviour of the water in overcoming
the block as 'intentional', though we may, if we wish, call it
'intelligent'. The intelligence lies in the nature of water and of
ground, and in the interaction between the two. In just the same
way the interaction between experience and a nervous system is
intelligent. Learning occurs, to pursue the analogy, through the
gradual wearing away of the lip of the hollow to facilitate the
behaviour inherent in the water - flowing downhill.

The difference between water, and animals, on the one hand,
and man on the other, is that the former do not have to defend
themselves against the transient arrest of their flowing and their
knowing; nor do they have preset 'beliefs' about the right way to
meet this new situation that may impede the actual discovery of
the right way. The water may have picked up, upstream, some
deposits or chemicals that will influence the way it wears away
the new obstacle. It will have some previous 'learning'. But this
modifies how it meets the blockage, it does not teach it ways of
avoiding or denying its existence. And this is the central problem
to be overcome if a person is to rediscover and release his inherent
ability to learn, his own natural adaptability and intelligence. He
has first to allow his experience to flow into areas that may arouse
fear or ignorance. He must dare to be incompetent or afraid, for
only if he does so can he discover whether the learnt fears (of
rejection, ridicule, madness, failure and the rest) that cause his
felt fear are real or imagined. He has to be helped to experience
for himself the fact that he will not die if he disagrees with his
parents, that his tears may elicit warmth and not derision. He has
to see that his way of coping when he was small was fine then,
but that he lives in a different world now; one in which he is no
longer dependent for survival on the kindness of others. He must
learn stingingly, to the heart, the truth of Henri Bergson's
deadpan assertion that 'the tools of the mind become burdens when
the environment which made them necessary no longer exists.'

In short, behind every limitation a man has placed on his consciousness and his behaviour lies the expectation of a painful consequence. Only by triggering and running that expectation, and
remaining fully sensitive to what actually happens, can he begin

to unlearn it. If at any point he breaks and runs, the result can be counter-productive, for his foray into his own fear has thrown up still more fear, and if that is where he stops, that is what he will have learnt. His years of avoidance will be vindicated. But he still will not know if the fear is grounded in present reality or in a history that lives on purely in his own mind.

We have seen that the ideas of ego and of will depend for their maintenance on those processes of selective inattention that lie at the root of the psychological sufferer's problem. It is no surprise, therefore, that efforts of will serve to increase the distress, not to alleviate it. 'Come on now, pull yourself together', and its allied criticism 'I don't know what you're making such a fuss about: things aren't that bad', reinforce the sufferer's struggle to deny the reality of his own miserable experience, and thus perpetuate his misery. Distress is not in itself problematic: it is the effort to escape it that exacerbates it and tightens the noose. I do not have problems: 'I' creates problems by attempting to repress and evade experiences that 'I' thinks it ought not to have. Jung knew this, as all effective therapists do. 'Problems are not solved, they are transcended or outgrown. This process cannot be conjured into existence intentionally or by conscious willing, but rather seems to be borne along on the stream of time.' And he went on: 'I only know one thing: when my conscious mind no longer sees any possible road ahead, and consequently gets stuck, my unconscious psyche will react to the unbearable standstill.' Struggling, we drown all the quicker; braking, we increase the danger of the skid. This is the law of inverse effort that is so alien to our common sense, and lies at the heart of the therapeutic process.

Conscious deliberation is an inappropriate strategy in the context of therapeutic learning for a number of reasons. First, it presupposes the dissociation that only the organism acting in concert can hope to heal. Second, it has to follow its own familiar logic which instantiates the limits that have to be put to the test. No amount of journeying in thought can change the tramlines of thought itself. Third, the very language of thought, its words and grammar, are unsuited to the task of opening oneself to new aspects of the experience which those words and rules express. Fourth, the intention to be aware produces a linear and over-focused mode of awareness that prevents the simultaneous activity of the many different facets and associations of a pool of exploration. It inhibits the vital attitude that Carl Rogers calls *openness to experience,* and which he describes as 'a lack of rigidity and permeability of boundaries in concepts, beliefs, perceptions and hypotheses. It means a tolerance for ambiguity where ambiguity exists. It means the ability to receive much conflicting information without forcing closure on the situation.'

Nowhere is the attitude of openness to experience, of living life as a learner, more eloquently expressed than in a letter to Jung from one of his patients, which he quotes in his 'Commentary on *"The Secret of the Golden Flower"'*.

Out of evil much good has come to me. By keeping quiet, repressing nothing, remaining attentive, and by accepting reality - taking things as they are, and not as I wanted them to be - by doing all this, unusual knowledge has come to me, and unusual powers as well, such as I could never have imagined before. I always thought that when we accepted things they overpowered us in some way or other. This turns out not to be true at all, and it is only by accepting them that one can assume an attitude towards them. So now I intend to play the game of life, being receptive to whatever comes to me, good and bad, sun and shadow for ever alternating, and, in this way, also accepting my own nature with its positive and negative sides. Thus everything becomes more alive to me. What a fool I was! How I tried to force everything to go according to the way I thought it ought to.

The person who enters therapy is embarking on a funny sort of journey in which he will learn to suffer less by suffering more. He will learn that 90 per cent of his mental dis-ease is self-generated: it arises from the misguided attempt to avoid the other 10 per cent of painful experience that is actually inevitable. He learns that his refusal to allow himself to be hurt has resulted in an accumulation of scarcely tested expectations of disaster that stay with him. He has become what he has resisted. And conversely he discovers that an experience fully lived is one that leaves no trace, and that does not drag on to contaminate and stultify the future. And he learns - and this is very hard to take, if one does not know its truth - that 'could you keep your heart in wonder at the daily miracles of your life, your pain would not seem less wondrous than your joy.' Hermann Hesse recorded the same discovery in his diary in 1918.

Suffering only hurts because you fear it. Suffering only hurts because you complain about it. It pursues you only because you flee from it. You must not flee, you must not complain, you must not fear. You must love. You know all this yourself, you know quite well, deep within you, that there is a single magic, a single power, a single salvation, and a single happiness, and that is called loving. Well then, love your suffering. Do not resist it, do not flee from it. Taste how sweet it is in its essence, give yourself to it, do not meet it with aversion. It is only your aversion that hurts, nothing else. Sorrow is not sorrow, death is not death if you do not make them so! Suffering is magnificent music - the moment you give ear to it. But you never listen to it: you always have a different, private, stubborn music and melody in your ear which you will not relinquish and with which the music of suffering will not harmonize. Listen to me! Listen to me, and remember: suffering is nothing, suffering is illusion. Only you yourself create it, only you cause yourself pain.

It is almost impossible for a person on his own to discover these truths, for they are disallowed by the processes through which he meets his familiar world. They cannot, as should by now be clear, be set aside by an effort of will. But if by chance he finds himself in a different environment in which these processes do not

work, and in which he can allow himself to experience their not
working, then, gradually, unlearning can begin, and he may, if
he persists, taste the wisdom of insecurity. Situations of this
sort we call therapeutic. We now need to identify what their salient
characteristics are. We will consider first the traditional one-to-
one meeting between a therapist and a single client.

The therapeutic situation contains two sets of influences that
are, in practice, blended together. The first are background
conditions that undercut the client's normal expectations about
how he must be with other people, what he must do and say in
order to win their approval, and what he must conceal. One such
expectation is a resistance against being helped or asking for
help, for this, he may have learnt, is a sign of 'weakness', and
therefore unacceptable. The first major step - which the voluntary
client will have already begun to take - is to accept this weakness
in himself; to realize that he cannot do it on his own. And this is
more than just a necessary condition for learning to take place:
it can be a powerful example, in its own right, of the way he has
been ham-strung by his fears of rejection and failure. To learn
that he has the freedom to say 'Please help me', and that others
have the freedom to say 'Yes' or 'No'; that some people will say
'Yes' and not think the worse of him for having asked; and that
when others say 'No' the sky does not fall in - all these things
may be valuable insights and provide ways in to the underlying
causes of his distress.

A second surprise he gets, as soon as therapy starts, is that
he cannot use his normal strategies and games to win the acceptance of the therapist, for he already has it. There is nothing he
can do because there is nothing he has to do. The therapist's
acceptance of him is unconditional. Brought up on a diet of
pleasing people, this may be very difficult indeed for the client
to learn, and give rise to exaggerated forms of his usual attempts
to win - being charming, witty, flirtatious, submissive, helpless,
managing, or whatever. The expectancy that there are right ways
of behaving is grounded in the belief that there are wrong ways.
Thus if the client is having trouble pleasing the therapist, he
may resort to trying to displease him - to being hostile, threatening, sarcastic, deliberately stupid, or rude - in an unconscious
and perverse effort to keep the belief alive that somewhere, somehow, something is wrong with him. Often clients swing backwards
and forwards between the attempts to seduce and to shock, dis-
playing considerable ambivalence. Just as a class goes through a
process with a new teacher of finding out what goes and what
doesn't, so one of the prominent elements of the early stages of
therapy is often this compulsive attempt to test out and chart the
limits.

At some stage this process triggers another. It seems to be a
natural reaction to the frustration of a well-established belief
for the person's behaviour to become more energetic: he becomes
'frustrated', upset and either frightened or more often angry.
If a pigeon is taught to expect that pecking a red spot will get

him food, and suddenly it stops working, he too gets upset, and
will often attack another pigeon if there is one to hand. In the
case of therapy, the client may not know how to please the therapist, but he arrives with a firm belief that there *is* a way, and -
if he is socially adept - with a battery of techniques for exploring
the social scene without raising too much dust until he uncovers
the hidden 'contingencies of reinforcement'. Thus as he threatens
the foundations of his client's social belief system, so at the same
time the therapist is generating feelings of fear or anger that are
themselves disallowed by the client's social learning. The ensuing
mixture of threat, distrust and frustration makes more desperate
the client's needs to be accepted, and to defend against the
unacceptable churnings inside. Out of this stew the good therapist
may help his client to learn much, by holding up to him a mirror
which reflects the confused and confusing mesh of his own con-
triving, in which he is caught. The specific methods that the
therapist has at his disposal for doing this depend largely on his
training and theoretical persuasion. They constitute the second
set of influences present in therapy, and we shall discuss them
in more detail when we look at particular therapeutic schools.

Some further background effects need mentioning. As well as
feeling ashamed of having to seek help, clients may have constricting beliefs about 'talking about themselves'. On the one hand
they may have been taught that it is boring and selfish to hold
forth about oneself. One often finds people in casual discourse
apologizing for 'going on about me and my silly problems'. Again
this springs from the feeling that I, just as I am, am not good
enough, and generates an incredulity that anyone - even someone
being paid to listen - could be genuinely interested in the details
of my life. On the other hand the client may have picked up lay
beliefs about the dangers of introspection or of being too analytical
about oneself, and have the vague impression that such activities
are unhealthy, and lead to narcissistic, introverted, self-conscious
and self-critical turns of mind. This is based on the confusion that
learning about yourself means thinking about yourself, and constitutes another barrier to progress that can only be overcome
through the experience of acceptance and transcendence. Finally,
the fact that talking about oneself is pleasurable may in itself be
sufficient to make the client feel guilty about doing so.

As well as bringing general expectations about social relationships, many clients have a specific expectancy about the therapist,
which is that he is the one who is going to do most of the work and
who will generate the insights and conclusions. Because he is so
used to being told by others what is wrong or right with him, he
anticipates that the therapist will do the same. So he is in for another shock to his belief system when the therapist, as well as
refusing to tell him how to behave, also refuses to tell him how to
get better. Of course if the therapist could help the patient in
such a straightforward way, he would. He is not in business, if
he is any good, to play hide-and-seek with his client's psyche.
But unfortunately he will have learnt that it usually doesn't work.

Jung again points out that advice-giving is as typical of modern psychotherapy as bandaging is of modern surgery, and goes on, in his 'Principles of Practical Psychotherapy' to explain why.

If I wish to treat another individual psychologically at all, I must for better or worse give up all pretensions to superior knowledge, all authority and desire to influence . . . This becomes possible only if I give the other person a chance to play his hand to the full, unhampered by my assumptions . . . The therapist is no longer the agent of treatment but a fellow participant in a process of individual development.

And most post-Freudian therapists agree. Winnicott, for example, argues that 'psychotherapy of a deep-going kind may be done without interpretive work . . . the significant moment is that at which the [client] surprises himself or herself. It is not the moment of my clever interpretation that is significant.' Some therapies do involve giving the client instructions, as we shall see, but in the main he will be disappointed, and once more frustrated, if he comes expecting to be passive: to be cultivated rather than having to do the digging himself. Thus learning that *he* is responsible for finding the solution is another important sine qua non of successful therapy. It also prepares the client for understanding that he is responsible for the problem itself, and that the real work that has to be done is getting into what seems to him to be the problem, and not evading it by looking elsewhere for an easy remedy. His life, social and material, may indeed be difficult, but he has turned it into a psychological problem. And he needs no Mr Fixit. The trouble is he is too fixed already.

The client tends to see himself as a victim, while the therapist sees him as the misguided creator of his own distress. The client arrives expecting not only a cure, but sympathy. But if he wants the therapist to commiserate with him, and collude in blaming his troubles on a harsh and hostile world, he is in for another disappointment. The therapist's job is not to agree that the weather is awful, nor to read to the client from travel brochures, but to provoke him into making the journey to sunnier climates and greener fields himself. And to do that he must get the client to give up his psychological paralysis and rediscover the use of his own legs. One way to do this is to help the client to see the reasons which caused him to develop his paralysis: what desirable consequences were obtained, or undesirable ones avoided, by the decision to behave or perceive in this restricted way. 'What are you getting by being depressed or agorophobic?' may seem a stupid question to the client who can see only that he is getting upset. It may produce anger, a disenchantment with the therapist ('You're just the same as everyone else') or even a flight from therapy itself. But if the sternness of the therapist does not exceed the resources of the client, the latter may come to see the point.

The broadcasting of one's attitude about oneself happens both ways in therapy. The client leaks information about his self-image to the therapist, and the therapist projects his own attitude of

self-acceptance to the client. This is another important ingredient
of the therapeutic brew, for the fact that therapy constitutes a
novel kind of relationship for the client is largely because there
is a rather different kind of person on the other end of it. He is
someone who has himself travelled the dark path that awaits the
client and has made friends with the demons along the way. He
knows and does not fear his own violence, sadness, sexuality,
guilt and anxiety, and so is able to look with understanding and
unfrightened eyes at those things from which the client flinches.
And in so doing he becomes a model of someone who has seen monsters and lived, and one from which the client can take courage.
Medusa is the reification of the client's own dark side; he believes
that he, too, would be turned to stone - petrified - if he looked
at her. Yet here in front of him is a real-life Perseus over whom
she seems to have lost her power. Unseen terrors derive their
terror from being unseen: with a glance and then a look, the
terror fades away.

Learning by example is a potent force in childhood and remains
so in the adult. Not only have the child's attempts at imitation
found favour with his parents; once learnt, imitation provides a
source of hints about how to cope with uncertain situations. I
may not know how to get something I want, but if I watch other
people getting it I may find out how it's done. And as the child
has picked up the fears and inhibitions of those around him, so
the adult may begin to unlearn them by modelling the acceptance
he sees in his therapist. Thus the therapist's congruence, his
authenticity, his willingness to live whatever feelings, clear or
confused, are ascendant in him, moment to moment, can be a
source of guidance and inspiration. At first it may seem a most
unlikely idea to the client that by allowing his blocks and fears
he will overcome them, but in his desperation he may be prepared
to give it a try.

A word about 'the therapist'. The picture I have painted of him
may sound too good to be true. He does not live in a problem-
free, euphoric state of grace; he has not arrived anywhere, he is
a more experienced, less reluctant traveller. As Sheldon Kopp
says 'the psychotherapist can only be of help to that extent to
which he is a fellow-pilgrim.' He need not have solved all his
problems, but in the course of encountering them he will have
learnt a lot about his own dissociation, and in so doing will have
begun to heal it. In fact his own lack of perfection may be a positive advantage for his work as a therapist, for he will feel closer
in time and spirit to the struggles of his clients, and he will not
be out of sight of them. Too whole, or holy, a therapist may be
either unrecognizable to the client, or a source of intimidation or
despair. Take one of the 'ultimate therapists', Jesus. If he were
to appear as a New York taxi-driver, he would be seen by almost
no one. His divinity, if he did not preach, would be detectable
only in his supreme ordinariness. On the other hand the teachings
of the real Jesus have put him way out of reach. Christianity has
been so much in awe of him that to take his life and teaching as

an exhortation to become like him, to realize our own Christhood, is a blasphemy. We have to take him as a dead declaimer of a moral code, not a live example of an achievable integrity. Thus it is that many of today's spiritual pilgrims have started in therapy, as either therapists or clients, and have only been able to see the greater revolution latent therein after lengthy struggles with their own neuroses. Religious ambition has to stand on the shoulders of a growing tolerance for one's own small, secular self. 'Though the patient enters therapy insisting that he wants to change, more often than not what he really wants to do is stay the same', says Kopp. But if he takes up the challenge that the therapist offers, and if he is lucky, he may emerge with an inkling of his own integrity, and a thirst for more.

Before we move on to look at psychotherapeutic techniques, note that much of the learning we have discussed in the last few pages has nothing to do with the particular tale of woe with which the client presents himself. He comes expecting an ordinary meeting distinguished by unusual subject-matter, his problems. What he finds is a situation of unusual form in which the therapist refuses to play by familiar rules; and much of the therapeutic learning arises from his efforts to come to terms with this. Gradually he acquires an alternative mode of social conduct which requires him to question the premises that have generated and sustained his distress. He does not, in the end, solve his problems: he learns, through being in therapy, a new approach to himself and his life in the light of which his problems begin to dissolve.

TECHNIQUES OF THERAPY

I shall concentrate here on what therapists of different persuasions say they do in therapy, not their justification for doing it. I want to show that the action of these techniques can be understood within the approach to therapeutic learning that I have just outlined.

Client-centred and Experiential Therapy
I start with these because they have focused most closely on the background conditions for therapy. The fundamental tenets of client-centred practice are widely known, and although, as Eugene Gendlin points out, they are almost equally widely misunderstood, it would be superfluous to spell them out in detail again. According to Carl Rogers, if the therapist is *congruent* (that is, his conscious awareness grows out of his tacit construing, rather than being imposed on it, and he feels free to communicate that awareness); if he exhibits unconditional positive regard, or *nonpossessive warmth*, for the client (that is, he accepts and values the client for what he is without any implicit conditions or provisos); and if he is *empathic* (that is, he makes a real effort not to interpret what the client says and does, but to get inside his world and feel as closely as possible how things are for him), and

if the client both perceives these attitudes and feels a need to change, then that change will happen 'automatically', and will be towards a fuller, more open experiencing by the client of his own situation, feelings, values and needs.

It will be clear that, according to my view, the three therapist conditions described by Rogers are indeed central. The congruent therapist provides the client from minute to minute with a model of someone whose words and actions are based on a non-fearful awareness of his tacit, intuitive wisdom and feelings, even though such feelings may at times be painful. By communicating to the client his own ability to accept all parts of himself, the therapist implicitly reassures him that it will be all right for him to do the same.

Unconditional positive regard - in a phrase used by Rogers in a seminar over thirty years ago, 'an absolute respect for the dignity and integrity of the client' - acts as another 'background' condition. We saw earlier that being closed to certain areas of experience is due to the fear of losing the love or esteem of significant others if these areas were to be acknowledged. 'Positive regard', whether from parents, peers or teachers, is very often conditional: 'I would love you, but . . . ', 'I won't love you, unless . . . ', 'I might love you, if . . . '. To experience being valued without reservation gradually teaches the client that nothing he can tell the therapist endangers their relationship. And as he loses the fear of losing the therapist's esteem, so he comes to accept and value himself more highly. 'Hey!' he begins to think to himself, 'Maybe it is o.k. to be me. Maybe I'm not such a louse after all.'

Yet it seems that these two attitudes on their own can do no more than set the scene for growth. If the client has no tacit 'programs' for processing certain kinds of experience, eliminating the circumstances that led to the deficit will not make them magically appear. Two further things must happen. The client must be able to bring the deficient constructs and beliefs into conscious awareness, and the relevant experience must be encouraged to appear, so that he has the opportunity to modify and elaborate the beliefs and evaluate his modifications. Trust and receptivity are necessary for the former; empathic responses from the therapist greatly facilitate the latter.

It is worth quoting at length Rogers's recent description of empathy.

[Being empathic] means entering the private perceptual world of the other and becoming thoroughly at home in it. It involves being sensitive, moment to moment, to the changing felt meanings which flow in this other person, to the fear or rage or tenderness or confusion or whatever, that he/she is experiencing. It means temporarily living in his/her life, moving about in it delicately without making judgements, *sensing meanings of which he/she is scarcely aware, but not trying to uncover feelings of which the person is totally unaware, since this would be too threatening.* It includes communicating your sensings of

his/her world as you look with fresh and unfrightened eyes at
elements of which the individual is fearful. It means frequently
checking with him/her as to the accuracy of your sensings, and
being guided by the responses you receive. You are a confident
companion to the person in his/her inner world. By pointing to
the possible meanings in the flow of his/her experiencing you
help the person to focus on this useful type of referent, to
experience the meanings more fully, and to move forward in the
experiencing.

To be with another in this way means that for the time being
you lay aside the views and values you hold for yourself in
order to enter another's world without prejudice.

It does not need stressing that this type of responding, if successful, fulfils the necessary conditions for growth. The therapist's responses must take off from, and continually return to,
the client's own experiencing, albeit experiencing of which he is
only dimly aware. To go beyond that into the realm of guesswork
and inference, however sophisticated, is to lose touch with the
client, and to try and pull him towards an external 'interpretation' of his dis-ease. Alan Watts too, in his comparison of Western
psychotherapy with Eastern approaches to liberation or 'enlightenment' called 'Psychotherapy East and West', stresses the importance of helping the client to explore his own meanings, and draw
out his own implications.

The way of liberation is the way 'down and out'; it is taking,
like water, the course of least resistance; it is by following the
natural bent of one's feelings; it is by becoming stupid and
rejecting the refinements of learning; it is by becoming inert and
drifting like a leaf on the wind . . .

There is an obvious parallel here with the philosophy of Carl
Rogers' non-directive therapy, in which the therapist simply
draws out the logical conclusions of his client's thinking and
feeling by doing no more than rephrasing it in what seems to
be the clearest form . . . The therapist himself is therefore
'stupid' and 'passive' like a Taoist in that he has no theory of
what is wrong with his client, or what he ought to become in
order to be cured.

Psychotherapy, suggests Watts, is more like judo than a fist-
fight. The way to help someone change the deep-seated, but ultimately crippling, assumptions by which he is living is not to
challenge them head-on, but to accept them and encourage them,
so that they are eventually brought down by their own momentum.

Just as this view of psychotherapy has little time for interpretation, so it gives equally short shrift to aetiology. Jung again:

Freud emphasises the aetiology of the case and assumes that
once the causes are brought into consciousness the neurosis
will be cured. But mere consciousness of the causes does not
help any more than detailed knowledge of the causes of war
help to raise the value of the French franc.

Although this is somewhat unfair to Freud himself, the general
point is sound. The client comes to psychotherapy because his

ways of construing, and repertoire of action strategies, are inadequate now, and even though these have arisen from traumas or subtler campaigns of attrition in his history, they have to be changed now. The goal of psychotherapy is a change in process, not in knowledge, and the latter by no means guarantees the former.

But having said that, there is one proviso, which we shall have to spell out clearly when we look at techniques like Kelly's 'fixed role therapy', or Behaviour Therapy. The proviso is that while we cannot initiate change by presenting a client with statements about his problem, we may be able to by giving his implicit (or explicit) commands about how he is to behave. We shall pick this up later.

Aldous Huxley has said 'Watching and receiving in a state of perfect ease is an art which can be cultivated, and should be taught on every educational level from the most elementary to the most advanced'. The work of Eugene Gendlin on what he calls 'experiential psychotherapy' represents the main attempt in Western psychotherapy to teach this art explicitly, so that clients can acquire for themselves a skill that usually remains with the therapist. It is worth noting both the 'Western' and the 'psychotherapy', for this art is well-known in the East, and in certain aspects of Western life that are not usually linked with psychotherapy.

Gendlin's main technique for doing this is called *focusing,* and is a direct attempt to teach people how to achieve that state of receptiveness described by Huxley. Focusing involves asking yourself 'What's wrong?' and then shutting up. Conscious awareness centres not on thought, but on that area of one's body where one usually feels things - often but not always the stomach. By attending to that place, in a quiet, non-selective manner, one allows a felt sense of a whole problem to emerge. Words and images may bubble up from this sense, but they must not be imposed on it. Such conscious products are not experienced simply as descriptions or conceptualizations of the problem, but as integral parts of its developing nature. If the concrete, bodily felt meanings, and their verbal or imaginal products are accepted in this way, then movement in the direction of greater clarity and release from the trap of one's own conceptualizations automatically occurs. And conversely, claims Gendlin, any therapy will be ineffective to the extent it fails to base itself firmly in this bodily experience, which brings feeling and thinking together in a creative union. Concentration on either the expression of feeling or cognitive insight alone is valueless. And the state in which this union can occur is wise passiveness.

What the client-centred or experiential therapist is after is not a solution to a problem, but a change in functioning. The 'solution' comes almost incidentally, as it were, as part of the much longer enterprise of giving to the client ways of assessing and 'playing with' his tacit constructs, and of giving back to him the confidence in his own needs, experiences, feelings, values,

intuitions and impulses that he lost when he was small. He needs
to be convinced of the truth of the first (and fundamental) Article
in Manuel Smith's 'Bill of Assertive Rights', which reads: 'You
have the right to judge your own behaviour, thoughts and emotions and to take the responsibility for their initiation and consequences upon yourself.' Rogers lists some of the changes that
occur in successful psychotherapy as the following:

> The person comes to see himself differently. He accepts himself
> and his feelings more fully. He becomes more self-confident and
> self-directing. He becomes more the person he would like to be.
> He becomes more flexible, less rigid, in his perceptions. He
> adopts more realistic goals for himself. He behaves in a more
> mature fashion . . . He becomes more acceptant of others. He
> becomes more open to the evidence, both to what is going on
> outside of himself and to what is going on inside of himself.
> He changes in his basic personality characteristics, in construc-
> tive ways.

It must be clear that Rogers's and Gendlin's approaches to
psychotherapy are very close to mine. They are, though, more
magical in that they make no attempt to explain how the conditions
of therapy lead to the observed outcomes, something I have been
at pains to do in this chapter. Rogers has not, I think, been
aware of the extent to which the client learns from the therapist
by modelling his authenticity and acceptance. Nor, following on
from this, has he stressed that therapy is not an absence of
usual rules and constraints, but a positively different situation;
and that the client learns a lot from learning how to handle it.

Where Gendlin improves on Rogers is in seeing that congruence,
warmth and empathy are necessary in therapy, and may be sufficient on their own: but if they are present then other, more
forceful, more directive interventions and suggestions by the
therapist can speed things up. Techniques and skills are no substitute for a genuinely warm and open personality in a therapist,
but a warm and open therapist may well use techniques to good
effect, if they arise from, and are constantly referred back to
the therapist's accurate and attentive understanding of the client's
experience. That is to say, the therapist who is 'moving about
delicately' in the client's world may find an impulse or suggestion
pop into his head. If he is already in his own head, trying to
think up a suitable technique, he cannot at the same time be sensitive to the flux of the client. The immediacy of the therapist's
intervention is vital, for the subtlety of its timing is usually much
more important than the sophistication of its content. Once he
gets caught up in thinking what to do, or trying to be congruent,
or savouring his own insight, his technique or his attempt at
genuineness will be phoney. It is his presence - in both senses
of the word - that lays the foundation for therapy.

It might well have been better for clients everywhere if Carl
Rogers had not put his finger so accurately on the qualities of
the person it is good to be with. For they are not things you can
do; they are only things you can be. Unfortunately once they

were written down as a description of the qualities that Rogers
saw in himself, they automatically became seen as prescriptions
for therapeutic efficacy, and thus another set of beliefs that
stand in the way of 'genuine authenticity'. Hemingway might have
been thinking of the Rogerian Trinity when he wrote: 'There are
some things which cannot be learned quickly, and time, which is
all we have must be paid heavily for their acquiring. They are
the very simplest things and because it takes a man's life to know
them the little new that each man gets from life is very costly and
the only heritage he has to leave' (from 'Death in the Afternoon').
Rogers's heritage is treasure indeed but paradoxically it has been
devalued by being unburied.

Psychoanalysis and Analytical Psychology
Many therapies have as a major ingredient the undercutting of
normal habits of interaction, and the psychoanalytic traditions
are no exception. If the therapist finds it helpful to suppress
the usual non-verbal signals of interest or approval, but cannot
trust himself to do so, one answer - the classical Freudian one -
is to sit where the client cannot see you. The client is then unable either to turn to the therapist for clues about what he should
be saying or doing, or to use the therapist as a source of changing stimulation with which to avoid himself. Unable to use any
actual clues about the therapist's mood or reactions, those that
he attributes to the therapist become more pure reflections of his
own habitual projections about other people - particularly people
who, like parents, seem to hold some psychological authority.
This encouragement of the client to exhibit and live his fantasies
in his relationship with the therapist - the so-called 'transference
neurosis' - is the most characteristic method, or anti-method,
perhaps, of classical analysis. Without telling the client that his
projections are absurd, the therapist can, in gentle ways, allow
the client to discover that he creates trouble for himself by
peopling his world with the ghosts of past disappointments. He
can then be helped to follow the strings that are hobbling his
perception back into the past where the fetters were first tied,
and, by exposing them to the corrosive power of awareness,
allow them to dissolve. Again we see the two-stage strategy of
creating a scenario that activates problematic beliefs, and then
easing the client's awareness towards their manifestations.
    While transference forms the foundation of analysis, two specific
types of thread are used to uncover the sources of distress: they
are free associations and dreams. 'Free' associations are free in
the sense that they are not determined by conscious or intentional
habits of thought: they are clearly not free in the sense of being
random. Imagine a chain of ideas, such as:

$$K \longrightarrow L \dashrightarrow M$$
$$L \longrightarrow N$$

in which K is 'safe' - i.e. neutral or unthreatening, L has come
to act as a signal for the uncomfortable or disturbing idea or
experience M, and N is a safe alternative to M, triggered by L,

which avoids the disturbance. Now in the normal course of events,
the flow would go from K to L to N, and M, the problem, would
never surface. But in the unusual circumstances of therapy,
where the therapist does not collude with or reinforce the evasion
N, and where the client's discomfort is acceptable, N may itself
be blocked, and the client find himself 'stuck' at L. L is thus
exposed as a possible antecedent of a threat, and if the client
can allow his blockage to exist, and not flee from it, awareness
concentrates at L and will eventually flow into the suppressed
area M, with accompanying fear and subsequent acknowledgment
and resolution. Thus it is, as analysts know, the words on which
a client halts or hesitates that are significant, not - as in the
party game corruption of free association - the idiosyncratic or
even bizarre nature of his association. Likewise, the value of the
process lies not in the exercise given to the therapist's or the
client's intellects in trying to puzzle out an ingenious interpretation of association or block, but in the experiential fact of being
stuck, and staying stuck. Jung, as usual, has an accurate diagnosis of the futility of these intellectual word games.

To 'analyse' the unconscious as a passive object has nothing
hazardous about it for the intellect - on the contrary such an
activity would correspond to rational expectation; but to 'let
the unconscious happen' and to 'experience' it as a reality -
that exceeds the courage as well as the ability of the average
Occidental. He prefers simply not to realize the existence of
the problem. The *experience* of the unconscious is, namely, a
personal secret communicable only with difficulty, and only to
the very few (from 'Integration of the Personality').

Unfortunately the products of the unconscious do, when they are
not too disturbing, pose fascinating challenges to our rational
powers of understanding that the educated brains of psychotherapists find difficult to resist. And if this applies to a client's
associations, it applies a fortiori to his dreams.

Although Freud and Jung disagree in claiming that dreams derive more from the client's past or present respectively, they are
certainly a rich source of information about the underlying nature
of his distress, which the client can be encouraged to take
seriously, and reflect on. Both Freud and Jung have, I think
rightly, been criticized for imposing too many of their own beliefs
and preconceptions on their clients' dreams. But my own suspicion is that this intrusion figured much more largely in their
theoretical writings than in their therapeutic sessions - and that
they were the more effective therapists as a result. Change in
the client is only imminent when he is confronted by his own
experience of his limitations and their symptoms. Thus for a dream
to be recounted and discussed is as beside the point as are simple
recitations of the client's woes. Unless the dream is not recalled
but relived, it lacks the charge, the energy and involvement that
is the potential source of salvation. Gestalt therapy, which we
turn to in a moment, has evolved ways for the therapist to help
the client re-experience his dreams, and to feel his way more

deeply into their significance. I have written further about an
alternative approach to dreaming in Chapter 9 and will not say
any more here.

In addition, Jung has given us the technique that he called
'active imagination', in which clients are encouraged to produce
creative works - poems, pictures, sculptures, etc. - on which
they can then reflect. Just as with dreams, these creatures contain much more than the creator either knew or intended: many
of their aspects reflect tacitly held beliefs. So here again we
have a way of gently confronting him with aspects of his performance that may well point to properties of just those misconceptions
or assumptions which underlie his distress.

Gestalt Therapy
Although the theoretical rationale of Gestalt therapy is strikingly
different from the psychodynamic therapies, some of the techniques it uses are similar - and as the purpose of this section is to
demonstrate a technical consensus between different therapies
underlying a wide theoretical diversity, it is on the techniques
that we shall focus.

Fritz Perls, like Freud, Jung and others before him, makes much
of dreams, assuming that they, like Jung's patients' creations,
provide externalizations of the products of the tacit 'construct
system' which can then be drawn into conscious awareness. His
distinctive contribution is a structured way of doing this: the
client is asked to recount the dream and then elaborate it by
taking the part of various elements, both animate and inanimate,
and both central and apparently incidental, and speaking for
them. Under the guiding hand of the therapist the tacit beliefs
and concerns behind the dream content are persuaded to dis-
close themselves to the client's conscious scrutiny. The therapist
does not claim to 'know' what the dream means, only how to help
the client to coax out his meaning; and like the client-centred
therapist he trusts in the therapeutic value of this activity in itself. 'Paradoxically, behavioural changes result from the acknowledgement and acceptance of how one is at any given moment
rather than through declaration of intention, promising oneself
or another to do better, etc.', wrote James Simkin in 1975.

As with the elaboration of dreams, the client may be asked to
hold fantasy conversations between two parts of himself, or himself and another. Again, to the extent that he 'gets into' the
exercise - i.e. can overcome self-consciousness - unconsciously
held beliefs may spontaneously appear. Psychodrama is effective
for the same reasons.

An interesting technique, peculiar to Gestalt, is gesture-
exaggeration. A client may be unconsciously crossing and un-
crossing his legs, sniffing, playing with his tie or prefacing his
utterances with a little laugh: the therapist picks such things
up and asks the client to repeat the action in an exaggerated
form. Often this prompts an insight when the client is forced
to confront head-on the previously tacit feelings and attitudes

that are leaking out in such gestures.

Behaviour Therapy and Fixed Role Therapy
We turn now to two examples of therapeutic practice that seem
rather different, behaviour therapy and behaviour modification,
and Kelly's 'fixed role therapy'.

First we may note that behaviour therapy shares a crucial
assumption with the humanistic therapies: that both the cause
and resolution of psychological distress are 'not really in one's
head or one's body, but in one's living' as Gendlin put it. One's
actions are jointly determined by one's situation and one's 'history of reinforcement contingencies' in similar situations. The
representation of this history inside the person is his map, or
construct system, as Kelly calls it. Skinner is at pains to point
out that the vast majority of this history is unavailable to conscious inspection: it is tacit. To attribute the causes of behaviour
to that fraction of our histories, and the feelings and thoughts
with which it is associated, which is available to consciousness
is a gross distortion of the truth. Behaviour therapy is theoreti-
cally not as different from other forms of therapy as is usually
supposed.

And, as one behaviour therapist put it, there is a growing
realization that, in practice, 'behaviour therapy is not as simple
and straightforward as its popular stereotype would imply. Clinical inference and sensitivity to a [client's] needs are equally
important. When used with sensitivity behaviour modification can
result in meaningful changes in a [client's] total functioning.'

How then shall we construe what behaviour therapy is and does?
One way is similar to Bannister and Fransella's characterization
of Kelly's 'fixed role therapy' in their book 'Inquiring Man'. If a
client is stuck in a conceptualization of himself as someone possessing certain fixed habits (stuttering, obsessional activities etc.),
which 'talking therapy' seems unable to shift, he is asked to
create and then act out a character that he finds plausible but
different from himself. In effect he is given a conscious set of
beliefs about himself that he has to substitute for his existing
ones - which were previously tacit, but which may, by this stage
in therapy, be partially available to consciousness. The principle
on which this technique rests is that not only do our constructs
determine how we act, but also how we act determines how we
construe ourselves. Thus although the client starts off playing
a conscious and alien role which he does not 'own', none the less,
if he is consistent, he has to come to construe himself, if not as
this new person, at least as someone who is capable of acting in
ways other than those issuing from the previous, stereotyped
self-image. And this may be enough to loosen these constructs
sufficiently for change to occur. 'We are what we pretend to be,
so we must be careful about what we pretend to be', as Kurt
Vonnegut warns in his Introduction to 'Mother Night'. And Michael
Frayn makes the same point in a more picturesque way in his
'Constructions'.

Tentatively - as a joke, because it's spring - the oak sapling throws out small shoots all over the place without a second thought. But in time the tree has to follow in all seriousness these paths which it has laid down for its own development, growing massively into their capriciousness, and so taking on the fantastic gnarled shape of its maturity.

Implicit in these quotations is a second reason why this way of prompting change is a potent one: it takes the onus of responsibility off the client. He does not have to decide when, where, why or how to act differently: he is told, and all he has to do is to go along with it, or not. Whether he does play his new role seriously depends presumably on the appropriateness of the alternative and the sensitivity and care (in both senses) with which the therapist offers it.

Construed in this way, the client's behavioural experiments are a means, not an end. The goal, just as with the techniques previously discussed, is the opening up and development of an impoverished and ossified area of tacit construing or belief. The 'humanistic' techniques attempt to do this by gently confronting the client with the spontaneously emitted behavioural symptoms of these tacit constructs. The 'behavioural' techniques persuade him to act 'artificially', and then help him to realize that (a) he is capable of acting in this new way, and (b) this way of acting is actually better than his old way. Modification of belief via conscious awareness of behaviour occurs in both cases.

Clearly this analysis can apply to behaviour therapy as much as to fixed role therapy: but are such convolutions necessary? Traditionally behaviour modification and behaviour therapy are seen as simple effects of conditioning, and talk of cognitive processes is superfluous. Fortunately it does seem as if some explanation in terms of 'higher mental processes' is needed. Brewer gives us his conclusion, based on a wide survey of the literature, in the title of his 1974 paper: There is no Convincing Evidence for Operant or Classical Conditioning in Adult Humans. His overall finding is that either subjects perceive what is expected of them, and collude with the expectation, in which case 'conditioning' occurs, or else they either do not perceive what is required, or they do, but decide not to go along with it, in which case no evidence for 'conditioning' appears. Whatever we do is a filtrate of awareness and belief.

Rational-Emotive Therapy

Although Albert Ellis's rational-emotive therapy (RET) stems from a philosophy that is quite close to the present one, its practice is quite different, being perhaps the most directive, almost bullying, of all therapeutic systems. Ellis himself describes the aims in a paper in 1975, as being 'to *confront* [the clients] with their magical philosophies, to explain how these cause disturbance, to *attack them vigorously* on logic-empirical grounds and to *teach* people how to change and eliminate disordered thinking' [my emphasis]. The transcript he presents shows the therapist,

who does nearly all the talking, haranguing the client on the
irrational basis of his problem. It is as if the therapist is trying
to force a change in the client's functioning by sheer verbal
strength, volume and persistence - a perfect example of the kind
of stand-up fight that most other therapies lean over backwards
not to be. Yet there is evidence that the violent actions of an
Ellis and the quiet reactions of a Carl Rogers can both promote
therapeutic growth. How come?

The first point to note about RET is that it is not just a rational
onslaught. Tuition is provided only in the context of, and in
relation to, the perceived problems of the client. Ellis is as aware
as anyone else that unless the teachings are planted in soil that
is rich in emotional nutrients, it will not 'take'. Secondly, the
insights that the therapist provides are followed up with exercises
designed to make their value apparent to the client through his
own experience. He may be shown in a therapy session, for
example, that he tends to 'awfulize' experiences of rejection that,
while unpleasant, do not actually provide good evidence for his
inference that he is 'a worthless, unlovable, no good bastard'.
His ability to differentiate between rational and irrational reactions
(defined as those that help or hinder, respectively, his discovery
of what is so, and what works in life) may then be developed
through exercises provoking shame in a therapy group, or through
homework assignments, somewhat like Kelly's fixed-role plays,
that require him to go through the situations he fears, and allow
himself to witness what happens, instead of being freaked by it.

Ellis does not beat about the bush. 'Emotional disturbance is
little more than another name for devout religiosity, intolerance,
whining, dogmatism, magical thinking and anti-scientism; . . .
if people rigorously follow the logical-empirical approach and
forego all forms of magic and absolutism it is virtually impossible
for them to be seriously disturbed.' One symptom of these
counter-productive traits is sloppy use of language: RET teaches
people to speak more accurately and honestly. 'I can't do it' becomes 'I won't do it'; 'You made me angry' becomes 'I made myself
angry at your performances and wrongly concluded that you were
a louse for doing them'; 'It is awful that this has happened' becomes 'It is highly inconvenient that this has happened'; and so
on. As with fixed-role therapy, a change in verbal habit does
not directly cause a change in the underlying cognitions and
beliefs, but it does so indirectly through a constant process of
friction. The new way of speaking becomes a constant rasp that
gradually wears down (we use the metaphorical expression 'grates
on') old habits of thought with which they conflict. One cannot
continue to see oneself as a victim if one is saying 'won't' rather
than 'can't'.

Perhaps the most valuable (and the most eastern) insight of
RET is that, whatever the person thinks his problem is, that is
not the problem. His reaction to his problems, his way of construing himself, his beliefs about failures or setbacks - these are
the problems. Thus RET 'is a form of psychological treatment

that usually aims for basic philosophical restructuring, hence for far-reaching personality change'. And its goal is not only to 'cure' the client of his symptom 'but to significantly minimize his or her disturbability and the consequent chances of the return of this or any other symptom'. Any apparent problem will do for the therapist to begin to show the client his tendency to turn events into problems by viewing them through a mask of archaic and inaccurate beliefs. As Ellis acknowledges, both his philosophy and methodology owe much to Kelly: his distinctive contribution is the explicitness, directness and rigor of the therapist's didactic attack on the client's bad theory about how he is or ought to be. At the same time, of course, he must be shown how to test his theory for himself, by (a) dis-identifying with his beliefs (they are all subject to experimental verification or falsification); and (b) reclaiming his ability to attend fully to the data on which those tests depend: his own experience.

Encounter
The last Western methodology of improvement we look at in this chapter differs in two ways from the therapies we have discussed up to now. First, encounter groups, as the original practical offering of the 'Human Potential Movement' to the world, were designed not to make distressed people less unhappy, but normal, 'healthy' people more happy. The ethos of encounter is not escaping but becoming, not push but pull. Second, an encounter group is a social situation more akin to a party than an interview. The declared aim is for participants to experiment with their beliefs about themselves and others by taking risks in their interactions with about a dozen 'ordinary' others. This is carried on, as a rule, with the assistance, support and direction (although this latter may be minimal) of a 'facilitator', as he is usually known. In the original format devised by Carl Rogers - what is now called the 'basic' encounter group - the role of the facilitator was merely to set the background conditions described earlier in this chapter, so that group members would simultaneously have their evasions undermined, and dare to express the fears, hurts and resentments that lay underneath. While people sometimes complain that the freedom of the encounter laboratory is artificial, it nevertheless provides a less insulated atmosphere than one-to-one therapy. The good facilitator, like a good parent or a good driving instructor, can be trusted to permit exploration, but also to ensure that the explorer does not do himself real harm. Yet within this security, a group member does have to take responsibility for his actions and the repercussions of those actions: they are 'real people' out there, with real feelings, taking real risks, just like him.

Encounter groups have had a mixed, and often hostile, reception in the world at large. To some they are a bizarre kind of circus in which an unqualified, Machiavellian, irresponsible and power-crazy ringmaster goads a group of people who don't know any better into parting with their money, and baring their teeth,

their souls and their bodies at each other. To others, as I have
described, they are warm and intimate havens within which a per-
ceptive, understanding and caring leader helps people to explore
and develop themselves and their relationships with others. The
truth is, as research has demonstrated, that at best they are the
latter, at worst - happily rather rarely it turns out - the former,
and often somewhere in between. There is no doubt that entering
therapy, especially an intensive experience like encounter, is a
risky business, for if the process is to work one must have some
degree of trust in the therapist/facilitator, and it is always possible for this to be misplaced. It is perhaps necessary to make a
few comments here on the dangers inherent in the search for self-
improvement to counter-balance any rosiness or over-enthusiasm
conveyed in this and the following chapter.

THE PILGRIM'S PITFALLS

Let us look a little further at how the relationship between the
seeker and his mentor can go wrong. (The word 'mentor' is as
near as one can get to a neutral descriptor for the therapist/
facilitator/guide/guru/Master.) First, the mentor may be a conscious villain, who is in the game for power, prestige, or, most
likely, money. The welfare of the seeker is quite secondary to
the achievement of these goals. Whether or not he has the ability
to deliver any goods, he lacks a personal commitment to doing so.
There are, of course, such cynical villains about, though far
more numerous are those who have deceived themselves as well
as their customers, and are convinced of their own rectitude.
Such people's commitment is to being helpful, but their skills are
inadequate and their real motives dubious. The seeker is in danger of being ripped-off financially and/or mucked-up mentally by
these shysters and zealots. For they will lead him out beyond his
normal limits into the volcanic waste of his own horrors and then
leave him there, either because they care not, or dare not stay
with him. And whenever a therapist or a guru's actions become
fogged by disintegration arising from his own desire or fear, he
becomes a liability.
  Therapists - especially analysts and psychiatrists - get very
tricky about this, and hide behind a barrier of 'professional
expertise' and jargon. A common twist is for any query about the
therapist's authority or motivation, or even any wish to know anything about him as a person ('Do you have any children?'), to be
taken as diagnostic of defensiveness, reaction or lack of understanding by the seeker ('That's interesting . . . I wonder why
you would want to know that?'). Such a response may be part of
a benign gambit. All too often it reflects an automatic set of Do's
and Dont's that the therapist brings to the encounter with him,
and that are no less rigid, counter-productive, self-preservative
and neurotic than those of his client. They enable him to keep
control and to hide. The professional smugness of these people,

their clever manipulativeness, their condescension and their unshakeable faith in their own rightness and benevolence is quite
appalling, and unrivalled by any other profession, including
medical consultants, lawyers and politicians. Their patron saint
must be Chaucer's Pardoner.

A further risk with these 'experts' is that they use their char-
isma to generate not autonomy in their customers but dependence
– a pitfall which many seekers are only too ready to fall into. The
convenient myth of the lengthy analysis – 'We can't really expect
any change in the first year' – keeps the money coming in and
the disciples at the feet. Signs of impatience or dissatisfaction
are again taken as aspects of the therapeutic 'work' rather than
legitimate charges from one adult to another.

If establishment psychiatry is infested with smooth men, the
newer therapies and the growth movement have the hairy ones.
They generate their dependency not by promising and delivering
a skilfully packaged nothing, but by substituting for therapeutic
growth periodic firework displays. After a week-end of telling
people what you don't like about them, crying, screaming and
murdering cushions, most people feel good – relaxed, cleansed,
receptive and honest. By Thursday they are wondering where it
all went, whether it was real, and when the next group is. There
is certainly an exhilaration in 'catharting', as there is in motor-
racing, deep-sea diving, hang-gliding or karate, and, for someone who has previously been incapable of crying, let us say, it
is significant to discover that he can do it. But that general recognition is just a beginning, an eye-opener, that lays the ground
for reclaiming and reintegrating a lost portion of one's capacity
into one's active self. To learn, as we have seen, one must be
receptive to an action and its consequences, and to get lost in a
solipsistic expression of emotion is as unproductive as to sit
around analysing why one feels depressed. Once one has the
ability to be a way, the bulk of the learning comes in finding out
the antecedents and consequences that attend being that way.
One of Gurdjieff's ploys was to bait one of his students into fury
and then suddenly say, 'Just watch! Continue being angry, but
be aware of what is happening; what is happening inside you and
in the room.' Instead of being swept away by the feeling, the
student became aware of it in its context, and it is this awareness, as we have seen, that is the necessary and sufficient condition for learning what is so. Many mentors, present and past,
have worked with feelings, but the good ones see that they are
a vehicle, not a destination. The Human Potential Movement has
been rightly criticized for being obsessed with emotionality as an
end in itself, and this has unfortunately bred a rather crude
anti-intellectualism. 'Get out of your head, man; get into your
feelings', has been the battle cry, and it has attracted more
people than it has helped.

Growth has become the growth industry, and therapies and
groups are advertised with the same enthusiasm and disregard for
the facts as snake oil. Heaven is just a weekend away, and This

Book Will Change Your Life. It is another pitfall to be seduced by
this glitter. Although I have criticized psychoanalysis for taking
too long, it is equally disingenuous to offer instant enlightenment.
To open oneself up to oneself, to experience and heal one's con-
tradictions and dislocations is not a quick or easy thing to do,
and the creation of false expectations can and does lead people to
follow the growth circuit, from one high-cum-disappointment to
the next, in search of the one that really works. And there is
plenty to choose from: encounter, bioenergetics, massage, pos-
tural integration, enlightenment intensives, rolfing, *est*, primal
scream, rebirthing (three kinds), transactional analysis, sufi
dancing, tai chi, Alexander, reflexology, shiatsu, transcendental
meditation, zazen, regression, Reichian bodywork, psychosyn-
thesis, gestalt groups, marathons, synanon, . . . the list is endless. Carried away by promises of increased self-confidence,
better orgasms and more satisfying relationships, it is hard not
to pick up the idea that the good life is eternally happy and
problem-free. This attitude generates good business for the
industry, because it makes the punter even more dissatisfied with
his own confused little life, and ensures his constant return. The
growth movement is successful because it appeals to people's
stupid idealism, escapism and need for security just as the football pools or fruit-machines do. The difference is the former pays
out happiness directly while the latter pay out money with which
you can buy happiness. The trouble is that people become so preoccupied with becoming some way, or stopping being some other
way they lose sight of the way things are. And seeing more and
more clearly the way things are, without any intention to have
them be different, is the only way in which they will become different. It is only through engaging with what is that I can find
out what works.
   An associated pitfall is mistaking the glitter for the gold, and
adopting the language, mannerisms and style of the particular
outfit one happens to be following while missing the essence. The
function of these styles is usually to affiliate the seeker to a
group of nice people he feels accepted by, and also to provide a
ready-made barrage of 'psycho-babble' with which to ward off
the philistines, and to defend oneself in general. The style is not
a way of being more open but a new way of staying closed. R.D.
Rosen's book called 'Psychobabble', and Cyra McFadden's 'The
Serial' ridicule the verbal and behavioural mannerisms of the
'groupies' delightfully. 'I'm coming from a really heavy anger
space right now' adds rather little to either the beauty or the
effectiveness of communication.
   The life-styles associated with different therapies and methods
vary widely. The encounter-culture tends to produce the Instant
Hug and the Deep Meaningful Look - both of which can become as
empty as 'How do you do?' and a perfunctory hand-shake. As
Rosen says, 'honesty or being "up front" is generally a good
policy but it can also become a nervous habit or a subtle petition
for someone else's confession to which one has no right.' The

followers of Bhagwan Shree Rajneesh, who have cornered the
growth movement in London at the moment, are keeping alive the
'beat zen', let-it-all-hang-out, follow-your-impulses, dress
scruffy and turn up late style of the Hippies. *est* graduates have
their own language and look like middle management. Transcendental meditation chaps look like junior management. Hare Krishna
freaks pretend to be crazy. 'Square zen' freaks have short hair
and are very, very quiet. All these trappings are irrelevant to
the real spirit and understanding which may or may not be present underneath. And unless one deliberately and consciously
adopts or is given a style as a therapeutic device, they are not
worth bothering about. But all paths have their wind-up walkie-
talkie doll products, playing at being grown-up, and becoming
one is a definite temptation that many seekers fall for.

Each of these traps for the seeker can also be a trap for the
sceptic, if he uses their existence as a way of denying the validity
of the search and the value of the aids completely. Even though
some therapies and processes cost a lot, and someone is making
a lot of money, it is still true that paying can enhance the participant's commitment and hence the benefit he obtains. Even though
he adopts a strange style of dress and he seems to his friends to
be submitting to an external authority, there may be a purpose
behind it that the sceptic cannot see. Even though the sceptic,
as much as the seeker, hankers for more joy and intimacy in his
life, he will not believe it if he sees it. A room-ful of happy,
laughing people who have just completed the *est* training, let us
say, will be viewed with deep suspicion. 'They must have been
conned', he will say. Or 'If they've paid £172 to be harangued
for two weekends, they've got to look happy, haven't they?' A
seeker's naive optimism is easily matched by a sceptic's naive
dismissals. He has just as much investment in protecting his beliefs that things can't get any better as the seeker has in believ-
ing that they can. After all, if sixty hours can transform your
life, his forty years of putting up with things must come under
the microscope, and it just might turn out that he is not unable
to do anything about his life, but unwilling.

5 LIBERATION FROM DE-LIBERATION:
The East and meditation

The psychotherapeutic quest becomes a spiritual one when the
assumption being questioned stops being 'I am bad' and becomes
'I am'. Instead of trying to become a better person, the process
of 'trying', the notions of 'better' and 'person', and behind that,
who is doing it all, these issues themselves begin to be problematic. For some people these fundamental questions begin to emerge
in therapy, as their increasing receptivity to the organism begins
to melt the image of who they thought they were. For others it is
triggered by intellectual enquiry. Whether one is battering away
at the philosophy of mind, relativity theory, the use of language,
the psychology of perception, the aims of education or the doctrine of the Trinity, sooner or later a question may emerge that
not only challenges an academic position but rattles the bars of
our intuition. Hidden deep inside quantum electrodynamics, or the
Gestaltist's approach to perception, is the stark fact that This
Means You. They are not just theories about the world, but refer,
alarmingly, to ways of experiencing it that are at odds with common sense.

For mainstream psychotherapy the primary concern is getting
on, managing, discovering what is workable. It focuses on particular obstacles or blocks to having one's life work, and sees itself
as successful when these are removed or circumvented. As a rule
it proceeds by the client's rediscovering and integrating into his
picture of himself much that he thought, or hoped, he wasn't.
It attends to the foliage of a life, snipping off twigs here and
polishing leaves there. It is direct, especially in its cruder forms:
if the client is unhappy at A and wants to be at B, it will devise
ways of getting him there, adjusted and relieved.

Therapy becomes spiritual when its concern becomes not getting
on, but getting in - when the workable becomes secondary to the
true, the veridical. The client sees more and more clearly that
'the problem' is not a detail of his life, the presence of a phobia
or the absence of a social skill, but the way in which he holds all
the details. He stops his fiddling with the leaves, and begins to
search for the roots. The puzzles and problems, far from diminish-
ing, start to multiply, as increasingly basic assumptions and
attitudes become questionable. Gradually he stops trying to clean
up these details, be they material, physical, social or psychological, and almost welcomes them as further pointers to the
location of the roots. Instead of trying to get from A to B, he
lets A be, sinks into it, and greets it as a teacher. Not 'Damn
you, you stupid bitch', but 'That's interesting, my stomach feels

tight and I can hear my heart beating fast and my smile is set in cement and my eyes won't look at you.'

The line between psychotherapy and religion is dissolving fast. Many of the modern therapists such as Rogers and Ellis are un- covering this indirect but radical trail. Where the wisdom of the Eastern Masters runs ahead of them is in seeing very clearly what the root is, in insisting that its severance is our only salvation and that nothing less will do, in devising techniques and situa- tions that dig directly to the root, and in spotting and fostering the subtle changes in the quality of people, their experience and action, as the search proceeds. It is these stages, changes and techniques that this chapter describes.

Enlightenment, the direct experience of one's connectedness and integrity, is a sudden event. It cannot be accumulated or developed by degrees. It is a 180° transformation in the experi- ence of one's life in which, to use an *est* metaphor, one stops being identified with bits and pieces in the stew and instead knows oneself, immediately, to be the pot. However one can help oneself to be accident-prone to this experience and to increase its frequency, depth and duration. Furthermore the experience itself very gradually transforms the experiencer, cleansing, strengthening and maturing him. Thus a quantum shift in experi- ence is enhanced (in probability and stability) by deliberate effort, and in its turn produces changes in the personality of the 'efforter'. This simple sequence of events has at times been mystified and misunderstood by people who have on the one hand insisted that spiritual growth is a continuous accumulation of vir- tue (and ignored the 'active ingredient' in this process) and on the other by those who have emphasized the jump at the expense of its antecedents and consequences. Provided the point is clear, we can go on to look at one description of the stages through which the spiritual seeker passes.

GROWTH IN DAILY LIFE

In the twelfth century a Chinese Zen master called Kuo-an (in Japanese, Kakuan) identified ten stages, borrowing an earlier Taoist pictorial metaphor of a herdsman's search for his ox or bull. Adding two more pictures to the original eight, and an interpretative foreword and a poem to each, he left us what are now known as the 'Ten Bulls of Zen'. Several versions of the pictures now exist, and some strikingly different translations of the fore- words and poems into English. There are also, interestingly enough, two commentaries on the Ten Bulls by living enlightened Masters. In 'The Search' Bhagwan Shree Rajneesh uses a trans- lation by Nyogen Senzaki and Paul Reps, while Master D.R. Otsu offers a more conventional (if such is possible) interpretation in 'The Ox and His Herdsman', translated, together with the Kuo-an poems, by M.H. Trevor. And D.T. Suzuki, while offering no interpretation of his own, gives us, in his 'Manual of Zen Budd-

hism' still another translation of the Kuo-an poems and preface,
and an alternative set of verses by Pu-ming.

Although the pictures are sometimes called the ox-herding, or
even cow-herding, pictures, the image of a wild, powerful, un-
governable bull is much nearer the mark, for it is a symbol for
man's dark side; the emotional energy and awareness that have
been dissociated from the clean, controllable, homogenized and
pasteurized aspects that constitute my 'I'. As the series progres-
ses, Man (ego) and Bull (repressed feelings and vitality) become
reacquainted, and eventually, in the rediscovery of integrity,
dissolve into each other completely. At first, only brief flashes
of integrity occur occasionally and unpredictably; eventually
integrity becomes a way of life.

The first picture is called The Search for the Bull. The seeker,
having heard or read something, or through his own experience
of catharsis or therapy, begins to get a hazy sense that things
are not quite as he had always taken them to be. He becomes
enthused and disturbed by the idea that his normal existence may
look flat and fraught from a higher plane - one which is in fact
attainable. The Kingdom of God, Buddha-nature, Tao, Brahman,
Enlightenment, Integrity, though incomprehensible, form an alluring counterpoint to a life of habit and deceit, obsessions and
possessions, which is beginning to make him sick. The examples
of Krishna, Buddha, Jesus, Moses, Mahavir, Suzuki or Krishnamurti shine before him: people who have Done It, Found It,
whatever It may be. He doesn't know what he wants, he may not
know what he is trying to escape - he almost certainly will not
suspect that 'want' and 'escape' are themselves the only causes
of his trouble - but the simple possibility of liberation may be
enough to start the search.

> *In the pastures of the world, I endlessly push aside*
> *the tall grasses in search of the bull.*

The problem is that the seeker at this stage is on a hiding to
nothing because he doesn't know where to look, nor would he
recognize the bull, the object of his search, if he saw it. He
assumes that there is something to be done, books to be read,
lectures to attend, disciplines to follow that will deliver the goods.
Knowledge, intelligence and effort are the tools that he instinc-
tively uses. However,

> *My strength failing and my vitality exhausted,*
> *I cannot find the bull.*

He sees the search as an achieving, not a dropping, an acquiring,
not a letting-go, and therefore searches outwards, not inwards . . .

> *Following unnamed rivers, lost upon the inter-*
> *penetrating paths of distant mountains.*

He certainly has no idea that 'The reason why the oxherd is not
on intimate terms with the bull is because the oxherd himself has
violated his own inmost nature' (Suzuki's translation of Kuo-an).

The second stage is Discovering the Footprints. Slowly it dawns
on the seeker that what he seeks is not on distant mountain tops
or in what Otsu calls 'the leftovers of learned meals', but right

at his feet. Through intellectual understanding of the writings
and teachings of the Masters, he appreciates that the bull is to
be found not in the world but in his reactions to it. 'The Kingdom
of God is within you', he reads, or 'Precisely in the midst of
worldly passions and erroneous opinions dwells the unborn original
self', as Hui-neng put it. Instead of looking for a grand conception he lowers his sights – and sees in the mud underfoot the
traces of the bull. Not yet the bull itself, just the traces, the
droppings. He reads descriptions of the terrain into which he will
be moving. He learns the things we discussed in Chapter 2: that
man's true nature is like a wave on the ocean, a transient and
dynamic form adopted by, and inseparable from, a greater Whole.
But he learns too that these philosophies are of no value in themselves, but are fingers pointing at a moon that he cannot yet see.
He comes to detach himself from the study of 'fingers', and to
realize that they serve only to direct his attention to the 'moons'
of his own true self, although they are still obscured by clouds.

Along the riverbank under the trees, I discover footprints!
These traces no more can be hidden than one's nose, looking
   heavenward.

Yet they are difficult to spot precisely because they are as close
to him, and as unnoticed, as familiar and as insignificant, as his
own nose. The seeker's attention is drawn to the processes of
his perception and action. What to do, what to study are super-
seded by the questions how do I know and act, and who is the
knower and the actor?

The scriptures emerge in a different light. Their authors are
not philosophers or theologians but cartographers and physicians,
and the scriptures themselves are at the same time guide-books,
recording the landmarks and the pitfalls of an experiential quest,
and prescriptions for dispelling the mists of the seeker's misconceptions, so that the vista can be seen. From now on the search
is an inward one, and new tools of awareness and courage must
be forged. The bull is understood to be the submerged complement of the ego, as the iceberg to its tip. The tip is attached to
the unseen nine-tenths below the water-line, and could not exist
otherwise; yet through its own delusion and unconsciousness it
has assumed itself to be the whole and to be autonomous. The
seeker must now summon up his blood, hold his nose, open his
eyes wide, and dive into the dark and icy water of his own fears
and desires.

The seeker who comes from therapy may already have taken this
plunge. But if he comes out of intellectual curiosity the transition from the warm armchair in his study to the perils of deep-sea
diving will be a traumatic one to make, if he makes it at all. Few
people do. There are certainly enough intellectual puzzles and
paradoxes in the literature to keep him cogitating and discussing
for a life-time. One of these, a central one, which the graduate
from therapy will have to come to grips with as well, concerns
the notion of acceptance.

Let us look at different reactions to moods or feelings that we

don't like and find uncomfortable. The most common is to avoid
it, either by repressing it internally, or by busying oneself with
physical distractions. The next - if the first one fails - is to
grapple with it: to tie myself up with the attempt to bring under
control that which I cannot avoid, and to suffer all the additional
feelings of frustration, impotence, anxiety, guilt or self-disgust
that are part and parcel of this absurd wrestling match with one's
own shadow. The third reaction, that a person may have learnt
while in therapy, is to try and accept whatever-it-is. To return
to Alan Watts again: 'Wisdom therefore consists in accepting what
we are, rather than struggling fruitlessly to be something else,
as if it were possible to run away from one's own feet.' So far,
so good. Accepting what I am sounds like a good idea . . . now
how do I go about it? And this is where the trouble starts, as
Watts goes on to explain. 'But if you cannot run away from your
feet, you cannot run after them either. If it is impossible to
escape from reality, from what *is now*, it is equally impossible to
accept or embrace it.' The idea of total acceptance is nonsense,
for accepting can only have meaning in the context of rejecting,
as Yes needs No and Good needs Bad. To accept everything is
effectively to have no reaction to it at all.

On the other hand if I attempt to accept any part of me, I can
only do that by rejecting another part. If I want to accept and
allow my anger or my depression, I can only do that by rejecting
and disallowing my non-acceptance of my anger. Both the anger,
and the unwelcoming reaction to it are aspects of me: yet I can
only own one, it seems. The scales can tip back and forth, but
the pans can never drop together. The only way out of this is
further in. This line of thought shows acceptance to be miscon-
ceived, for it continues to presuppose dissociation. 'I' cannot
'accept' 'myself', it is not anything that I can do at all. Rather
acceptance is that state of mind that arises when I and myself
are united: when the tip realizes its true relationship to the iceberg. It cannot accept it - it is it. Chewing over the problems of
effort and will also leads to the same intellectual indigestion, and
relief is again forthcoming with a redirection of attention from
the head to the proper organ of digestion, the stomach. When the
problem becomes visceral, its solution becomes possible.

In the third stage, Perceiving the Bull, the seeker moves from
understanding the nature and whereabouts of the bull into direct
experience. Any hopes about being passively led to the truth by
an external authority have to be dropped. He recognizes that
from here on, the way lies in an increasing openness to all aspects
of his own nature. The bull is present in his every thought, feeling, perception and action, as inseparably as salt dissolved in
water. Thus there is nothing he can do to encourage the appearance of the bull: the only effort he can make is to become increasingly attentive and receptive to what is already the case. This
receptivity has to be cultivated, and has to become ever more
non-selective and non-judgmental, so that every single one of his
habits, prejudices, and attitudes, everything he has ever taken

for granted, can be put to the test of experience. This is the beginning of meditation, and meditativeness: it is where the search starts in earnest.

Unfortunately, as we have seen, the requisite change in the direction and intensity of awareness cannot be achieved by an effort of will, for will presupposes man's dissociation and pre-judges what is to be attended to, and in what way. All he can do is start to allow himself to enter in to certain areas of experience that he had previously learnt, more or less successfully, to avoid. These include doubt, disappointment, anxiety, frustration, em-barrassment, uneasiness, shame, hurt and guilt: all of them can now be treated, if not with pleasure, at least with interest, for they are all pointers to aspects of himself that he has chosen to ignore. Early on, for example, the seeker will be forced to admit how little of his own experience and action he actually controls. Physiological processes proceed of themselves. Far more worrying, the appearance of thoughts, feelings and moods turns out to be things I can do little about. 'Why am I having just this thought just now?' 'How come I usually feel tired when Julie comes over except tonight I don't?' 'What a weird train of thought: I wonder where that came from?' A million questions like this are askable everyday, and not one of them, if we are really honest, answer-able with any degree of certainty at all. As Irmgard Schloegl says, in her excellent little book 'The Zen Way',

> Having been courageous and honest enough to have seen this happen time and again, the inevitable conclusion must be that I am at least sharing the 'house' I live in, of which I thought myself the master, with something unknown, something stronger than I, and acting in a way which seems to me to be without rhyme or reason.
>
> My disquiet upon finding such a mate is bound to be serious. This is why I prefer not to be aware of him, and go to great lengths to avoid seeing him. Unfortunately in turning my back so as not to see him, I actually give him special power over me. For the stronger I resist something, the more that something fascinates me, gets hold of me.

And so the seeker's love-hate relationship with the bull-that-is-himself develops.

Side by side with the stirrings of the bull, the developing sen-sitivity to ignored aspects of self, comes an enhanced scepticism about what the self thought it was. Nothing is certain any more. The seeker sees just how much he has been adding to and dis-torting his perceptions, how selective and dishonest an instru-ment his reason has been, to what extent his psychology has been moulded by his neurotic needs to maintain or deny reality. He experiences for the first time the wide disparity between his be-liefs and what his experience tells him is so, if he will let it. A potent example is that made famous by Douglas Harding: in belief, I have a head, but in my immediate experience I am headless. I can point to anything in my environment and see both the finger pointing and the object, but when I point at my own face, all

there is is the finger. If I tell the truth, my 'head' right now
consists of the desk, the papers, a moving hand, a window frame
and the fields beyond, the sound of the birds and the traffic. I
say I can see my face in a mirror - yet what would I be seeing if
all the mirrors in the world were distorting ones? (In fact they
are!) My 'face' is a construction, a hypothesis, a short-hand for
a mass of sensations. To feel that one has no head, that one has
swapped a meatball for infinite space, is a profound and shocking
insight, whereas to entertain the thought 'I have no head' is so
obviously false as to be absurd, at best a rather facile play with
words. To suspend what is 'obviously' true or false, and look with
innocent eyes at what is so, is what the seeker's task now becomes.

Taking the risk, again and again, of being naive and stupid,
of becoming as little children, brings the seeker to the next stage,
Catching the Bull. As his courage and tolerance grow, so the
bull gets more and more fierce and uncontrollable. From time to
time he bursts out with full force, in feelings of terror, rage or
lust, sweeping the seeker away.

I seize him with a terrific struggle.
His great will and power are inexhaustible.
He charges to the high plateau far above the cloud-mists,
Or in an impenetrable ravine he stands.

The most frightful facets of the bull are certainly the feelings of
assertiveness, fear and sexuality that the seeker has excluded
from himself since childhood. Once he begins to allow his awareness back into those areas, he may be astonished at their explosive force. Trevor translates part of Kuo-an's foreword as,
'Stubborn self-will rages in him and wild animal nature rules him.'
For the seeker these encounters with himself are, to start with,
dramatic and cathartic in the extreme. His feelings are no less
intense than those of a man diving into the Arctic Sea, or a
novice literally facing a charging bull in a corrida.

For most spiritual seekers, at most times in history, the bull
has been only too ready to burst out of his confinement, and display the forms and intensity of his primitive, infantile energy.
For the contemporary Western seeker, however, the bull may be
so stupefied and cramped that the intention to attend to him is
not enough, and he has to be goaded out. Recently, certain
spiritual traditions have begun to borrow from the Western growth
movement intensive techniques for promoting catharsis. Habits
of inattention have to be breached forcibly by throwing the seeker
into just those extreme situations that, if they had occurred
spontaneously in his normal life, would have sent him into therapy.
With the guidance and support, as well as the provocation, of a
Master, though, this stage can be entered and traversed without
the agony being prolonged. If the seeker can surrender to the
Master, he can more easily surrender to himself. If he can allow
himself to be a helpless witness to the inferno that rages within,
rather than trying to fight with it and suppress it, the accumulated repressions can burn themselves out, and the herdsman

and the bull both become cleansed by the fire.

There is a pitfall here, as we saw in the last chapter. Catharsis in itself is not the point. It is strong medicine, a purgative, for dissolving away some major blocks to awareness. Latent fears that I will go mad, kill somebody, be totally rejected if I give way to my passions; that if I ever let the bull out of his pen, even for an instant, I will never be able to control him again; that once he gets loose in the china shop of my self-image, I shall be completely and irrevocably destroyed; all these can only be defused by allowing them to become manifest in the act of catching the bull by the tail, and seeing, feeling, tasting, experiencing the fact that I survive. At first I may become lost in a flood of feeling. Later man and beast know each other well enough to co-exist, and they can begin to incorporate each other. Once the big 'meta-fears' are exorcised, I can be more attentive to my experience, whatever it is and wherever it may lead. There is no longer any need to act out the passions: I can contain and watch the fire burn within, neither expressing nor suppressing it.

There are other ways in which the seeker can lose track at this stage. He may become so enthralled with his new-found energy and power, his abilities to cry, to shout, to let it out, that the bull is appropriated by the herdsman, and paraded as a fair-ground attraction. His bellow doesn't frighten me any more, but I can use it to intimidate others. Man and bull can tolerate each other, but their relationship does not ripen, and it bears only egotistic fruit. A variant of this is where the seeker, instead of avoiding his feelings, now clings to them: he becomes attached to the pyrotechnics of his emotional highs, and rejects the flat normality of routine interactions. He does not see that his purpose is to be able to enter into his highs and lows as they arise, not to have to cultivate them.

The seeker may also become attached to novel experience of a different, even more alluring, kind. In the aftermath of his struggles he may feel the lightness, even ecstasy, that follows a release of tension and the discovery that one of his fears is a phantom. Deep despair may flip into an irrepressible belly-laugh, and a feeling that it is all O.K., or all absurd, or that he is at the same time perfectly vulnerable to all his sensations, and perfectly invulnerable, in a perfect balance that nothing can disturb. These peak experiences or 'mini-satoris' give him his first real taste of what he has only read about before: the effortless presence and omnipotence of the man of Tao or the adept in Zen. He begins to know what the mystics are talking about. The trouble is that these experiences cannot be sought or caught, for they occur only in the complete abandonment of any effort to get or keep things a certain way. Enlightening never strikes twice in the same place, so it is no use looking for it where you found it before.

After the fireworks comes the fifth stage, the slower, more meticulous process of Taming the Bull. Now

The whip and the rope are necessary,
Else he might stray off down some dusty road.

The whip and the rope are interpretable in many ways, but the
commentators agree that they refer to the need for some support
and structure to help the seeker avoid the pitfalls, to consolidate
and broaden the increased awareness that he has sampled, and to
resist the constant temptation, all the stronger because so automatic, to slip back into the deep-rooted habits of inattention and
objectification of perceptions. By the latter I mean the constant
tendency to attribute one's reactions to 'the world', to blame one's
suffering on circumstances, to construe oneself as a victim, instead of persisting with the realization that I create the world I
inhabit and the values and attitudes I hold. 'There's nothing good
or bad but thinking makes it so' must be more than a motto: it
must become an ever-present component of the machinery through
which I perceive and act. Time and again the seeker slips unconsciously into the stream of his experience, and time and again he
has to haul himself out and sit quietly, watching, on the bank.

Bhagwan Shree Rajneesh has used the whip as a symbol for
awareness, and the rope to refer to discipline. Both are needed
together, though superficially one might think them to be in
opposition. Awareness after all is supposed to be an unrestricted
receptivity to whatever is the case, while discipline necessitates
a restricting of what is possible. But by this stage there is no
conflict, for discipline refers only to what one does, to action,
and the seeker is now clear that the two realms of awareness and
action are separable, and that who he really is has everything to
do with the former and nothing with the latter. Discipline without awareness leads to a zombie-like following of codes and precepts that reduces alertness and responsibility. The effort to be
aware without a discipline to support it is very difficult, for
attention will be constantly channelled and subverted by old habits
of thought and behaviour. A tailor-made environment which, for
example, continually grates on the likes and dislikes of the ego,
or undercuts, as therapy does, the normal patterns of evasion
and defence, is one that keeps the bull restless and the herdsman
discomfited, and throws them together time after time. In this
process of 'gradually letting the holy body grow', as Zen calls it,
the special moments of insight become more ordinary, more permanent in daily activity, less fragile and less momentous. While
feelings and moods continue to come and go, the seeker keeps his
balance in the midst of them. Knowing himself to be the ocean,
and dropping his identification with the waves, an unshakeable
peace and watchfulness pervades his activities. Having to be less
wary about where his experience might lead, he enters fully into
whatever present is actual. And as an integral part of the same
development, the thought processes of planning and regretting,
rehearsing, analysing and surmising become less compulsive and
begin to drop away. In everyday life, as well as in special periods
of inactivity, the seeker's mental state becomes quiet and meditative.

At this stage the presence of a Master is very important. Each
seeker's barriers and trials are different, his resolve may waver,
he may fall prey to what Chogyam Trungpa calls 'spiritual materialism' as his reflexes of desire and pride attempt to appropriate the
changes in his being that are occurring. All those traps and idio-
syncrasies the Master is able to spot and neutralize with his own
special bag of tricks, meditations, tasks, shocks, lectures and
example. Eventually we may say of the bull, with Kuo-an,

Being well trained, he becomes naturally gentle.
Then, unfettered, he obeys his master.

The sixth stage is the last one I shall discuss here: the last
four go into realms that I cannot begin to comprehend. In Riding
the Bull Home, the struggle between ego and id, herdsman and
bull, is over. The illusion of their separation is broken, and
each sinks into the other. Together they form a strong, sensitive
and compassionate unity. The seeker does not have to perform to
please others, yet his authenticity and naturalness inspires awe
in them. All his attachments have been penetrated and deflated -
to body, to mind, to possessions, to status, to enlightenment
itself, to life. He is no longer a cloud but the sky, not the reflection but the mirror, not the wave but the ocean, not the stew but
the container. His perception is so complete, his bliss so unshakeable, he fits so exactly with his surroundings, so completely in
accord with nature and himself, that his actions have a startling
economy and effectiveness and his inactions a deep serenity. He
is not a perfect person, yet he is always perfectly himself.

Life, according to the *est* training, is a roller-coaster. It goes
up and down, and there is nothing anyone can do about that.
There is only one choice. Either you get dragged along behind
the car, by a rope around your neck, kicking and screaming,
lagging going up and leading coming down, but always attached.
Or you can climb into the car and choose to have things be exactly
the way they are, whether you like them or not, whether they
hurt or not, whether you can intervene in any way or not. By
the sixth stage, the seeker is firmly in the car.

MEDITATION

The two ingredients of the spiritual search that are the most
obvious, and the most mysterious, to the outsider are the practice of meditation, and the relationship of the seeker to his guru,
the Master whom he has chosen to be his guide and mentor. We
will look at these in turn.

The discipline of meditation, like all religious discipline, has no
value in itself. Many established religions err in presenting their
disciplines of prayer, fasting, abstinence or contemplation as being intrinsically worthy activities. It is simply 'good' to observe
them, and the only answer to 'why?' is 'It is ordained. God/Jesus/
Mohammed/Krishna/Buddha/The Pope says so.' Unfortunately,
with this attitude the observance is mechanical and the point con-

sequently missed. As we saw above, the practical object of these
practices is to become more alert, more alive, more aware. And
unless awareness is invested in them there will be no dividend.
Thus meditation is a temporary device, a course of treatment,
which supplements and facilitates the changes occurring in daily
life, and which will eventually be dropped when its purpose is
accomplished. It provides an intense period of awareness that
serves as a training for being aware during the rest of the day.
It is an exact mental parallel to the physical discipline of doing
some exercises in the morning in order to improve one's all-round
fitness. But though the aim is simple and pragmatic, the techniques
themselves are many and varied, some straightforward and some
rather sophisticated, some for beginners and some suitable only
for people who are mentally fit and strong already. Perhaps we
can get a feel for this variety by looking at a few contrasting
forms of meditation.

Transcendental Meditation, perhaps the form most widely believed to be prototypical in the West, requires the practitioner
to sit quietly in an upright chair, eyes closed, for twenty minutes
repeating silently a special word-like sound called a mantra. Each
person is given his own personal mantra at his initiation which he
must keep secret, though it appears that nearly everybody gets
one of the same two or three. As attention keeps wandering away
from the mantra so one keeps bringing it gently back. There is
no effort or strain to keep the mantra in mind: just whenever you
notice you've stopped saying it, you start again.

Several other common types of meditation are similar, in having
a preferred object of awareness which is repeatedly chosen, but
not clung to. The object may be visual, as in the contemplation
of a mandala, or physiological, as in *vipassana*, or insight, meditation, where the natural rhythm of one's own breathing acts as
the constant reference point.

The beginner to *zazen* also watches his breath, counting his
exhalations from one to ten again and again. It differs from vipassana, let us say, in requiring the meditator to put as much effort
and concentration into this counting as possible. Whereas vipassana has a more *tantric* attitude to experience, accepting without
judgment whatever comes, zazen to start with takes the *yogic*
attitude of a wilful attempt to train one's mind in a particular way.
There is also in zazen much fuss made about the posture. Lotus
position, left leg on right, spine vertical, ears in line with
shoulders, chin tucked in, eyes half open looking at the floor
about two metres away, left hand on right hand, thumbs raised
with tips touching to form a large oval space . . . all must be
correct. Deviations through weariness or forgetfulness are greeted
with a hearty crack on the head or across the shoulders with a
big stick, the *keisaku*.

There there is prayer, both petitional and devotional, which is
a potent form of meditation if it does not lapse into empty recita-
tion on Sundays and empty chatter at bed-time. Christianity has
ultimately done God a disservice by representing Him as a Person.

When people forget that God the Father is a metaphorical finger pointing at an ineffable Moon, prayer loses its power to transform. A series of routine enquiries, apologies and compliments directed at something that I conceive of as like me only better falls on deaf ears, for 'I and the Father are One'. When I know myself so thoroughly that we merge, precisely in the moment of meeting I know God: until then I do not know Him at all, and I am better off admitting it.

If prayer does not consist in the mindless replaying of old, old tapes, it equally has nothing to do with intellectual comprehension or clear communication. Even if God were a Person, He would certainly speak seventeenth-century English as well as He speaks today's, and there is little doubt that He would derive more pleasure from the full-bodied and elusive eloquence of Thomas Cranmer's Book of Common Prayer than the flat and tasteless businessman's lunch of the modern versions. The words are not important, except that they should help to foster a meditative frame of mind. This is achieved far better by a stately and mysterious poetry, that creates a deep resonance, than by clear, unambiguous prose, which engages the unwanted gears of rational thought. The purpose of prayer, as of all meditation, is to transform the pray-er; worshipping God is a device of provoking the realization of one's own Godliness. Unfortunately the executors of Christ's will have lost all sense of this: they are curators and bureaucrats, and their only magic is to turn His living heritage to dust. Small wonder that those who have a nose for things of the spirit are following the scent eastwards.

Meditation is usually thought of as a sedentary activity: there are, however, many forms of meditation in action. In t'ai chi the focus of awareness is on very slow, elegant movements: it looks like a cross between karate and ballet at a hundredth of normal speed. At the other extreme is the whirling of the Sufi dervishes and the 'dynamic meditation' of Bhagwan Shree Rajneesh. This latter is worth describing, because at first sight it looks nothing like meditation at all. Dynamic meditation lasts an hour and consists of five stages, the first three of ten minutes each and the fourth and fifth a quarter of an hour. In the first stage the meditator stands and breathes through his nose as hard and as fast as he can, using his whole body to force the air out of his lungs. If he pushes himself to the limit and beyond, his experience changes from him doing the breathing to the breathing doing itself, with him left watching the crazy display that his body is putting on. Quickly he discovers that he can lose control of his physiology and let out a physical bull that has more power than he could imagine. He learns to get over his fright, and is able to witness its rampaging with a detached interest. This makes possible the second stage, where he does the same thing with the even more scary area of his emotions. He may shout, scream, laugh, cry - follow whatever channel the liberated energy takes - provided only that he again allows himself to enter into it totally. After this catharsis, he reverts to an exhausting physical routine

in the third stage, jumping up and down with his hands in the
air and expelling the sound 'Hoo' from the pit of his stomach.
Nothing is held back until the end of this stage when a voice calls
'Stop!'. He freezes instantly in whatever posture he happens to
be, and stays there, without moving a muscle, for fifteen minutes.
In this silence, having thrown out some of his accumulated madness and repressions, and having loosened, albeit only temporarily, the stranglehold of his ego on his experience, he witnesses his larger self. Finally, to some gentle, floating music, the
meditator dances in celebration of his aliveness and his capacity.
Bizarre as this sequence may seem, it is not hard to make sense
of it in terms of the bull analogy. He is goaded, released and
observed, and the alchemy of observation transmutes his base-
ness. The more I know him, the less he runs my life.

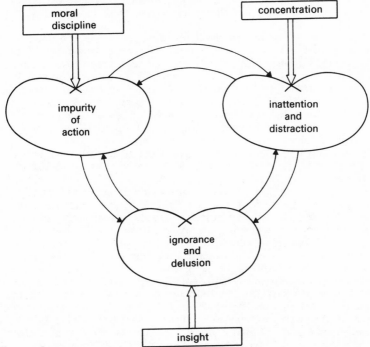

Figure 3

All meditations, from the quiet humming of Tibetan Buddhists
to the whirling of the dervishes, the Jesus prayer of the Christian mystics to the 'self-remembrance' of Gurdjieff, the ritualized
love-making of Tantra to the physical privations of the Hindu
Samana, the passive devotion of the Bhakti to the 'choiceless
awareness' of Krishnamurti, all have a central purpose which is
insight into oneself. And all have a central method which is a redirection and expansion of awareness. They differ, though, in

how this retraining is best achieved. We can follow their logic
with the aid of Figure 3. Dissociated Man may be thought of as
having three aspects to his dissociation, each of which is sustained by, and helps to sustain the others. One is the ineffective-
ness and immorality of his behaviour. The second is his inability
to control his mind – the rag-bag nature of his consciousness, his
literally scatter-brained and whimsical attention. The third is his
ignorance and delusion about himself and the world. Ignorance
prevents him seeing how poor his action is. He simply does not
perceive many of the ways in which his life doesn't work. Inability
to concentrate inhibits the extent to which he can inspect his
beliefs. His rituals and routines ensure that his beliefs are rarely
if ever brought to light by unexpected events. It all fits nicely
together into a shock-proof package. The job of a spiritual discipline is to prise the package open, and the disciplines vary in
which, and how many of, the three points they focus on, and in
what order.

Many start by trying to clean up thought, word and deed by
imposing on the seeker a moral code. Orthodox Buddhism, Hindu-
ism, Islam, Judaism and Christianity all take this route, as do
many of the monastic and esoteric schools as well. However, it is
interesting that four of the contemporary Masters best known in
the West, Gurdjieff, Bhagwan Shree Rajneesh, Krishnamurti and
Maharishi Mahesh Yogi, have not made any great moral demands
on their followers. Perhaps to counter the ossified codes of the
Western religions, they all stress that 'right doing' is not a pre-
requisite for 'right being', but a product of it. What makes an
action good is the quality of the doer, not the objective nature
of the act.

The second way out of the vicious cycle of impurity, inattention
and ignorance is through gaining control of one's attention, so
that one is able to hold an object, thought or sensation in focal
awareness without wavering. Many meditations are aimed towards
this goal of 'one-pointedness', though the object of attention may
be a mantra, a prayer, a mandala, the photo of a guru or a lover,
a flower, a movement, or the rise and fall of the breath. As the
meditator's concentration improves, the preferred object comes to
hold centre stage in his consciousness, while the rest of his experience continues on the periphery. The early Christian monks,
for example, were instructed to repeat the 'kyrie eleison' silently
throughout the day 'until it became as spontaneous and instinctive
as breathing', as Thomas Merton says in 'The Wisdom of the
Desert'. The meditation object becomes a constant thread that
runs through the meditator's experience, providing a still point
around which his world turns. Once this is achieved, most schools
move the meditator beyond the artificial discipline of concentration
into a more direct attack on ignorance and delusion through non-
judgmental observation, or 'witnessing', of the mind and its
activities.

The danger with all the techniques of moral discipline and concentration is that they initially strengthen the ego, by insisting

that part of me can stand aside from, control and change another part. Even though the seeds of the ego's destruction are inherent in the 'path of will', if the seeker falters or is not guided carefully, any changes or abilities that accrue from his practice will be claimed by 'I' as further evidence of its power and control. To avoid this, some schools and some Masters play down the value of technique, insisting that change cannot be produced directly. The only way, they say, is to aim for insight, for experiential understanding, and that this is the only way in which change will happen, because it can only happen of itself. Ramana Maharshi used to say the only way to solve life's problems is to see who has the problem. The 'technique', if such it can be called, of the 'path of understanding', requires no activity or effort but only the gradual cultivation of a passive receptivity, which Krishnamurti described nicely to a group of Indian children.

You have to watch, as you watch a lizard going by, walking across the wall, seeing all its four feet, how it sticks to the wall, you have to watch it, and as you watch, you see all the movements, the delicacy of its movements. So in the same way, watch your thinking, do not correct it, do not suppress it - do not say it is too hard - just watch it, now, this morning (quoted by Daniel Goleman in his book 'The Varieties of the Meditative Experience').

The most open-ended non-technique of watchfulness requires simply that most difficult of attitudes: a willingness to allow oneself to experience whatever is the case. Slightly more circumscribed versions require the seeker to create special situations in which to witness his reactions, or to set himself to be triggered into witnessing by certain types of experience as they occur in the normal course of events. The 'Vigyana Bhairava Tantra', a tantric scripture over four thousand years old, provides a compendium of 112 techniques of meditation that contains examples of each type. 'Wherever your mind is wandering, internally or externally, at this very place, *this*' or 'Wherever your attention alights, at this very point, *experience*' are the most simple and most impossible. Others suggest switching on to certain specified events. 'At the start of sneezing, during fright, in anxiety, above a chasm, flying in battle, in extreme curiosity, at the beginning of hunger, at the end of hunger, be *uninterruptedly* aware.' 'See *as if for the first time* a beauteous person or an ordinary object!' 'When eating or drinking, become the taste of the food or drink, and *be filled*.' 'On joyously seeing a long-lost friend, *permeate this joy*.' While in others, a particular experience is provoked, and then observed. 'Pierce some part of your nectar-filled form with a pin, and gently *enter the piercing*.' 'Roam about until exhausted and then, dropping to the ground, in this dropping *be whole*.' (The 'Vigyana Bhairava Tantra' is translated by Paul Reps in 'Zen Flesh, Zen Bones'.)

The purpose of mindfulness, and the way in which it works, we have already discussed. To repeat Bhagwan's concise formulation, 'Observation is alchemical.' In the very moment of becoming aware

of an attitude or feeling, the habits of thought and behaviour
that underlie them are put to a test of their validity and effectiveness. Clear observation of a sequence of experience automatically,
alchemically transmutes one's prior expectations, beliefs and
habits with respect to that sequence.

But we need to ask as well: what are the effects of practising
one-pointedness? How does this narrowing-down of attention
develop into an opening-up? How does it work? First, most con-
centrative meditations occur in quiet surroundings in which the
variety of stimulation available for awareness to snap at is significantly reduced. Just as on the psychoanalyst's couch, the stream
of the person's consciousness becomes an unavoidable reflection
of his own intrinsic patterns of construing and interpretation.
The content of awareness cannot be blamed on 'out there': it becomes more and more obvious that it is my own production. Thus
even though a primary object of attention is specified, the objects
that keep distracting me are potentially more relevant and informative to me than a concert on the radio or a conversation in the
pub. The thoughts and sensations that intrude are not irrelevant
nuisances, though they may at first seem that way. At the same
time as one's concentration develops, so, surprisingly perhaps,
does one's equanimity towards this flotsam drifting about on the
surface of the mind.

In fact the attempt to fix the concentration on a single object
ensures that the distractions will break through. Psychological
experiments show that an image fixed on the eye automatically
fades; a word constantly repeated seems to come and go, and to
change its sound and meaning. For the beginner, therefore, there
is no way that one-pointedness can be achieved. As meditation
proceeds, things change. The quantity and urgency of the
thoughts that the mind throws up diminish. At the same time,
the perception of the object becomes more sensitive, more differentiated and refined. It is no longer constantly the same mantra,
let us say, that is repeated. Every time the small differences in
pace, pitch, intonation and stress are noticed - like all the little
details of Krishnamurti's lizard. The sound becomes full of interest
and potential. And as the organism becomes more finely tuned, so
his 'recognition' of the object is continually suspended, and it
ceases to fade in the way it did before.

Second, the period of concentration provides, as Robert Ornstein calls it in 'The Psychology of Consciousness', a 'holiday'
from the constant rush-hour travel of everyday perception, in
which the senses must be turned down or bust. When one goes
back into the world, one is willing and able to let more of this
sensation in. Instead of a dark filter being placed around awareness indiscriminately, so that the detail in which one perceives is
unrelated to the object of perception, now the meditator is able
to turn the gain up and down selectively. He becomes the master
of his own insensitivity, not its prisoner. So as well as changes
occurring within the period of concentration itself, a complementary increase in the breadth of receptivity happens when the dis-

cipline is removed. This kind of contrast, or rebound effect is
again very well documented in experimental psychology, and
reflects basic physiological characteristics of the central nervous
system.

The third consequence of meditation is the most subtle, but
ultimately the most important. One of the chief characteristics of
thought is the extent to which it is self-propagating. One sight
or sound, the smell of a madeleine biscuit or the firmness of a
handshake can send us off for minutes on end (or in Proust's
case, for twelve volumes), on an internal saga of past or future
that occupies conscious awareness totally. Tacitly we keep tabs
on the present: consciously we sample it just every-so-often. All
types of meditation aim to undercut this inattention by providing,
in conscious awareness, a continuous thread that ties whatever
else one is aware of to the present moment. A picture might help.
In the centre of each of the circles of Figure 4 lies those features
of experience that are activated by the present. In (a), thought
can take off from that and follow its own patterns and obsessions

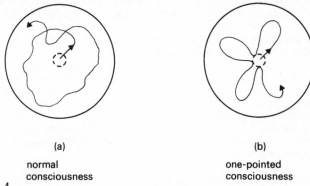

(a)

normal
consciousness

(b)

one-pointed
consciousness

Figure 4

for hours. Where it goes is determined by the tram-lines that
exist, and by the desires and fears that are represented in the
mechanisms of thought. The words and images that pop up reflect
the autonomous churnings of this system, and do not incorporate
information about the present situation, and about what actual
possibilities exist right now. Preoccupied with pipe-dreams of
sexual conquests, or fantasies of rejection, the real woman slips
by unseen. (Thus it is that the wise passivity of the meditator
will eventually flower into a crisp and spontaneous vitality, in
which that which can be done is done, immediately, without fuss
or flap.)

In (b) the object of meditation burns in consciousness throughout the day, providing a reference point, a hub around which the
rest of experience turns, and which continually connects thought
with the organismic sensations that are running alongside it.
Flights of fantasy are punctured before they can get under way
as the activity that would have sustained them is drawn back,

through the focal point of the mantra, prayer or picture, into the realm of the present. In insight meditation, the cultivation of mindfulness, self-remembering, choiceless awareness, wise passiveness, witnessing - whatever you like to call it - increases one's presence of mind without employing the artificial bridge of the meditational object. The result, the goal, is the same. The obsessional internal monologue drops away, to be replaced by a feeling of relaxed readiness, peacefulness and immediacy. Detachment and involvement grow side by side.

There is one other kind of spiritual technique that is more active, more like an intellectual wrestling match with oneself than the retraining of awareness that I have considered so far. Instead of working on the form and direction of attention, it tackles the content, the habits of more or less rational thought, head on, and eventually brings them down through a reductio ad absurdum of their own efforts. The most well-known example of this approach is the kōan system originated and still used extensively by the Rinzai sect of Zen Buddhism. The seeker is set a question that looks at first sight amenable to a verbal solution: 'What are you?', 'Does a dog have Buddha-nature?', 'You see the smoke from your cigarette - which is moving, the smoke or the breeze?', 'How can a man gain Enlightenment in a supermarket?', Or he is given one of the many odd Zen stories to unravel:

Nansen saw the monks of the eastern and western halls fighting over a cat. He seized the cat and told the monks: 'If any of you says a good word, you can save the cat'. No one answered. So Nansen boldly cut the cat in two pieces.

That evening Joshu returned and Nansen told him about this. Joshu removed his sandals, and, placing them on his head, walked out. Nanson said: 'If you had been there you could have saved the cat'.

Or a modern equivalent:

'I think I'll go and meet her,' said Alice . . . 'You can't possibly do that,' said the Rose: 'I should advise you to walk the other way.' This sounded nonsense to Alice, so she said nothing, but set off at once towards the Red Queen. To her surprise she lost sight of her in a moment.

Again and again the seeker presents an answer to the Master, who greets every attempt with a peremptory rejection. Gradually the kōan stops being merely an intellectual puzzle and invades his whole life. It becomes, as Zen puts it, like a red-hot ball of iron that the seeker has swallowed and cannot spit out. Eventually, having exhausted all possible approaches to the problem, yet still gripped by the throat by it, he surrenders, admits his helplessness, and in that moment achieves a qualitative change in his being which is itself the only possible solution. The mechanism of the kōan has been widely discussed by Watts, Ornstein, Narranjo, Suzuki, Schloegl and others: I do not intend to beat it to death here.

Like Mahesh Yogi's 'transcendental meditation' and Rajneesh's 'dynamic meditation', the kōan system has also been packaged for

the impatient consumers of the West. A total three, five or seven
day immersion in a kōan is available in what is known as the 'enlightenment intensive'. A group of people are divided into pairs.
Partners sit opposite each other alternately taking five minutes
to answer the question: 'Tell me who you are.' After a total of
forty minutes, there is a five minute break, and then the participants repeat the process again with a new partner. This is kept
up continuously for three days, let us say, punctuated only by
short, infrequent breaks for eating, bathing and sleeping. Except
when answering the question, the whole time is spent in silence.
After working through all his ideas and abstractions about who
he is, his memories from the past, his fantasies about the future,
the ready-made answers drop away and the participant becomes
identified not with his concepts any more but with his immediate
experience. Eventually, if he has committed himself to the process
sufficiently, he gains a direct perception of who he is: neither
ideas nor sensations, but the space, the potentiality, the void,
in which *all* experience takes place.

THE MASTER

The spiritual quest is one of seeing through and transcending
one's inappropriate limitations. The enlightened one still has his
limits - he cannot fly, nor live without air - and his preferences -
he continues to choose tea rather than coffee - but these are now
fully integrated into the equation of his life. Conversely he has
dropped all attachments and aversions that are not existentially
based, all the spurious variables that for most people prevent the
solution of the equation that combines want and can and produces
do. He is quite literally under no illusions about himself: he is
free of his psychological limits, and free to contend only with the
biological and physical limits that are left. He is not continually
trying to get things right so he can be satisfied: he comes from
a constant state of satisfaction, overflowing in such a way that
whatever he does gets things right, because they were never, in
fact, otherwise.
    The Master is such a one who has travelled the path to his own
liberation and has come back to do what he can to help others
along their own paths. This is a most difficult undertaking for
the ways in which the seeker frustrates his own understanding,
are deep and devious, and the Master has to be even more devious
in his attempts to trip up the neurotic dance we lead ourselves.
Not all enlightened beings become Masters, as not all healthy beings become doctors. What, then, are the special skills and functions of the guru?
    There are a number of metaphors for the Master, some of them
more appropriate than others. He is not, for example, a philosopher or a theologian - not primarily. His chief concern is not to
devise accurate theories about Reality or God, but to lead people
to direct encounters with them. Intellectual formulations are never

an end for him, though he may use them as a means. Consequently very few Masters write: nearly all the scriptures were originally spoken, and only later transcribed and published by disciples. Words come, are uttered at a particular time and for a particular purpose, and their job is then completed. The Master knows that the truth he is trying to broadcast cannot be caught in a net of words, however fine its weave. Yet his problem is to try time and again to find a way of saying what cannot be said.

Because he is not in the business of telling the truth, his utterances have a sharpness and a kick that is not to be found in the learned journals and the fat tomes: his language would be less out of place in a working-man's club than a university department of religious studies. The activities that go on in the latter, and in his name, are as beside the point as an analysis of the carbon copies of the prescriptions of a dead doctor. One is free to follow such academic pursuits, of course, but one had better be clear that they have nothing at all to do with one's own health.

The image of a Master as a teacher is also misleading. It is impossible to produce a change in someone's being, in their spontaneity and intuition, perceptions and impulses, by telling them things, however insightful or profound the tellings may be. Rational understanding is part of the problem, not the path to a solution, so the only thing that a teacher gets his audience to be is taut: if the head gains wisdom without taking the body with it, disparity and dissociation are multiplied. And by the same token the Master is not directly concerned with his disciples' doing better – though he may, as we have seen, use moral discipline as a device for provoking some necessary change. As he is not concerned to teach better knowledge, so he is no preacher of good behaviour, though he may both inform and instruct to achieve specific effects.

The most helpful metaphor is, as I have intimated already, that of a physician or therapist: enlightened Masters are, we might say, the Ultimate Therapists, for they focus their benign attention not on problems but on the very root from which the problems spring, the problem-sufferer and solver himself. The Master deploys his therapeutic tricks to one end: that of the exposure and dissolution of the fallacious self. His art is a subtle one because the illusions cannot be excised with a scalpel, dispersed with massage, or quelled with drugs. He has to work at one remove by knocking away familiar props and habits, and sustaining the seeker's courage and resolve through the fall. Only thus can the organism cure itself. His techniques resemble those of the demolition expert, setting strategically placed charges to blow up the established super-structure of the ego, so that the ground may be exposed. Yet he has to work on each case individually, dismantling and challenging in the right sequence and at the right speed, using whatever the 'patient' brings as his raw material for the work of the moment.

The guises in which these masterly physicians present themselves may change alarmingly, depending on who and what they

are working with. Their prescriptions have to be tailored to the
dis-ease. It is no surprise therefore that Masters are often out-
rageously inconsistent in what they say and do. If people view
them as philosophers, of course, this creates a lot of annoyance
and confusion: but this reaction stems from the mistaken analogy.
We would not censure a doctor for recommending rest to one
patient and exercise to the next: on the contrary, eyebrows would
be raised if he were consistent, prescribing 'fresh air and exercise', or any one cure, for headaches, broken legs, colds and
pregnancy alike.

Sometimes the Master appears as a guide, suggesting meditations
or practices in a friendly sort of way; sometimes a sergeant-major,
publicly berating a disciple for faults real or invented. Which he
chooses will depend on his intuitions about the disciple's personality, his resilience, commitment, stubbornness or acquiescence.
When appropriate he may appear as a cartographer. Having
listened to someone's fearful and garbled account of an experience
during meditation, he may reassure them by providing a framework within which they can comprehend what is happening to
them. On such occasions the Master may sound as if he is teaching, whereas his intention is quite different. Whether what he
says is true, or even sensible, is secondary to the question of
whether it will allay the seeker's intellectual turmoil long enough
for him to follow through a therapeutic chain of events from which
he might otherwise flee in terror. At times the Master may even
become a con-man, ignoring the truth entirely in order to create
a useful situation or reaction. Bhagwan tells the story of a father
who came home to see the ground floor of his house on fire, and
his children playing happily upstairs. Thinking quickly he
shouted, 'Come and see the fantastic presents I've brought you
from town' and they immediately came rushing out, though he
was lying, and had no presents for them at all. Had he told them
the truth which they could not have understood, they might well
have stayed put, and been burned to death. The lie that they
could understand saved their lives. Just so, Bhagwan says, our
house is on fire, but we are deaf to the truth, and the Master
has to use whatever he can to get us out of the house. Once outside, we can see what he was up to, and the compassionate con
will be appreciated, not resented.

These con-tricks are especially necessary to the Master when he
is in the role of fisherman. His problem is that until people know
what he is talking about - through experience - they do not know
what he is talking about. By holding out the promise of presents
of material and intellectual kinds, people can be persuaded to put
themselves at risk; they can be goaded outside the house of their
own ignorance into a clearer atmosphere of understanding that
becomes its own reward. Maharishi Mahesh Yogi, for example is
a salesman, he sells meditation to people brought up to pay and
to consume. So he charges a good price and promises a good return. 'Half a week's income, eh? . . . That's forty pounds. It
must be good.' What the punters don't know is that when they buy

their mantra and their forty minutes a day, they are sowing in
themselves the seeds of destruction of the very motives that led
them to invest in the first place. Other Masters like Krishnamurti
and Bhagwan Shree Rajneesh bait their hook with words; their
art is that of the sophist. They catch people through their desire
to achieve not material but intellectual possessions. Here again,
people are reeled in through their need to understand: but having
swallowed the academic hook, they find that the line and the sinker
of personal involvement, and the confronting of the limitations of
rational thought, soon follow. The bait must be palatable: it needs
to have enough of the truth to be satisfying, yet easily digestible.
If the truth, as Buddha put it, of 'suffering and the end of suffering' is exposed (in so far as it can be) too rapidly or too
harshly, many people will either be repelled or frightened by it,
or will just not understand at all. Thus it is that many Masters
and traditions conceal the pill in a spoonful of honey, using jokes,
anecdotes, fables or parables. It often turns out that people are
reached more effectively in this indirect way than by being beaten
over the head with the hard facts or forced to swallow the bitter
truth. Still other Masters, like Jesus, as we shall see in a minute,
and like some Indian yogis, present themselves as magicians,
trapping those who believe in the 'supernatural' with tricks and
miracles. Whatever the bait, be it the power of flight, intellectual
arguments, or sleight-of-hand, its sole purpose is to attract
people to the Master. If many of them leave again, disappointed
or disillusioned (i.e. with their illusions still intact), some will
stay. They will begin to sense the power of the Master and his
real purpose, and will allow themselves to surrender to his healing schemes.

Perhaps even more important than the disguises which the
Master can take on is his indefinable quality underneath, that
provides a constant inspiration and example to the seeker, and a
mirror of his own state. However much he despairs of ever being
free of his fears and of reconciling man and bull, the presence of
the Master reminds him that it is possible. The quest is long and
dark, and discouragement and failure are constant companions.
With a Master in whom he trusts, though, the seeker can always
see a speck of light at the end of the tunnel. As well as the bare
fact of the Master's existence, his manner and bearing, insight
and wisdom provide an example, a source of nourishment on which
the tacit learning processes of the seeker can feed. By sitting in
the Master's presence, aware of him without thought or judgment,
the seeker begins to imbibe and manifest the same quality of
clarity and stillness. There is, as Zen says, a direct transmission
outside the scriptures, heart to heart. The Master is a queen bee
around which the community of seekers - in Buddhism the *sangha*
- gathers to drink his essence.

And the Master is a mirror too, in which the seeker sees, if
he will, his own reflection. In 'The Psychology of Consciousness'
Ornstein quotes some testimony to this. In Omar Khayyam we
read: 'I am a mirror, and who looks at me, whatever good or bad

he speaks, he speaks of himself.' And Shunryn Suzuki Roshi, a
Zen Master now in America, says 'The perfect man employs his
mind as a mirror, it grasps nothing, it refuses nothing, it receives
but does not keep.'

JESUS

The mysterious mastery of the Zen patriarchs and abbots is well
documented these days. Perhaps it might be of more interest to
use Jesus as an example of a Master, both to show how the characteristics I have outlined appear in action, and to shake a little of
the dust off the Gospels. What support do they provide for the
view of Jesus, not so much as 'the only begotten Son of God',
and 'King of the Jews', but as one of a small band of Remarkable
Men doing his best to goad, irritate and drag other people towards
their own enlightenment?
   There is no doubt that he was a masterly fisherman: he even
uses the metaphor himself. He holds out the carrot of some
heavenly state just around the corner ('The kingdom of heaven is
at hand')* and does not go out of his way, when speaking in public, to explain to people that this is a rather different kind of
kingdom, and he a rather different kind of king, than they might
have imagined. Working on the principle that 'many are called but
few are chosen', and that those who cannot drop their materialistic
motives are in for a disappointment, he initiates a very successful
advertising campaign for 'the Kingdom of God' and 'everlasting
life'. Jesus was also a consummate magician. Living in superstitious
times, he realized, as he said rather sorrowfully to a man in
Galilee: 'Except ye see signs and wonders, ye will not believe.'
So signs and wonders he provided, giving dramatic public demonstrations of his powers as a psychotherapist by relieving people
of hysterical symptoms, and doing party tricks at wedding recep-
tions. Though some of his magic seems a bit cheap, it was necessary and effective. After his training with the spiritual sect called
the Essenes, and his prolonged delving into himself in solitary
meditation, he turned out to be an astute psychologist: 'But Jesus
did not commit himself unto them', John noted on another occasion,
'because he knew all men. And needed not that any should testify
of man: for he knew what was in man.'
   Two general points about his teaching are noteworthy before we
look at the actual conventions of the map which he used to guide
his followers. First like a good physician, he contradicts himself.
Compare: 'Honour thy father and mother', 'Blessed are peace-
makers', and 'But I say unto you, whosoever is angry with his
brother without a cause shall be in danger of the judgment . . .
whosoever shall say, Thou fool, shall be cast in danger of hell

---

*I shall take the easiest option of assuming that the four Gospels
are what they claim to be: accurate records of Christ's ministry.

fire' on the one hand, with: 'Think not that I am come to send
peace on earth: I came not to send peace, but a sword. For I am
come to set a man at variance against his father, and the daughter
against her mother in law. And a man's foes shall be they of his
own household.' Or the unequivocal call, recorded by Luke: 'If
any man come to me, and hate not his father, and mother, and
wife, and children, and brethren, and sisters, yea, and his own
life also, he cannot be my disciple.' Strong words from a Man
whose Father is still visualized as a Victorian householder.

The other outstanding feature of Jesus' teaching is his reliance
on parables, in which he uses the everyday vocabulary of agri-
culture, planting, sowing, wine-making and so on, as innocuous
cloaks for his revolutionary truths. He explains to his disciples
very clearly why this subterfuge is necessary. 'Therefore I speak
to them in parables: because they seeing see not; and hearing
they hear not, neither do they understand . . . For this people's
heart is waxed gross, and their ears are dull of hearing, and
their eyes they have closed; lest at any time they should see with
their eyes, and hear with their ears, and should understand with
their heart, and should be converted, and I should heal them.'
So he cannot tackle them head-on, but must slide his knowledge
into them, a little at a time, when they are not looking.

His teaching, when we take the lid off it, contains several very
familiar ingredients. The possibility of the attainability of God-
hood by every individual is there, although it has sunk to the
bottom over the course of two thousand years. In John, for instance, we find:

> Jesus answered them, Is it not written in your law, I said,
> Ye are gods? If he called them gods, unto whom the word of
> God came, and the scriptures cannot be broken; say ye of
> him, whom the Father hath sanctified, and sent into the world,
> Thou blasphemest: because I said, I am the Son of God?

And in Luke the famous suggestion where to search:

> The kingdom of God cometh not with observation; neither shall
> they say, Lo here!, or lo there! for, behold, the kingdom of
> God is within you.

Like a mustard seed, indeed, that needs discovering and slowly
nurturing. How do we go about this cultivation? The directions
also have a familiar ring.

> Judge not, that ye be not judged. For with what judgment ye
> judge, ye shall be judged: and with what measure ye mete, it
> shall be measured to you again. And why beholdest thou the
> mote that is in thy brother's eye, but considerest not the beam
> that is in thine own eye? Or how wilt thou say to thy brother,
> Let me pull out the mote out of thine eye; and, behold, a beam
> is in thine own eye? Thou hypocrite, first cast out the beam
> out of thine own eye; and then shalt thou see clearly to cast
> out the mote out of thy brother's eye.

The image fits exactly with the diagnosis of man's condition that
we find in the East: the problem is one of attention, of awareness,
and not just of what we see, but of the way we see, impediments

in the process of vision itself. That is why the disease is so difficult to spot, for we know no alternative to our cloudy sight,
and taking it for normal, cannot see what the fuss is all about.
Yet if we do not see what is so, we are divided, living in a distorted and dissociated world.

Every kingdom divided against itself is brought to desolation;
and every city or house divided against itself cannot stand.
Once we achieve that redirection of attention, the motes begin to
dissolve, so that instead of accumulating more and more illusions,
the process is reversed.

For unto everyone that hath [illusions] shall be given [more
illusions], and he shall have abundance: but from him that hath
not shall be taken away even that which he hath.

Perhaps the biggest lacuna that we have, says Jesus, is the
belief that we can do anything to save ourselves, to ensure our
own security through clinging to friends, possessions, home,
even life itself. 'If any man will come after me, let him deny himself, and take up his cross, and follow me. For whosoever will
save his life shall lose it: and whosoever shall lose his life for my
sake shall find it.' The only security is to be found in trust, in
letting go of those 'treasures that moth and rust doth corrupt'.
Birds and plants do not take out life insurance or hire security
guards, 'wherefore, if God so clothe the grass of the field, which
today is, and tomorrow is cast into the oven, shall he not much
more clothe you, O ye of little faith? Therefore, take no thought,
saying, What shall we eat? or What shall we drink? or Wherewithal
shall we be clothed? . . . for your heavenly Father knoweth that
ye have need of all these things. But seek ye first the kingdom
of God, and his righteousness: and all these things shall be added
unto you.' Nor need you worry about what to say or do. 'Take
no thought how or what ye shall speak, for it shall be given you
in that same hour what to speak. For it is not ye that speak, but
the Spirit of your Father that speaketh in you.'

The enlightened man, the Son of man, the Man of the Spirit, is
he that lives perpetually and naturally in this trust in the Father,
Nature, the Tao. 'The foxes have holes, and the birds of the air
have nests, but the Son of man hath not where to lay his head.'
And 'The wind bloweth where it listeth, and thou hearest the
sound thereof, but canst not tell whence it cometh or whither it
goeth: so is everyone that is born of the Spirit.' For such a man,
trust is effortless, for he knows there is no alternative. The
idiocy of the ego's attempts to get the world just right has been
fully exposed and the attempts abandoned, so that he now lives
as an indissociable part of the greater Whole that produced and
sustains him. St John records several instances of Jesus's acknowledgment of his own lack of autonomy: his understanding
that actions come through him, not from him. 'Verily, verily, I
say unto you, The Son can do nothing of himself, but what he
seeth the Father do: for what things soever he doeth, these also
doeth the Son likewise', and again: 'I can of mine own self do
nothing: as I hear, I judge: and my judgment is just; because I

seek not mine own will, but the will of the Father which hath sent
me. If I bear witness of myself, my witness is not true. There is
another that beareth witness of me; and I know that the witness
which he witnesseth of me is true.' This last statement is perhaps
the clearest indication in the Gospels of Jesus's surrender, of his
realization in his own life of *wei-wu-wei*, action through inaction,
that is so familiar in Taoism. 'When ye have lifted up the Son of
man, then shall ye know that I am he, and that I do nothing of
myself; but as my Father hath taught me, I speak these things.
And he that sent me is with me: the Father hath not left me alone;
for I do always those things that please him.' And the same realis-
ation is available to anyone: all that is required is that they get
out of their own way. 'If any man will do His will, he shall know
of the doctrine, whether it be of God, or whether I speak of myself.'

If all people are capable of being at one with the Father, they
must be capable of being at one with each other, of coming to see
their unity, their ultimate connectedness with all things and all
creatures. 'Neither pray I for these alone, but for them also
which shall believe on me through their word; that they all may
be one; as thou, Father, art in me, and I in thee, that they also
may be one in us: . . . I in them, and thou in me, that they may
be made perfect in one.'

In order to achieve this surrender, to recapture one's innocence
and at-onement, one must drop all the psychological possessions
that add up to the sense of an independent self: all the beliefs,
desires, fears and conditionings that do not have any basis in
reality. One must die to one's familiar lies before one's integrity
can be reinstated. Jesus is not alone in using the metaphor of
death and resurrection to describe this process. 'Verily, verily,
I say unto thee, Except a man be born again, he cannot see the
kingdom of God.' Nor in comparing the innocence of the man who
has lost his life and found it again, with that of the infant who
has yet to lose it. 'Suffer little children to come unto me, and forbid them not, for of such is the kingdom of God. Verily I say unto you, Whosoever shall not receive the kingdom of God as a little
child shall in no wise enter therein.' Or in a different Gospel:
'Except ye be converted, and become as little children, ye shall
not enter into the kingdom of heaven. Whosoever shall humble
himself as this little child, the same is greatest in the kingdom of
heaven.' Just as a small child trusts in his father, so does the
enlightened man trust in existence.

The trouble is that there is no way to surrender, because it is
not a doing but a relinquishing of doing. Time and again disciples
ask 'How?' - how to surrender, how to attain the kingdom, how to
see the Father, as if it might be a matter of sending in a curri-
culum vitae and waiting for an appointment. But 'how' already
denies the seamlessness of things: it presupposes that 'I' can step
in and, through its own intelligence and efforts, get things better.
The core of the problem is in the impulse to ask the question.
Nevertheless Masters have to give in to the continual clamour for

methods and techniques, because the ego cannot be brought to a
confrontation with its own stupidity directly. It must be led
around by the nose for a while first. While Jesus would, if he
could, have given people the eyes to see, he too has to dance his
followers about. What methods does he offer?

First, he encourages his audience to surrender to him. If they
cannot drop their baggage and sink into the Father, they might
be prepared to taste surrender to themselves through surrender
to the Son. 'All things are delivered unto me of my Father: and
no man knoweth the Son, but the Father; neither knoweth any
man the Father, save the Son, and he to whomsoever the Son will
reveal him.' And he immediately goes on to show 'how' to know
the Son: 'Come unto me, all ye that labour and are heavy laden,
and I will give you rest. Take my yoke upon you and learn of
me; for I am meek and lowly in heart: and ye shall find rest unto
your souls. For my yoke is easy and my burden is light.' This is
the miracle of surrender: that by adding the apparent burden of
obedience and subordination to the Master to the already intoler-
able weight of one's own life, the load is not increased but dissolved. Though one might think that this is achieved through
simply dumping one's cares on to the guru, the process is not
that at all. Responsibility is not abrogated; it is entered into
fully and accepted in a way that has never happened before. The
burden is found to be a product of misconception – like walking
by trying to lift up and move your legs with your hands one by
one. When seen into through the experience of helplessness, it is
given up at once.

Second, Jesus encourages people to pay attention to his example:
not to particular actions or words but to the quality of his own
being. Masters know the power of their own presence to enlighten
and transform their neighbours. The disciple does not have to do
anything, to copy or imitate. Just by being near, he picks up,
unintentionally and unconsciously, some of the Master's grace.
Jesus uses the metaphor of feeding for this process: feeding not
on the dry bones of his teaching but on his living example, his
flesh and blood.

Verily, verily, I say unto you, Except ye eat the flesh of the
Son of man, and drink his blood, ye have no life in you. Whoso
eateth my flesh, and drinketh my blood, hath eternal life; and
I will raise him up at the last day. For my flesh is meat indeed,
and my blood is drink indeed. He that eateth my flesh, and
drinketh my blood, dwelleth in me, and I in him. As the living
Father hath sent me, and I live by the Father: so he that eateth
me, even he shall live by me.

While in the Holy Communion service we find the three elements
of surrender (faith), ingesting Christ as an example (feeding),
and the lightness and bliss (thanksgiving) that results, brought
together: 'Take and eat this in remembrance that Christ died for
thee, and feed on him in thy heart by faith with thanksgiving.'

Third, Jesus, like all Masters, stresses the intrinsic value of
the four 'a's': alertness, aliveness, awareness and attention. In

John's Gospel, he uses the image of light for awareness: 'light
is come into the world, and men loved darkness rather than light,
because their deeds were evil. For everyone that doeth evil hateth
the light, neither cometh to the light lest his deeds should be
reproved. But he that doeth truth cometh to the light . . .' In
Luke, Jesus says:

> Let your loins be girded about and your lights burning; and
> ye yourselves like unto the men that waiteth for their lord,
> when he will return from the wedding; that when he cometh
> and knocketh they may open unto him immediately. Blessed are
> those servants who the lord when he cometh shall find watch-
> ing . . .

And in Matthew:

> But know this, that if the goodman of the house had known in
> what watch the thief would come, he would have watched, and
> would not have suffered his house to be broken up. Therefore
> be ye also ready: for in such an hour as ye think not the Son
> of man cometh.

Fourth, and perhaps most characteristic of Jesus, are what we
might call his 'kōans of action': impossible tasks that he sets
people, which, if they strive mightily to complete, will result in
the explosion of the 'doer'. In Zen the disciple struggles with an
impossible problem in thought. In Christianity he struggles with
an equally absurd problem in action. The two most powerful
kōans are these: 'Thou shalt love the Lord thy God with all thy
heart, and with all thy soul, and with all thy mind. This is the
first and great commandment. And the second is like unto it,
Thou shalt love thy neighbour as thyself.' The disciple is instructed to will his love - 'Thou shalt' - for a God-figure he cannot
comprehend, and for all his fellow men, many of whom inspire
only irritation and contempt. And the problem is even worse, because nothing less than total sincerity will do. 'Woe unto you,
scribes and Pharisees, hypocrites! for ye make clean the outside
of the cup and of the platter, but within they are full of extortion
and excess . . . Woe unto you, scribes and Pharisees, hypocrites!
for ye are like unto whited sepulchres, which indeed appear
beautiful outward, but are within full of dead men's bones, and
of all uncleanness.' It's no use faking it: your love must be spontaneous, genuine, constant and right from the heart. What a
beautiful Catch-22! The only way out is to try to do everything
you can to comply, and in the ultimate moment of despair to open
oneself at last to the gift of love: a love of God and of man that
is everlasting and overflowing when the 'lover' is missing. The
point is missed now, as it was then, by turning this bone-
crunching device for transformation into a half-hearted and gut-
less morality; because the point is not the keeping of the commandments, but the friction that the attempt to keep them necessarily produces, a friction that burns away the barriers to our
unity.

Part II

6 INTEGRITY IN
   CONTEMPORARY PSYCHOLOGY

In Part I we explored the notion of Integrity; its ontology, the
experience of self that lies at its centre, and the loss and recapture of that experience - Paradise, Paradise Lost and Paradise
Regained. We found that man is brought up to experience himself
and his world through a theory or a map that is in certain crucial
respects profoundly misleading. King among these misapprehen-
sions is the belief that he is the map rather than the experiential
terrain on which it is overlaid; for once this assumption is made a
person cannot question the map without simultaneously questioning himself. A threat to the theory becomes a threat to his own
survival, if a man sees himself as the theory. Thus the other
fallacies that the map contains become insulated from all those
aspects of experience that could find them wanting. They become
almost - though happily not quite entirely - beyond question. The
most important of these fallacies concern the self: they project a
picture of man as independent, separate, autonomous, persisting,
and as the source or cause of many of his actions. They lead him
to see his thought as holding executive power over his behaviour,
and thus to get upset when mental authority seems to be ignored
by wayward flesh. The extent of his intimacy and mutuality with
the world beyond his skin is seriously underestimated. Much of
himself is denied access to his picture of himself, and to conscious
awareness, thus constraining his development and preventing him
sloughing off old skins of habit and belief that are no longer fitting. Most of the time, therefore, man is out of sync, out of kilter
with his body, his feelings and his circumstances, a fact of which
his awareness varies on a scale ranging from 'not at all' to 'acute'.

So to point out these errors of judgment, even to suggest that
there might be room for improvement, is not to diminish man. To
deprive man of his active and controlling self is not to leave him
incomplete - ruptured and rudderless, less substantial and less
potent. In fact, it doesn't make any difference at all to the way he
works, for we have only robbed him of an idea, a conceit. And in
the realm of his experience he ends up not poorer but infinitely
richer: no longer trapped inside a meatball, jousting with a hostile
world, but heir to the entire universe. Not 'a stranger and afraid,
in a world I never made', but at ease and at home everywhere
because he knows himself to be both architect and host.

The quest in Part II is for a psychology of Integrated Man to
replace the Self-ish one we have rejected. How can we account for
the way man really works if his own account, his second nature,
cannot do the job? So the plan is to come up with an account of

integrated functioning that conforms to the principles we have established, and then road-test it on a fair selection of everyday activities and phenomena in the psychological domain and see how it performs.

The starting point will be a look at some of the dominant theoretical traditions in contemporary psychology to see what help we can derive from them. To the extent that their underlying models of man are acceptable, we may be able to pilfer some of the bits and pieces we will need from stores, as it were, in order to cut down on the number that have to be specially manufactured. Chapter 6 sees us out on this scavenger hunt, and we will then be able to try to bolt together a working model in the home workshop that we will set up in Chapter 7.

Right at the outset we are faced with a problem, though. Psychology is not one beast but many, each with a different concern, level of rigour and philosophical base. At one end we have the 'whole-person' psychologies of the humanistic and psychodynamic schools; at the other the technical theorizing of cognitive psychology and the minute observations of the behaviourists. These tacitly agreed divisions of level and labour are a headache, for on the left wing we have the commendable relevance and regrettable woolliness of the humanists, and on the right the enormous precision about tiny functions of the others. And each resists and resents the modus operandi of the other.

For example, we already have considerable knowledge about the full human-ness of man from authors in the humanistic and psychodynamic traditions but they give us little idea about the detailed workings of the human organism. Their general attitude seems to be that to demystify those aspects of human beings that are most human is necessary to dehumanize them: to treat people as objects, albeit objects of interest, and thus to insult and belittle them. As soon as one starts to talk of computers or retrieval of information from memory, or visual information processing, their eyes glaze and their lips curl. Not all, it's true - Fritz Perls has been known to use computer analogies to explain aspects of human functioning - but most. Whereas I believe that this dehumanization is not an inevitable companion of clear understanding, although the very limited nature of cognitive psychology has, until recently, made it so. As Skinner says in 'Beyond Freedom and Dignity', 'science does not dehumanize man, it de-homunculizes him', and that is both legitimate and valuable. It is an article of faith for me that it is possible to understand and to model man-in-his-richness (however inadequately we can, at the moment, do it); that this ambitious project is the only one of importance in psychology; and that wilful romanticism may be aesthetically satisfactory, but it takes you no place. On the other side of psychology, in the behavioural cognitive, experimental streams, we have masses of nitty-gritty models of man's performance, but all of them stemming from, and applicable to, an extremely narrow subsection of the total range of thoughts, feelings, impressions and actions of which man is capable. The antagonism between these two approaches constitutes the

deepest and most abiding split in psychology, and it is a necessary preliminary to a model of Integrated Man to bridge it; to
make some progress towards an integrated psychology.

In this chapter we shall rummage through the writings of four
of the senior figures in psychology, representing contrasting,
but potentially useful approaches to the person. They are George
Kelly, Carl Rogers, Erich Fromm and 'B. F.' Skinner. From
George Kelly and his theory of personal constructs comes a careful analysis of the conventional nature of the knowledge that we
use for construing and interpreting the world. From the psychoanalytic theory of Freud and its development by Erich Fromm
derives an appreciation of that side of man's nature that is normally denied to conscious awareness. Skinner's behaviourism
balances the view of man as self-inventing and self-directing that
characterizes Kelly and others with an appreciation of the extent
to which we are formed by our natural, involuntary dealings with
environment. Carl Rogers forces us to see the importance of our
internal, bodily sensed feelings and emotions in learning and
development.

I should say that in no sense is the intention of this chapter to
provide exhaustive surveys or critiques of these authors. On the
contrary, I shall in most cases be basing my comments on a small,
selective part of their output, usually just those papers or chapters where they have been at their most philosophical and/or
speculative, and where their comments strike me as being most
relevant to the development of a model of Integrated Man within
the traditions of twentieth-century psychology.

GEORGE KELLY

My sources for discussion of Kelly's Personal Construct Theory
(PCT) are Kelly's major work, 'The Psychology of Personal Constructs', and the popular exposition of his views by Bannister
and Fransella, 'Inquiring Man'.

The point from which Kelly starts is that what a person does in
a situation depends on how he construes it. We all possess a
theory about the world - which includes ourselves - and this determines all our dealings with it; how we perceive it, think about
it, feel about it and react to it. 'We can only make assumptions
about what reality is and then proceed to find out how useful or
useless these assumptions are' (Bannister and Fransella). We
operate in the world with our theories just as a scientist operates
in the laboratory with his. On the basis of the theory we predict
what is going to happen next, and in what way our actions will
influence what happens next. By continually comparing what we
expect to happen with what actually does happen we can develop
our theory so as to be ever more accurate. Kelly says,

> Man looks at the world through transparent patterns or
> templates which he creates and then attempts to fit over
> the realities of which the world is composed. The fit is

not always very good. Yet without such patterns the world appears to be such an undifferentiated homogeneity that man is unable to make any sense out of it.

Thus there is at the very basis of PCT a recognition of the difference between the map and the territory that we discussed in Chapter 2. Furthermore, in order to compare the map with the territory, and thereby improve the former, it is necessary to be aware of *both*, in just the same way that a scientist can only develop his theory by noticing things that it cannot yet account for. Yet Kelly does not discuss the considerable problem of how one can be aware of something that one cannot construe; a problem which any model of man that accepts the basic map/territory view must consider. We shall see later that this issue of the modifications of a construct system by a reality that it cannot yet incorporate is the crucial one in accounting for significant learning.

Kelly also agrees with the view of Integrated Man in seeing nature, and man within it, as processes rather than structures. His attitude is definitely tuneful rather than pebbly. For example, he says: 'Another important prior conviction is that the universe ... is continually changing with respect to itself ... within our universe something is always going on. In fact that is the way the universe exists: it exists by happening.' And he goes on to apply this particularly to living creatures:

By assuming that matter is composed basically of static units it becomes immediately necessary to account for the obvious fact that what was observed was not always static but often thoroughly active. What made the units active? Why 'energy' of course!

Instead of buying the prior assumption of an inert object, either on an implicit or an explicit basis, we propose to postulate a *process* as the point of departure for the formulation of a psychological theory. Thus the whole controversy as to what prods an inert organism into action becomes a dead issue. Instead the organism is delivered fresh into the psychological world alive and struggling...

For our purposes man is not an object which is temporarily in a moving state but is himself a form of motion.

Bannister and Fransella put it this way:

Suppose we begin by assuming that the fundamental thing about life is that it goes on. It isn't that something *makes* you go on; the going on *is the thing itself*. It isn't that motives *make* a man come alert and do things; his alertness is an aspect of his very being.

Kelly here makes exactly the same neat switch that Newton made in thinking about the motion of inanimate bodies. 'A body will remain at rest or travelling with constant velocity unless acted upon by an external force.' Motion itself is not a problem any more; it is a given. What needs explaining is not activity but change in activity. We can see men not as being prodded into activity but as 'open systems of energy exchange which exhibit activity intrinsically, and upon which stimuli have a modulating, but not an initiating effect', as J. McV. Hunt puts it.

Kelly has also seen the importance of the interconnectedness of things. 'The universe that we presume exists has another important characteristic: it is integral. By that we mean it functions as a single unit with all its imaginable parts having an exact relationship to each other ... it all works together like clockwork.' But although this sounds very similar to the position described in Chapter 2, Kelly's nerve is already beginning to fail. For in his telling analogy to clockwork, the cogs and levers are separate things fitted together. For Kelly the world is an intricate assembly of things: for Buddhism and sub-atomic physics the things themselves do not exist as separate entities at all. They only 'exist' in the sense that an arbitrary boundary is placed round some portion of the world for the purposes of description. The 'thing' referred to is a composite, an abstraction, an approximation to the territory. Things are created by people for their convenience; they are not discovered or dug up like an old pot. Korzybski's famous dictum 'Whatever I say a thing is, it is not', and Max Clowes's 'There is no seeing, only seeing as' present this truth neatly packaged. When I see something as a particular thing, its identity derives in part from its relationship with other 'things' in its context. When I change the context, the things themselves change. And I myself form a very important part of the context, so that any change in me brings a corollary change in my perception of the things around me. Bannister and Fransella have presumably seen this, for they quote Bertrand Russell saying, 'The observer, when he seems to himself to be observing a stone, is, if modern physics is to be believed, observing the effects of the stone upon himself', with obvious approval. Yet this recognition does not inform the writings of George Kelly in the way that, understood 'with the heart', it would have to.

Kelly's use of clockwork as an analogy also belies his belief in an intrinsically dynamic universe; for clockwork has to have a motor, some focused sources of energy that moves the rest of it. The motor or spring in a sense stands outside the system of which it is part. It is connected, but it is not influenced by the rest of the system in the same way as the rest of the system is influenced by it. And sure enough, we find in Kelly that there are such motors in his universe: centres of activity that are more influencing than influenced. They are living creatures.

One part of the universe, the living creature, is able to bring himself around to represent another part, his environment ... Because he can represent his environment he can place alternative constructions upon it, and, indeed, *do something about it* if it doesn't suit him. To the living creature then the universe is real, but it is not inexorable unless he chooses to construe it that way ... Men can play active roles in the shaping of events. [My emphasis]

Kelly sees man as rather like a traffic policeman directing and controlling the cars - the events - around him. He does not see that the policeman is just as much controlled by the cars as they by him. His basic mistake, where he breaks faith with the principles he claims to accept, is in assuming that because man is able to predict events, sometimes with a high degree of success, he is therefore able to control them. He is quite explicit about this: 'As a scientist man seeks to predict and *thus to control* the course of events.'

From Buddhism's point of view this simple piece of false logic is basic to our illusory conception of our own nature. Remember the man sitting on the bank of a river, who gradually comes to notice certain patterns and consistencies in the sequence of objects floating past. To amuse himself the man begins to play a game with himself called 'I Did It', which relies on him pretending to ignore the corks (which he has noticed predict bottles), so that he can apparently conjure bottles out of thin air. Unfortunately, he becomes so enthralled with his game that he takes it for the truth, and forgets that his feeling of control rests solely on noticing regularities in a world over which he has no real control at all. The only difference between this sad figure and the rest of us is that our 'world' is not 'out there' like the river, but is the stream of thoughts, feelings, perceptions and movements that flows in and through us. We are both the stream and the watcher.

Why Kelly is so insistent on control is revealed very clearly later on in his book. 'To abandon the notion of control, with respect to any behaviour whatsoever, is to abandon the notion of lawfulness.' And he has already pointed out that without lawfulness, the world is chaotic, 'an undifferentiated homogeneity'. No wonder he is frightened to let go, like a man who has to breathe with the utmost deliberation lest he stop breathing, or another who cannot trust himself to float if he stops thrashing about. But the laws are not imposed by us on nature, or on our own behaviour, as the instrument of our control; they are our conceptualization of regularities that exist of themselves. If we change our conceptualization, our law, our view of what and how we control, that alters the object of the law not one whit. The feeling that predictability depends on control (rather than vice versa) is the source of Kelly's fear – as it is, at bottom, the source of fear in every one of us.

Perhaps the clearest expression of the way PCT presents the person to himself is to be found in Bannister and Fransella:

It is argued you consider yourself a person in that:
1. You entertain a notion of your own *separateness* from others; you rely on the privacy of your own consciousness.
2. You entertain a notion of the integrality or completeness of your experience, so that you believe all parts of it are relatable because *you are the experiencer.*
3. You entertain a notion of your own *continuity over time*, you possess your own biography and live in relation to it.
4. You entertain a notion of the *causality* of your actions, you have purposes, you intend, *you accept a partial responsibility for the effects of what you do.*

5. You entertain a notion of other persons by analogy with
    yourself, you assume a comparability of subjective
    experience.

In summary you see yourself as *self-inventing*.

I have italicized those key ideas that are essential to construct
theory's view of the person, and alien to Integrated Man. In fact,
far from helping to put man back together, Kelly fragments him
further. Consider this passage:

does a man control his own destiny? Our anwer to that is
that he may control it to the extent that he can develop a
construction system with which he identifies himself and
is sufficiently comprehensive to subsume the world around
him. If he is unable to identify himself with the system, he
may be able to predict events determinatively but he can
experience no personal control.

Now we have not just the familiar 'I' and 'myself', but we have
a 'construction system' as well – and a curious process of 'identifying', which 'I' effects between 'myself' and 'my construction
system'. It looks as if all three are separate, but that somehow
the first persuades the second to view itself as if it were the
third.

There is an obvious and attractive way out of this, which is to
say that the construction system is not just 'identified' with myself, it is myself. They are two different ways of talking about
the same thing. However we are not free in PCT to make this
simple move. In Kelly's definition of guilt, for example, as 'the
dislodgement of the self from one's core role structure', the two
are clearly different: otherwise how could one be 'dislodged' from
the other? Kelly himself is unacceptably cavalier about the problem of self in relation to the construct system. A letter to Bannister
in 1965 (quoted in Bannister and Fransella, pp. 145-6) on the subject concludes a variety of ill-thought-out speculations with the
observation 'Perhaps the self-concept is not a concept about the
self but rather the set of concepts perpetrated by the self. How's
that for confusing the issue?' 'Self' remains as ambiguous and
elusive as ever.

Kelly also addresses himself to the philosophical issue of determinism. He recognizes quite correctly that a kind of determinism
'is implied in our idea of an integral universe. The universe as it
flows along is not essentially divided into independent events like
cars on a railroad train. It is an essential continuity. Because of
this continuity we may consider that there is a determinism operating between antecedent and subsequent events.' Here he almost
gets it right. What he fails to see again is that the whole notion of
determinism as construed in opposition to free-will is only sensible
if the determiner and the determinee can be isolated. And, as he
says, they cannot. One does not need to side with determinism
against free-will: the conflict is resolved by being transcended.

More important than this, though, is that Kelly refuses to see
the radical implications of his logic for man's view of his own
nature. Again he baulks, calling this sense of determinism

'relatively unimportant', and preferring to concentrate on his own definition of determinism in terms of the subordination of constructs to each other. 'Since no event could possibly have happened otherwise and still have been itself, there is not much point in singling it out and saying that it was determined.' While one can agree with this narrow statement, it is a lame justification for dismissing the whole issue as unimportant!

Despite these criticisms of PCT, there are a number of useful points we can pull out that orient us in the right direction, and that are carried through in the development of the theory. One is that a person's construct system is ultimately not just a basis for understanding the world but is the source of action. 'A theory provides a basis for an active approach to life, not merely a comfortable armchair from which to contemplate its vicissitudes with detached complaisance.' And another is the grounding of a person's construing in the significance that events have for him. The theory is a basis for action, but the acting is itself purposeful, and derives from internal needs and desires, both transient and lasting. A person's theory 'is an essential chart for his personal adventures, not ... a self-contained island of meaning in an ocean of inconsequentialities.' Both these points are important, for, as we shall see, they are conspicuous by their absence in contemporary models of cognition, and need to be built back in before such a model can begin to be an adequate account of human experience and behaviour.

While we are anticipating the cognitive models that we shall discuss in detail shortly, it is interesting to note that Kelly himself anticipates the form that these models have taken, and suggests, albeit very perfunctorily, how PCT can be envisaged in these terms. 'We conceive a person's processes as operating through a network of pathways ... The network is flexible and frequently modified, but it is structured and it both facilitates and restricts a person's range of action.' And, further on, we find: 'When a person scans the events with which he is surrounded he 'lights up" certain dichotomies in his construct system. Thus construct systems can be considered as a kind of scanning pattern which a person continually projects upon his world. As he sweeps back and forth across his perceptual field he picks up blips of meaning...' It is a pity from our point of view that Kelly did not feel inclined to explore these metaphors further. He was content 'simply to invite attention to the fact that the personal construct system can be viewed cybernetically', and leave it at that. We shall see how close these throw-aways are to the spirit of John Anderson's ACT system, which they antedate by more than twenty years.

One feature crucial to Kelly's development of the theory of personal constructs is the notion of 'bipolarity'. Roughly, a construct is represented as a pair of autonyms, and if being used to construe an object or event - another person, let's say - then that person cannot be simultaneously construed with respect to both ends, or poles, of the construct. That is, we may see this other person either as kind, or unkind, or we may not apply a kind-unkind construct at all. But we cannot see them as both kind and unkind, loved and hated, friendly and hostile, virginal and sexy.

In one sense this is true, for calling something 'X' necessarily creates some contrast 'not X', which the thing is not. If the thing is both X and not-X, then no contrast has been created, and we have said nothing. This is true in the world of maps. But on the ground itself things are not X or not-X, they are just there.

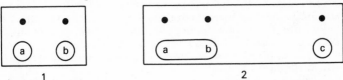

1   2

Figure 5

We can choose to create a grid through which to observe, like Figure 5.1, which makes *a* and *b* in opposition. The frame defines area *a* as 'X' and area *b* as 'not X'. But we could also choose a frame like Figure 5.2, in which *a* and *b* are the same two areas, but are jointly construed as 'X', and contrasted with a third area *c* which is 'not X'. Buddhist scripture is full of warnings like

If you say the world is One, you are mistaken.
If you say it is Many, you are mistaken.
If you say it is both One and Many, you are mistaken.
If you say it is neither One nor Many, you are mistaken.

which point to the fact that the categories and logic of Kellean and Aristotelian thought are conventions on the map, not cuts in nature. I will argue later that a prime function of poetry is to demonstrate to us that the map neither captures not controls reality, by using language to generate 'impossible ideas', like a conjunction of sexuality and spirituality, for example, that can be felt but not understood.

It is true that in the formation of a construct, there must be the implied contrasting of A and B, which are alike in some respect, with C, from which they differ. A and B are smooth, warm, pretty or trustworthy, while C is jagged, cold, ugly or shifty. It is also true that there is an implied contrast whenever a term is used. But it does not follow that constructs are stored inside the head in antonymous pairs; that we should treat all constructs themselves, rather than their usages, as being contrastive. A construct represents a central tendency of meaning, 'fuzzy' at the edges, that has developed from a whole host of contrasts, all of them siightly different. When I call someone an idiot, it may, depending on the particular other person and particular circumstances, have roughly the meaning of 'reckless' (in contrast with 'suitably careful') or 'delightfully spontaneous' (in contrast with 'dull and conventional') or 'stupid' (in contrast with 'clever'). The first and third are critical, negative things to say; the second is a compliment. I cannot select one of 'careful', 'dull' or 'clever' as being the contrast pole to 'idiotic'. It depends.

My image of construct theory's model of the mind is row upon row of those little 'houses' with two figures on a swivel that tell you what the weather's going to be like. If it is going to be fine, the bikini-clad figure is out; if wet, the other one, with umbrella and wellies. There is a kind of logic, or psycho-logic, that ties these pairs of figures together: if Mrs Sunny is out, then Mr Warm and Mr Gardening-Weather are likely to pop out as well. But the disjunctive premise on which this battery of baby meteor-ologists is based is too limited to do justice to the intricacies and inter-dependencies of human cognition. Constructs are used con-trastively, but (a) a particular pole may not have a permanent, well-defined contrast; and (b) the contrast implied in any par-ticular usage is a function of the term chosen and the context in which it is thought or uttered.

Kelly's views on learning are also potentially useful. His claim is that 'learning is not a special class of psychological processes, it is synonymous with any and all psychological processes. It is not something that happens to a person on occasion; it is what makes him a person in the first place.' Thus not only is man a form of motion; the form that he is is continually altered and dev-eloped by the motions he performs. If it were possible to confront a man with the same event twice he could not react the same way the second time, for the processes in terms of which he reacts will have been altered by the first experience. In ordinary speech we make a distinction between those experiences in which we just 'behave', and those in which we 'learn' - and like any distinction it is a useful approximation. But its failure to acknowledge that every interaction with the environment produces some lasting change can lead one into such errors as assuming that a failure on a child's part to learn what you have deemed to be important reflects a failure to learn anything, or worse, a general reluctance to learn at all (the curious phenomenon of being 'unmotivated', to which we shall return later).

To acknowledge that all experience is learning experience, how-ever, is not to say that everyone learns the same things, or at the same rate. Matthew Arnold used to speak of a school inspector colleague of his who claimed to have had thirteen years' experience. 'On the contrary', asserted Arnold, 'it was patently clear to all who knew him that he had had the same year's experience thirteen times.' And Aldous Huxley in the same vein once remarked that 'It is not what experiences a man has, but what he *makes* of those experiences, that matters.' This is important, for it suggests a basic parameter of learning: what Kelly calls *permeability*. 'A con-struct is permeable if it will admit to its range of convenience new elements which are not yet construed within its framework.' In other words, for the construct system to develop, it must in some way be sensitive to aspects of experience that it cannot yet con-strue. This, as we have seen already, is perhaps the central prob-lem in accounting for learning within this kind of framework. The construct system determines one's experience - yet one's exper-ience also determines one's construct system. How can these two statements, which appear to be contradictory, but both of which seem to be generated by the same underlying view, be resolved? Kelly's answer, in terms of permeability, is not too helpful: it relabels the problem rather than tackling it. It is another of his intuitively appealing but ultimately unhelpful metaphors, for there is in PCT no clear idea of what it is that the construct system must be permeable to. Before we can provide an adequate answer to this we need to draw on Carl Rogers's discussions of the same issue, for he can take us a little further.

But first let me give two quotations from Kelly which are helpful, and with which I agree. The first concerns the place of language in PCT:

> It is not possible for one to express the whole of his construction system. Many of one's constructs have no symbols to be used as convenient word handles. They are therefore difficult for ... the person to manipulate or to subsume within the verbally labelled part of his system. [This] makes it difficult for a person to be very articulate about how he feels, or for him to predict what he will do in a future situation which, as yet, exists only in terms of verbal descriptions.

But to amplify this we should perhaps set it alongside Aldous Huxley's succinct analysis of the pros and cons of language in 'The Doors of Perception':

> Every individual is at once the beneficiary and the victim of the linguistic tradition into which he has been born - the beneficiary in as much as language gives access to the accumulated records of other people's experience, the victim insofar as it confirms him in the belief that reduced awareness is the only awareness and as it bedevils his sense of reality, so that he is all too apt to take his concepts for data, his words for actual things.

Kelly sees that part of the construct system is verbally labelled and part not, and sees also the difficulty in trying to predict a hypothetical (i.e. only verbally specified) future. Huxley sees beyond this to the influence that language has on the construct system as a whole, both in determining its formation and in ossifying and limiting the system once formed.

The second quotation is to do with the origin of neurosis, or suffering:

> Ultimately a man sets the measure of his own freedom and his own bondage by the level at which he chooses to establish his convictions. The man who orders his life in terms of many special and inflexible convictions about temporary matters makes himself the victim of circumstances. Each little prior conviction that is not open to review is a hostage he gives to fortune: it determines whether the events of tomorrow will bring happiness or misery. The man whose prior convictions encompass a broad perspective, and are cast in terms of principles rather than rules, has a much better chance of discovering those alternatives which will lead eventually to his emancipation.

Again we can set this beside Huxley's dense and eloquent insights, which this time agree more closely.

Me as I think I am and me as I am in fact - sorrow, in other words, and the ending of sorrow. One third, more or less, of all the sorrow that the person I think I am must endure is unavoidable. It is the sorrow inherent in the human condition, the price we must pay for being sentient and self-conscious organisms, aspirants to liberation, but subject to the laws of nature, and under orders to keep on marching, through irreversible time, through a world wholly indifferent to our well-being, towards a decrepitude and the certainty of death. The remaining two-thirds of all sorrow is home-made and, so far as the universe is concerned, unnecessary.

Both concur with Buddhism's Four Noble Truths in seeing much of human suffering as springing not from an unkind world, but from an inadequate theory which identifies itself with reality and thus must ever deny its own limitations.

The final point that we can take from Kelly concerns the way of construing emotions and our awareness of them. Although he postulates, as we have seen, several inhabitants of the human frame, he is at pains to deny one particular split, that between the rational and the emotional, thoughts and feelings. To quote Bannister and Fransella, 'For Kelly [the rational/emotional] dualism is a badly articulated attempt to cope with the fact that man is a process, and that at different stages in the process very different modes of experience and activity obtain.' His way of integrating feeling and construing is, at least for certain key 'emotions', to redefine them in terms of awareness of certain kinds of transition in the construct system. The prototype is anxiety, which is defined as 'the awareness that the events with which a man is confronted lie mostly outside the range of convenience of his construct system'. If we can de-jargonize this, it means that anxiety is the feeling you get when you don't know what to do next, and when you must therefore conduct a behavioural 'experiment' which is not guaranteed to succeed. It is not something bad, or to be avoided: it is a useful signal in awareness that there is some learning to be done. Unfortunately we are brought up to think that incompetence is something reprehensible, to be concealed or denied, and thus the biological signal of incompetence - which is actually an integral part of being alive - is construed negatively. It is possible to reconstrue anxiety as a reflection in conscious awareness of what myself-in-the-world is up to, and therefore to welcome it. But because this involves becoming aware of the illusions of which we spoke in Part I, it is rather difficult to do.

The reinterpretation of anxiety is interesting but not the most important point here. The central insight is the replacement of a cognition/affect dualism by a construct system and a concept of awareness of certain current or threatened states of that system. We will take this idea and develop it considerably in Chapter 8.

Let us summarize what we can take forward with us from our raid on Kelly. He agrees in principle with the ideas of man as a pattern of processes; of his being an integral part of an undivided world; and of divisions being imposed on the world by an acquired set of concepts, constructs and categories that are largely social or conventional in origin. He does not, however, follow these ideas through fully. He still retains the illusion of man as a separate agent who controls and chooses as well as predicts. This is reflected in the confusion between the self and the construct system, which is never resolved. There is some idea of man divided within and/or against himself, but no explicit description of what an 'ideal' person would be, which one finds in many psychotherapeutically derived writings. There is a useful notion of awareness introduced and related to emotions, but there is little concern with the quality of this awareness. Although PCT is a theory of whole people it views them, in the spirit of traditional psychology, very much from the outside by ignoring the immediacy of experience. One does not feel oneself reflected from the pages of George Kelly as one does from authors like Rogers, Maslow or Fromm. There is no discussion of degrees of awareness, or of consicous and unconscious processes - although one finds pointers like 'a habit can be seen as a convenient kind of stupidity which leaves a person free to act intelligently elsewhere.' The postulation of non-conscious processes in Integrated Man is, as we shall see, essential.

It may seem that I have reviewed the philosophy behind PCT only to be harsh with it. On the contrary, I hope it will be clear that there is a great deal of value, and I have concentrated on the points where its adequacy breaks down in order to see how far it will go, and in which directions one needs to move on.

CARL ROGERS

One thing that is missing from Kelly is any development of the idea that the 'normal' is abnormal - i.e. that there is a natural, healthy, integrated way of being that is almost unknown, and unacknowledged, particularly in Western society. While this idea reaches its fullest elaboration, as we have seen, in Taoism and Buddhism, there are traces of it in the writings of Trigant Burrow, and of the humanistic psychologists such as Abraham Maslow and Carl Rogers. There is, I suspect, no good reason for selecting Rogers as the chief spokesman, but I met his work first, and still find his insights the most personally meaningful and simply and elegantly expressed. His view of the 'fully functioning person' (together with Maslow's 'self-actualizing man') is as near as psychology has got to Integrated Man. It is therefore worth while exploring his characteristics a little. The quotations are mainly drawn from the two papers that comprise part IV of 'On Becoming a Person'. The section is called A Philosophy of Persons, and the two papers are To Be That Self Which One Truly is: A Therapist's

View of Personal Goals, and A Therapist's View of the Good Life:
The Fully Functioning Person.

First, Rogers stresses that the fully functioning person is a
certain kind of process, not a special product. He is characterized by movement, not by any state. 'The good life is not any
fixed state. It is not, in my estimation, a state of virtue, or con-
tentment, or nirvana, or happiness. It is not a condition in which
the individual is adjusted, or fulfilled, or actualized. To use
psychological terms, it is not a state of drive-reduction, or tension
reduction, or homeostasis.' Rogers is clearly in agreement with
Kelly about man's being a form of motion, and in this, as he
points out, they are taking a rather different premise from that
usually implicit in academic psychology. But he goes beyond Kelly
in suggesting that the most healthy people are those who are most
fully in motion - whose constructs, in Kelly's terms, are most permeable. Rogers elaborates his vision like this:

> The person who is psychologically free moves in the direction
> of becoming a more fully functioning person. He is more able
> to live fully in and with each and all of his feelings and
> reactions. He makes increasing use of all his organismic
> equipment to sense, as accurately as possible, the existential
> situation within and without. He makes use of all the inform-
> ation his nervous system can thus supply, using it in aware-
> ness, but recognizing that his total organism may be, and
> often is, wiser than his awareness. He is more able to permit
> his total organism to function freely in all its complexity in
> selecting, from the multitude of possibilities, that behaviour
> which in this moment of time will be most generally and gen-
> uinely satisfying. He is able to put more trust in his
> organism in this functioning, not because it is infallible,
> but because he can be fully open to the consequences of each
> of his actions and correct them if they prove to be less than
> satisfying.

There are a lot of things to note about this. First, this is a
description of trends that Rogers claims to have observed in his
psychotherapeutic clients when certain conditions of safety and
understanding are experienced. Although it sounds like a list of
nice things that people should move towards, in fact this is how
people do move, when they experience themselves as free to move.
'The good life, from the point of view of my experience, is the
process of movement in a direction which the human organism
selects when it is inwardly free to move in any direction, and the
general qualities of this selected direction appear to have a certain
universality.' This is of course extremely contentious. Rogers
construes his role in therapy as removing some commonly present
constraints which then allows the client's natural tendency towards healthy growth to manifest itself in the ways described.
One could equally say that Rogers is conditioning his clients to
behave in certain ways, albeit with a very subtle and ostensibly
'non-directive' set of cues and rewards. We considered this in
detail when we looked at the role and ploys of various kinds of

master or guru or therapist in Part I: suffice it to say here that
Rogers's way of looking at growth in terms of the reassertion of
inherent, natural tendencies is very similar to that contained in
the Eastern traditions.

Second, perhaps the central characteristics of the fully functioning person are his openness to experience and trust in his
own organism. Rogers distinguishes between a person's experience,
which is 'everything that is going on in his nervous system', and
his awareness, which is the sub-set of that experience that is
present in consciousness. The fully functioning person is one in
whom there is a high degree of congruence between those two
levels: that is, there are no psychological blocks that prevent a
person becoming consciously aware of states of activity within
him. Like Integrated Man, the Rogerian person is able to accept
into consciousness whatever is happening in him and in his surroundings regardless of whether it happens to accord with his
consciously conceived purposes or not.

There are two things to note about this. The first is Rogers's
slightly unfortunate use of language. He uses the term 'experience'
to refer to states of the nervous system that may influence behaviour but of which one may be quite unconscious, as when you
have been driving a car, or ironing, or washing up, and you
'come to' - the unconscious activities and stimuli suddenly become
consciously recognized. Yet a common use of the word entails
consciousness - as in 'I experienced a sudden shock.' In contrast,
by 'awareness' he means only conscious awareness, whereas I find
no anomaly in the idea of unconscious awareness. Nor does one
find in Rogers's theoretical formulations any recognition of degrees
of awareness: he speaks as if one either were or were not conscious of an event. Common sense and common language on the
other hand attest to the fact that we may be 'dimly aware',
'slightly aware', 'partially aware' and so on, up to 'intensely' or
even 'exclusively aware'. Our picture of the mind of Integrated
Man needs to contain a sliding scale of awareness to subserve
these different degrees of focus or concentration.

While Rogers's labels are slightly unsatisfactory, it is difficult
to find alternatives. I do not like 'consciousness' as a substitute
for 'awareness' for it connotes an object or structure inside the
head, like 'short-term memory' into which thoughts can be placed.
I prefer to construe different kinds or degrees of awareness in
process terms: that is, as reflections of different transient states
of activity within the mind. Therefore I choose the terms *conscious*
or *focal awareness* to include all the degrees of what Rogers just
calls awareness; and *tacit awareness* to refer to those aspects of
current stimulation that are represented in terms of activity in the
central nervous system, but which have not, for one reason or
another, become consicous. These terms are taken from Polanyi
and follow his usage quite closely.

The acceptance of this distinction between tacit and focal awareness is important for our understanding of Integrated Man, for it
will help explain the differences and relatednesses between 'I' and

'myself-in-the-world', the map and the territory of myself. Fromm, in his essay 'Zen Buddhism and Psychoanalysis' says: 'Experience can enter into [conscious] awareness only under the condition that it can be perceived, related or ordered in terms of a conceptual system and of its categories.' And, in talking about the origin and effects of this system, he goes on, 'Every society, by its own practice of living and by the mode of relatedness, of feeling, and perceiving develops a system of categories which determines the form of awareness. This system works, as it were, like a *socially conditioned filter*; experience cannot enter [conscious] awareness unless it can penetrate this filter.' This filter - Kelly's construct system - both limits and distorts the true organismic experience. Thus conscious awareness will fail to contain some of those aspects of the world of which one is tacitly aware, and may also contain aspects that are not present in tacit awareness. The stage is now set for the internal conflict that we spoke of at length in Chapter 3. We become at war within ourselves - the brain desiring things which the body does not want, and the body desiring things which the brain does not allow; the brain giving directions which the body will not follow, and the body giving impulses which the brain cannot understand.

The second comment about Rogers's concept of 'openness to experience' concerns a possible misunderstanding. He sometimes speaks as if to be open to experience is to allow into conscious awareness all current stimulation, in a raw, uninterpreted state. For example:

If a person could be fully open to his experience however, every stimulus - whether originating within the organism or in the environment - would be freely relayed through the nervous system without being distorted by any defensive mechanism ... whether the stimulus was the impact of a con-figuration of form, color, or sound in the environment of the sensory nerves, or a memory trace from the past, or a visceral sensation of fear or pleasure or disgust, the person would be 'living' it, would have it completely available to awareness.

You find the same kind of thing in Watts as well, where he talks of 'the basic mind which knows reality rather than ideas about it', or the Zen experience as being 'completely sensitive to each moment, in regarding it as utterly new and unique, in having the mind open and wholly receptive.' It is possible to read these dec-larations as saying (a) there is a separate reality; and (b) human beings are capable of being completely conscious of the total momentary complexity of this reality; (c) in a way that does not impose any 'interpretation' or construction on it. Clearly this is nonsense. There are basic physiological constraints or 'interpre-tations' that limit our sensory world most severely, just because we have a nervous system that is insensitive to many forms of energy. As we saw with the example of the rainbow, the world that any organism inhabits is a joint function of nature and his nature. And the upper bound of that world is set by his genes.

There must be selection between the (hypothetical) 'reality' of All Possible Stimuli - the Universe, Cosmos, call it what you will - and the potential, experience-able reality for any organism, which we might call the *Pristine Potential Reality*. While many mystical writings speak of 'cosmic consciousness' and the like, it is quite impossible to interpret this within the present framework in terms of any kind of perception of a separate reality that breaches the physiological limits I have discussed.

In fact there are several more stages of selection that limit our phenomenological world even further. Let us go back to the stone rolling down the hillside that we used as an example before. It starts at the top with a certain structure that predisposes the stone to 'behave' in a variety of ways. This is its pristine state. But as it rolls we saw that this structure is modified to facilitate its passage through the kind of environment that it has already experienced. It becomes specialized, and in so doing, some of its options are closed. Its *Developed Potential Reality* is different from what it was when it started.

The same happens to living organisms as they rub along in their social and physical worlds. Nervous tissue is modified by experience in ways that are much more complicated than the smoothing off of a stone - many specializations remain reversible for at least some period of time, for example - but not different in principle. A baby is born with the potential to learn any human language. But after he has learned one it is more difficult to learn the second, and it will be learned in a different way. His potential capabilities for construing and acting become tuned to the environment of which he is part. This Developed Potential Reality sets the actual limits to what an organism, at a particular point in its life, is capable of doing or experiencing. And it continues to develop until the moment of death.

This is still not the reality with which the organism itself can be in touch however, for it would be impossible for the total Developed Potential Reality to be active at once. If it were, this would mean that all one's accumulated knowledge and skills were in awareness together, and if one were to propose this, it would make nonsense of the idea of awareness. That part of the Developed Potential Reality that is active at any moment (and we shall specify more closely what this means in the next chapter) is the *Organismic Reality*: it is the overall pattern of activation in the nervous system. If the Developed Potential Reality is the library you have built up, the Organismic Reality is the book you happen to be reading now.

Part of the Organismic Reality enters conscious awareness, and part does not. I am now aware of the sight of my pen moving across the paper, and (as I come to think about it) the pressure of my feet on the floor, but not of my heart beat or of the digestion of my bowl of Shreddies. That sub-set of the total process that constitutes my Organismic Reality that is represented in conscious awareness I call the *Conscious Reality*.

It might make these different levels of 'reality' clearer if we

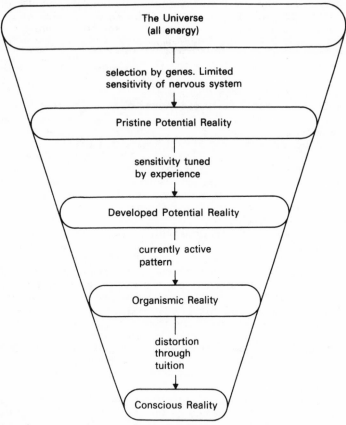

Figure 6

think of them in terms of a computer. The reality of All Possible
Stimuli is the same for the computer as it is for us, for it exists
(by definition) independently of any observer. The Pristine
Potential Reality is the computer fresh off the production line. Its
limits of sensitivity and capability are set by its 'hardware' - its
mechanical and electronic constitution. The Developed Potential
Reality refers to the computer later on in its history when it contains many programs that it can call on, and much data to work
with. In contact with its particular environmental demands (running psychological experiments for one; calculating wages and income tax for another) it has acquired particular specializations.
(In general the computer differs from a person in that (a) all its
knowledge is received by tuition, none by direct induction; and
(b) the accumulated programs ('software') do not alter the hardware, so that the acquisition of one program does not interfere
with the acquisition of any other.) The Organismic Reality refers

to the momentary internal state of the computer, i.e. which parts
of the data-base are active, what instruction is currently being
executed etc. The Conscious Reality we may imagine as the last
statement to be printed out by the computer, or the set of symbols displayed on its cathode ray screen. These are particular
kinds of product, interim statements, of the rapidly changing
Organismic Reality. They reflect it; they do not influence or control it.

We shall be very concerned with the relationship between the
Organismic and Conscious Realities in what follows. It is sufficient
at the moment to point to three different types of relationship. In
the first, an aspect of Organismic Reality is capable of pretty
clear and accurate representation in Conscious Reality: it has easy
access to consciousness. It may or may not be consciously attended
to now, but it can enter conscious awareness whenever it becomes
activated. The second are those aspects where the appropriate
methods of representation have not been developed through lack
of exposure to an environment that would stimulate their development. I may be unable to see certain significant differences between two X-ray plates, or taste the difference between two fine
wines, or tell whether a piece of music is by Haydn or Bach,
where others, with greater experience than mine, do not even
have to think. These aspects of the Universe cannot enter my
conscious awareness because they are not part of my Developed
Potential Reality. My nervous system has not been tuned to pick
them up.

The third and most important class of concept is that which can
be present in Organismic Reality, but whose entry into Conscious
Reality is blocked or distorted, for these are the aspects of our
internal realities that can generate the conflict. Carl Rogers's
'openness to experience' is not a swamping of the nervous system
by the Universe: it is a close correspondence between the Organismic and the Conscious Realities. To be open to experience is to
be non-defensive, not non-selective.

One step on the road to openness to experience is to realize that
one's functional reality is much wider and more complex than the
restricted consciousness with which we normally identify ourselves -
to realize that there is more to me than meets the 'I'. Having
recognized the existence of this intruder in 'my' house - the Bull
of Buddhism - one can then go on to discover that he is actually
wiser, more realistic and more trustworthy than 'I', the host. 'As
I observe the clients whose experience in living has taught me so
much, I find that increasingly such individuals are able to trust
their total organismic reaction to a new situation because they
discover to an ever-increasing degree that if they are open to
their experience, doing what "feels right" proves to be a competent and trustworthy guide to behaviour...'

As well as openness to experience and trust in one's organism,
Rogers identifies what he sees as a third central aspect of the
fully functioning person - existential living. This means living
fully in the moment, being absorbed in the present, free from

plans, desires or regrets. In such a state,
> A man with no form, no shadow
> Turns into a rice pounder_
> When he pounds rice. (Sosho)

Or, in Rogers's own words, 'the self and personality emerge *from* experience, rather than experience being translated or twisted to fit preconceived self-structure. It means that one becomes a *participant in and an observer of the ongoing process of organismic experience, rather than being in control of it.*'

This is a most significant statement, for in writing it, Rogers leaves Kelly behind. While Kelly Man is terrified that loss of control will lead to an inability to function in a chaotic, undifferentiated world, the fully functioning person realizes that his organism can cope on its own. He does not need to know what's going to happen next, indeed he cannot, because 'What I will be in the next moment, and what I will do, grows out of that moment, and cannot be predicted in advance either by me or by others.' He even finds this a source, not of terror, but of pleasure and fun. One of Rogers's clients says, 'Things are sure changing, boy, when I can't even predict my own behaviour in here any more. It was something I was able to do before. Now I don't know what I'll say next. Man, it's quite a feeling ... I'm just surprised I even said these things ... I see something new every time. It's an adventure, that's what it is - into the unknown ... I'm beginning to enjoy this now, I'm joyful about it, even about all these old negative things.'

Rogers sees, too, where Kelly does not, the implications of his position for the free-will *vs* determinism debate. The fully functioning person '*wills* or *chooses* to follow the course of action which is the most economical vector in relationship to all the internal and external stimuli, because it is that behaviour which will be most deeply satisfying. But this is the same course of action which from another vantage point may be said to be *determined* by all the factors in the existential situation ... The fully functioning person ... not only experiences but utilizes, the most absolute freedom when he spontaneously, freely, and voluntarily chooses and wills that which is absolutely determined.' But the person who is defensive, who is incongruent, whose consciously conceived wills and desires are not grounded in a clear, unified awareness of his Organismic Reality, but in a patchwork of distortions and delusions, this person finds that he is unable to carry out the dictates of his own volition, and descends on the slippery spiral of internal conflict and impotent frustration into depression and self-contempt.

In his description of the fully functioning person, Rogers comes very close to Watts's 'adept at Zen' (quoted in Chapter 2) or to the descriptions of the man of Tao that one finds in Lao Tsu or Chuang Tsu:

> Do not seek fame. Do not make plans.
> Do not be absorbed by activities.
> Do not think that you know.

Be aware of all that is and dwell in the infinite.
Wander where there is no path.
Be all that heaven gave you,
But act as though you have received nothing.
Be empty, that is all.

The mind of a perfect man is like a mirror.
It grasps nothing. It expects nothing.
It reflects but does not hold.
Therefore, the perfect man can act without effort.

It should be clear that the 'acceptance' of the fully functioning person, Integrated Man, or whatever, is not a passive fatalism, but on the contrary a tremendous source of realistic power. As Don Juan, the Yacqui Indian sorcerer says in Carlos Castaneda's 'Tales of Power', 'A warrior takes his lot, whatever it may be and accepts it in ultimate humbleness. He accepts in humbleness what he is, not as grounds for regret, but as a living challenge.' The emaciated Indian swami sitting on his fundament meditating while all around are dying of hunger or cholera is no more the prototype of Integrated Man than is a pin-striped accountant on the 8.23.

Although Rogers goes further towards Integrated Man than does Kelly, none the less there come a point where he reins in. That point is the acceptance of complete unity both within a person and between the person and his environment. It is striking, in the summary of the fully functioning person we have quoted, how obviously in the driver's seat is a 'he' who is able to make use of 'his' nervous system, to permit 'his' organism to do things, to experience 'his' feelings, and so on. It does not seem as if Rogers is here reluctantly succumbing to the dominant forms of language: the feeling is that he does wish to maintain a separation of experiencer from experience, knower from known, actor from action, thinker from thought - a separation which, as we have seen, is denied in Buddhist philosophy.

Two other comments, one positive, one not. The first refers to Rogers's notion of satisfaction, which is very unsatisfactory. He says, you recall, that the fully functioning person is 'able to permit his total organism ... to select ... that behaviour which in this moment of time will be the most generally and genuinely satisfying.' Now if this is true by definition, then the idea of satisfaction is vacuous and redundant: he is just saying 'you do what you do'. But if there is some way of talking about satisfaction independently of what somebody actually does, then it may be useful. As far as I know, though, Rogers does not ever try to do this. It is, I think, something that needs to be done: we need some way of approaching the problem of why one action is selected over another - and this is one area in which behaviourism is helpful - but simply to say 'because it's more satisfying' begs the question.

The second, related, point that Rogers throws in at the end of the first quotation, is that openness to experience means openness not just to the antecedents of behaviour, but to the behaviour itself, and to its consequences. Learning must depend on an ability to evaluate the success of actions, and to modify them in the light of that evaluation. Here Rogers draws attention to the knotty problem of the role that conscious awareness plays in learning, a problem to which we will return later.

ERICH FROMM

Of the authors discussed in this chapter, Fromm is the one who has most involved himself with the Eastern philosophies, and his essay 'Psychoanalysis and Zen Buddhism' is a deliberate attempt to explore the parallels between Zen and his own developments of Freudian theory. In fact Fromm's 'psychoanalysis' is much closer to Rogers than it is to Freud. Like Rogers he believes in the basic trustworthiness of man - or the natural, original, integrated man within. Like Rogers he believes that the 'best' actions are characterized by such 'biological' words as natural, fitting, adaptive and harmonious, rather than the 'ethical' canons of good, right, moral, kind, etc. Morality is a consequence of a deeper kind of 'right living'; to try to be good misses the point in the way trying to be spontaneous does: it increases the conflict within man that is itself the source of immorality. 'Neither Zen Buddhism nor psychoanalysis is *primarily* an ethical system ... They do not tend to make a man lead a virtuous life by the suppression of the "evil" desire, but they expect that the evil desire will melt away and disappear under the light and warmth of enlarged consciousness.' The largely unconscious Organismic Reality includes, and is therefore necessarily in harmony with, nature: in that sense its actions are good and 'live'. But when the person is split, this natural goodness is lost, and actions become 'evil' - the reverse of 'live'. The effect of trying to be good is to increase the split, and so increase the evil. Like Rogers (and Kelly) he sees life as a continual process, not a succession of states. 'Birth is not one act, it is a process. The aim of life is to be fully born. To live is to be born every minute. Death occurs when birth stops.' And like Rogers he has a clear idea of psychological well-being.

Well-being is the state of having arrived at the full development of reason: reason not in the sense of a merely intellectual judgment, but in that of grasping truth by 'letting things be' (to use Heidegger's term) as they are. Well-being is possible only to the degree to which one has overcome one's narcissism; to the degree to which one is open, responsive, sensitive, awake, empty (in the Zen sense). Well-being means to be fully related to man and nature affectively, to overcome separateness and alienation, to arrive at the experience of oneness with all that exists... Well-being means to be fully born, to become what one potentially is; it means to have the full capacity for joy and for sadness, or, to put it still differently, to awake from the half-slumber the average man lives in, and to be fully

awake. If it is all that it means also to be creative; that is,
to react, to respond to myself, to others, to everything
that exists - to react and respond as the real total man I
am to the reality of everybody and everything as he or it
is. In this act of true response lies the area of creativity,
of seeing the world as, it is *and* experiencing it as *my* world,
the world created and transformed by my creative grasp of
it, so that the world ceases to be a strange world 'over
there' and becomes my world. Well-being means finally to
drop one's Ego, to give up greed, to cease chasing after
the preservation and the aggrandizement of the Ego, to be
and to experience oneself in the act of being, not in having,
preserving, coveting, using.

Nearly all the aspects of Integrated Man are present in this
eloquent passage: the re-combination of intellect and affect;
acceptance of reality as it (and you) are; openness to experience;
awareness of one's interdependence with all other people and
things; living in (but not just for) the moment; the idea that one
'creates' the world out there; experiencing one's self not in terms
of achievements, acquisitions or social labels, but as the momentary totality of feelings, thoughts, percepts and actions that one
is. Of incidental interest is that both Fromm and Rogers couch
their model man in terms of an expanded conception of reason or
rationality. Fromm's well-being is the fullest development of
reason, while we find Rogers saying: 'I have little sympathy with
the rather prevalent concept that man is basically irrational ...
Man's behaviour is exquisitely rational, moving with subtle and
ordered complexity toward the goals his organism is endeavouring
to achieve.' For both of them, true rationality inheres not in logic
but in integrity.

Freud shared some beliefs with the Eastern traditions, such as
the powerful effects that self-knowledge can have not just in
informing but in transforming us; and of course, he 'believed
that our conscious thought was only a small part of the whole of
the psychic process going on in us, and, in fact, an insignificant
one in comparison with the tremendous power of those sources
within ourselves which are dark and irrational and at the same
time unconscious.' His broadcasting of the existence and importance
of unconscious process is without doubt the most useful of his
achievements from our point of view. But we must follow Fromm in
going beyond Freud's conception in two main respects. First,
Freud's idea is of 'the' unconscious as a store for parts of our
autobiography. 'The unconscious is perceived as being like a
cellar in a house, in which everything is piled up that has no
place in the superstructure; Freud's cellar contains mainly man's
vices; Jung's contains mainly man's wisdom.' Secondly, as Fromm
says, Freud's unconscious is the home of the dark, violent,
beastly, unacceptable side of man's nature. Fromm's improvements
are to see that 'the content of the unconscious ... is neither the
good nor the evil, the rational nor the irrational; it is both; it is
all that is human'; and to choose 'to speak of conscious and

unconscious as states of awareness and unawareness, respectively, rather than as *"parts"* of the personality and specific contents.' In terms of the psychoanalyst's avowed aim of making the unconscious conscious, this now means not taking a memory from one bit of the personality and putting it in another, but of removing blocks to awareness. This shift enables us to see growth in process terms; our autobiography is not a warehouse of memorabilia, but is represented as changes of process that enable us to cope better (or worse) with areas of our perceived and felt worlds. Bringing certain processes into awareness is a precondition for their modification, and we shall see that we can use the concept of awareness as a shifting flow of activity or control in the nervous system to provide a much more detailed account of psychotherapeutic growth, and significant learning in general, than Freud was able to.

A third sense of 'conscious', different from the structural and functional ones we have looked at so far, needs as Fromm notes, to be kept distinct. This is the identification of conscious with 'reflecting intellect', and unconscious with 'unreflected experience'. From the point of view of our functional analysis both of these are legitimate types of conscious awareness. I may be aware of my breathing, or I may think about it: these are alternative styles of consciousness.

In one respect we have to disagree with Fromm, though: he tends, like Jung, to glorify the unconscious. For example, 'the Unconscious is the whole man - minus that part which corresponds to his society. Consciousness represents social man, the accidental limitations set by the historical situation into which an individual is thrown. Unconsciousness represents universal man, the whole man rooted in the Cosmos...' This simple identification of the unconscious with what I have previously called Organismic Reality is not good enough. The unconscious is not all 'naturally good' because much of the socialization to which we have been subjected, much of what Fromm earlier called the socially conditioned filter, is itself unconscious. Our Organismic Reality itself has been contaminated from childhood with all kinds of precepts and prohibitions which permeate every aspect of behaviour from bowel control to voice quality, from the choice of trousers to the choice of lovers.

So far this chapter has explored some descriptions of the internal world from the phenomenological point of view: how we conceptualize our own experience, its origins and functions. What we are at any moment is a bundle of nervous tissue, tuned to react to and construe certain patterns of externally and internally arising stimulation in certain ways, of which some part is currently active. This Organismic Reality may result in overt action, or in internal states of conscious awareness of different kinds - feelings, thoughts, memories, dreams, perceptions - or both, or neither. While these states may appear to be discrete and/or persistent, they arise from and reflect organismic processes that are continuously changing from birth till death. And although this conscious

print-out does reflect unconscious activity, it reflects it in only
a partial and distorted way, for consciousness has its own language (verbal and non-verbal), conventions and symbols, like the
contour lines on a map, that have no counterpart in Organismic
Reality. In addition, as a result of certain learning experiences,
or their lack, particular features of Organismic Reality - such as
those which would give rise to the states of awareness that we
call 'rage' or 'lust' - may be denied to consciousness altogether.
For many reasons we see ourselves in consciousness only 'through
a glass, darkly'.

The rediscovery of integrity is a slow and tortuous business
precisely because it requires the cleansing power of conscious
awareness to be turned on such dark and tangled corners of our
process in order to wash out the many pockets of social fiction
embedded in the fabric of organismic fact. First, though, we must
understand more clearly the nature of this organismic fact and
this behaviourism can help us to do.

B. F. SKINNER

We need to confront Skinner on two counts: he is actually very
relevant to Integrated Man, and he is also the universal Aunt
Sally for anyone with humanistic tendencies - and therefore, like
all Aunt Sallies, widely oversimplified, misinterpreted and maligned.
The two clearest statements of the nature of behaviourism are his
recent books 'Beyond Freedom and Dignity' and 'About Behaviorism', from which the quotations are drawn.

I pointed out in the Preamble that any theory has a 'focus of
convenience'; that is to say there is a certain limited set of phenomena which the theorist is interested in, and which his theory is
designed to account for in the first instance. Subsequently, of
course, the theory may be helpful in accounting for a much wider
set of things (its 'range of convenience') but its form is permanently set by the focus. One of the reasons Skinner has been
maligned is that his focus is different from that of most of the
more humanistically inclined authors. Rogers's theory of personality, for example, originates in a concern with how people
experience themselves - particularly in interaction with others.
Kelly's own personality theory is initially an attempt to account
for how people explain that experience to themselves: it is a shot
at making explicit people's implicit theories about their own perception. Skinner's primary concern is not with experience or
perception, but with the causes and control of action, and particularly in these two books with people's implicit theories about the
causes and control of their own actions. His aim is to show that
our theory - at the centre of which stands the old bogey 'Self-as-
Agent' - is unnecessary, anti-scientific, and misleading. As this
aim is also mine, Skinner's analysis of and solution to the problem
deserve attention. They are, as it turns out, pretty inadequate;
but we shall learn useful things from the exercise.

Let us start with Skinner's opening shot at what he calls the
theory of Autonomous Man.

The function of the inner man is to provide an explanation
which will not be explained in turn. Explanation stops with
him. He is not a mediator between past history and current
behavior, he is a centre from which behavior emanates. He
initiates, originates and creates, and in doing so he remains,
as he was for the Greeks, divine. We say that he is autonomous - and, as far as a science of behavior is concerned,
that means miraculous.

In more positive terms he states in 'About Behaviorism', 'A person is not an originating agent; he is a locus, a point at which
many genetic and environmental conditions come together in a
joint effect.' In statements like this, Skinner becomes a Buddhist -
though I doubt whether he knows it, or would like the idea if he
did. Alan Watts could certainly have written that sentence (remember his saying 'I am neither a passive and helpless witness ...
nor an active doer and thinker ... Inside the skull and the skin
as well as outside there is simply the stream flowing along of itself') - as could Hui-Neng or Suzuki. 'I' is not the name of an
agent or a cause, but of a place in space and time where a certain
unrepeatable combination of action and awareness is happening.

It is fascinating to watch Skinner and Watts, from quite opposite
sides of the American establishment ('mechanistic reactionary' vs
'religious freak') and the American continent (Cambridge, Massa-
chusetts vs Sausalito, California) agreeing on the fallacious nature
of man's theory of himself, and also diagnosing the same causes.
We have seen how Watts attacks our noun-based view of the world
as denying the facts of unity and change. Here is Skinner: 'We
tend to make nouns of adjectives and verbs, and must then find a
place for the things the nouns are said to represent. We say that
a rope is strong, and before long we are speaking of its strength.
We call a particular kind of strength tensile, and then explain that
the rope is strong because it possesses tensile strength ... A
state or quality inferred from the behavior ... begins to be taken
as a cause.' This tendency to infer an internal cause for behaviour
of a particular kind, the only evidence for which is the behaviour
itself, is difficult to spot because it is so pervasive. A man learns
cricket fast and we say he 'has an aptitude' for it. He circles the
right letters on a card and he 'is intelligent'. The circling of the
letters is the evidence for the intelligence, which then suddenly
becomes something separable from the behaviour, and able to
cause or control it. To say that an organism eats because it is
hungry is only to say that it eats when it is ready to eat. The so-
called causal explanation of an event is only the description of the
same event in other words. And the view is given the august
endorsement of Wittgenstein: 'At the basis of the whole modern
view of the world lies the illusion that the so-called laws of nature
are the explanations of natural phenomena.'

The stimulus for this ubiquitous absurdity is the fact that we
cannot always, in our simple-minded way, identify an external

cause for our actions. From the fact that we cannot point to an external cause, we infer (fallaciously) that there is no external cause; and from that we infer (again fallaciously) that we must have 'done it ourselves'. The fallacy comes from a failure to appreciate the selective nature of conscious thought. Skinner himself says 'An organism behaves as it does because of its current structure, but most of this is out of reach of introspection.' The state of the nervous system that results in an overt movement is much more complex, and incorporates many more influences from the external and internal environments than can possibly be represented in a conscious thought – or even a long stream of conscious thought. And worse: as we saw when discussing Fromm, conscious awareness not only fails to capture more than a distorted fragment of tacit awareness; it also contains elements that have no basis in personal experience at all. Thus it is that we offer ourselves motives for our own actions (sometimes in good faith, sometimes not) that are complete fabrications. You do not have to be a psychoanalyst to see how people delude themselves about their own motivation.

The idea of will-power follows from the same false logic. If my conscious wish is to do one thing, and I find myself doing something that I think I want to do less, I am puzzled. Instead of acknowledging that my actions are influenced by factors that my consciousness cannot, or is not currently, representing – that the heart has its reasons of which reason itself knows nothing – I invoke the magic of the will to preserve the illusion. Skinner's Autonomous Man is our Dissociated Man, approached from a slightly different angle, for the illusion of autonomy leads inevitably to the feeling of dissociation between a controlling 'I' and a wayward 'me' who must be constrained, directed and harnessed.

Skinner's answer to this is behaviourism, which he defines in the following passage.

A behavioristic analysis rests on the following assumptions. A person is first of all an organism, a member of a species and a subspecies, possessing a genetic endowment of anatomical and physiological characteristics, which are the product of the contingencies of survival to which the species has been exposed in the process of evolution. The organism becomes a person as it acquires a repertoire of behavior under the contingencies of reinforcement to which it is exposed during its life-time. The behavior it exhibits at any moment is under the control of a current setting. It is able to acquire such a repertoire under such control because of processes of conditioning which are also part of its genetic endowment.

Skinner's emphasis on the automatic role of the environment in the development and exhibition of a behavioural repertoire is important. The idea of an indissociable organism-environment field which acts as a whole, and in which the cause of, or responsibility for, action cannot be attributed to either aspect alone, is implicit throughout his philosophy. Yet when he gets near to this central

issue, Skinner becomes unbelievably confused. First of all we find
the whole weight of responsibility transferred from the inner man
to the environment. 'Whatever we do, and hence however we perceive it, the fact remains that it is the environment which acts
upon the perceiving person, not the perceiving person who acts
upon the environment.' Then we find the responsibility back in
the person again. 'Human behavior ... is a form of control. That
an organism should act to control the world it inhabits is as characteristic of life as breathing or reproduction ... we can no more
stop controlling nature than we can stop breathing or digesting
food.' So who's controlling what? (Or what's controlling whom?)
The solution, as we have seen, lies in transcending the organism-
environment duality: from the higher perspective of mutuality, it
is clear that each controls, and is controlled by, the other, and
that to speak of control is to take a partial and distorted view of
what is a unit.

Skinner finally retreats into the absurdity of two 'selves'; one
is controlled by the environment and the other controls it. Sure,
I'm controlled by the environment, he says, but I can set up the
environment so that it will control me to do what I want. 'The
individual controls himself by manipulating the world in which he
lives ... The controlling self must be distinguished from the controlled self, even when they are both inside the same skin, and
when control is exercised through the design of an external
environment, the selves are with minor exceptions, distinct'
('Beyond Freedom and Dignity', pp. 201-2). I give the complete
reference for those who refuse to believe that such an enormous
and confused volte face is possible. It is interesting to see the
lengths to which a 'self', even B. F. Skinner's, will go to preserve the illusion of its own identity, agency and autonomy.

Despite Skinner's failure to flush Autonomous Man out of his
own thinking, it is worth while to look at his answer to the question of how man and world interact, and especially at how the
mechanism whereby they do so develops and changes. The medium
through which interaction takes place is called a 'contingency of
reinforcement', which is the record that an organism keeps of
what it did, when it did it, and what happened as a result. Skinner labels these three components of the record Response, Stimulus and Reinforcement: I shall call them Antecedent, Behaviour
and Consequence. As a result of experience and maturation, it
possesses a repertoire of behaviours together with a record of
what the result (consequence) has been of producing those
behaviours in particular contexts. We can describe this accumulated knowledge as being of the form 'If in situation A I do B,
then (if things are running true to form) C is likely to result.'
If I am tired and can see a chair (A), and I sit down on the chair
(B), I will be less tired (C). If my trousers are ripped and I can
see a needle and thread (A), then I can sew them up (B), and the
rip will be repaired (C). If I feel like making love and I know that
my wife is angry with me (A), then stroking her bottom (B) is
likely to get me a clout (C). In the next chapter I shall make use

of this simple description, but developed and interpreted in ways rather different from those Skinner allows himself. It is worth noting here four of these developments. First, A, B and C refer not to unique actions or events but to classes of actions or events. No pattern of activity in the sensory nervous system is ever repeated exactly, nor is any pattern of excitation in the motor system. In order to be any use the ABC information must have generality: it would be better described as 'In situations of the type A, actions like B will probably result in consequences like C.' This of course creates the problem of how the nervous system represents this kind of information but represent it it must. Skinner sidesteps the issue by (a) refusing to speculate about internal representations, and (b) insisting that stimuli, responses and reinforcements (to use his terms) are 'classes of externally observable events'. But identifying these classes in the outside world is - except in such simple and artificial cases as a rat in a box - an even more difficult task.

Second, both antecedent and consequent are, in my usage, total patterns of activity in the central nervous system (CNS), and are compounded of excitation from both inside and outside the body. Roughly speaking, information from outside tells the animal what is possible; from inside, what is desirable. The conjunction of these determines what action will occur. Thus perception, motivation and action are utterly indissociable: this is the basic message of Skinner's behaviourism. It is one that is essential to our model of Integrated Man, and is conspicuously ignored in the theory and practice of much 'official' psychology.

Third, information is not only abstracted, and generalizable, but probabilistic. There is no guarantee that a consequence that usually follows A and B will always follow A and B, because the external world is not under one's control. A bomb may drop, the wires may be down, the batch of pills may be dud, the Prime Minister may tell the truth. This feature of uncertainty must be designed into Integrated Man.

Fourth, although Skinner will not talk about physiology, he makes a most important point about the way 'contingencies of reinforcement' are represented in the CNS, which is a blow to most contemporary theories of memory in cognitive psychology. In 'About Behaviorism' we find:

> A person is changed by the contingencies of reinforcement under which he behaves; he does not store the contingencies. In particular he does not store copies of the stimuli which have played a part in the contingencies. There are no 'iconic representations' in his mind; there are no 'data structures stored in his memory'; he has no 'cognitive map' of the world in which he has lived. He has simply been changed in such a way that stimuli now control particular kinds of perceptual behavior.

And in equally strong terms in 'Beyond Freedom and Dignity':

> The environment is often said to be stored in the form of memories: to recall something we search for a copy of it

which can then be seen as the original thing was seen. As
far as we know, however, there are no copies of the environment in the individual *at any time*, even when a thing is
present and being observed.

Skinner, in talking about memories and percepts as 'copies' of
the outside world, seems to be talking about simple-minded theories of perception and cognition that nobody these days would
defend. The thrust of his criticism runs the risk of being ignored
and losing contemporary relevance. However his point applies to
any theory that talks of, or presupposes a 'memory' in which
'representations' - of whatever kind or degree of sophistication -
are stored. All such conceptions see memorizing in terms of an
addition to content, which may be subsequently retrieved or
reactivated. Skinner wishes the same acts to be construed as
alterations to process, in which any event leaves its mark on a
person in terms of a functional modification of his nervous system,
such that a future experience of a similar event will be followed
by certain behavioural and phenomenological states that we call
'responding appropriately', or 'remembering'. All learning is seen
as not essentially different from the learning of the stone rolling
down the hillside, that we discussed earlier. Just as the structure
of the stone is altered, quite naturally and 'unintentionally', by
its encounters, so is the structure of a nervous system altered by
its encounters. The structure of the nervous system is infinitely
more plastic, and its scope for modification consequently much
greater than that of the stone; and certain states of the nervous
system are accompanied by awareness, a phenomenon that as yet
we are not obliged to attribute to stones. Yet, Skinner is assert-
ing, there is no fundamental difference between the two in the
way their behaviour is controlled and executed, and their behavioural repertoires are acquired.

Skinner is a fascinating case: his philosophy is like that of a
hawk with several smuts in its eyes. The vision is acute and clear,
but interrupted and limited by large blind spots. Having laid the
ground for an improved psychology of memory, he refused even
to consider how it might develop. The sole reason is that 'a model
or system continues to turn attention inward, away from genetic
and personal history'. Because Autonomous Man is an inadequate,
mystifying model, all models must go. Not only has the baby gone
out with the bathwater: like an incensed landlady he has banned
bathing completely. This alternative leaves human nature just as
mysterious, its mystery preserved not by magic this time, but
taboo. When we turn to the details of learning (as opposed to the
execution of already learned actions) in Skinner's system, the role
of the Consequence becomes of paramount importance.

The environment not only prods and lashes, it *selects*. Its
role is similar to that in natural selection, though on a very
different time scale, and was overlooked for the same reason.
It is now clear that we must take into account what the
environment does to an organism not only before but after it
responds. Behavior is shaped and maintained by its consequences.

Here we find Skinner in bed with another slightly surprising partner - George Kelly this time. For Skinner's organism, like Kelly's, is a scientist. When he knows what to do, he does it. When he doesn't, he experiments, emitting an action whose a priori probability of success is uncertain and monitoring (or in less mentalistic language, being sensitive to) the consequences that accrue. While Skinner would not approve of the florid tones of Kelly's fundamental postulate - 'a person's processes are psychologically channelized by the ways in which he anticipates events' - they agree that people are in business to predict, and that they spend much of their time learning to predict better. Where Skinner's analogy to natural selection is helpful is in denying that there is a 'self' that sits at the controls of the learning process, deciding what things mean, what to learn, and what predictions to make. Just as it is in the nature of organisms to move, so it is to predict and to learn. There is no need for a person inside the organism to 'do' the predicting; rather predicting is just a label for describing in part what organisms are.

These are the central insights and flaws of Skinner's philosophy: a couple of more minor points before we leave him. First, Skinner, like Kelly, Rogers and Fromm, is concerned not only with diagnosing the condition of contemporary man, but treating him. Skinner's remedy lies in a rational technology of behaviour - although he does realize the dangers in this. 'It is certainly not difficult to point to the unhappy consequences of many advances in science, but it is not clear how they are to be corrected except through a further exercise of scientific power.' He does not connect at all the problems of the self with the problems of reason. For the greatest illusion of the abstract ego is that it can do anything to bring about a radical improvement either in itself or in the world. To put all your eggs in the basket of reason, intervention and control is to perpetuate the internal dissociation that is itself the root cause of our trouble.

Second, Skinner's account of awareness and consciousness is pretty limited. He has nothing to say about the function of awareness, for example. He would deny that it has any function, for how, he would ask (quite properly) can a mental state determine, or even influence a physical system? But the issue can be recast in terms of what is the functional difference between those physical states that are accompanied by conscious awareness, and those that are not. And to this question he does not address himself. A further problem is that, while he exposes Autonomous Man as an illusion having no organismic basis, his alternative psychology cannot account for either the origin or the nature of the illusion itself. A complete psychology must have things to say both about the way we really are and the way we think we are. Luckily Kelly fills this gap.

Finally, it must be said that part of the reason why Skinner is misunderstood is that he is hard work to read. Despite quoting from a list of authors that reads like (suspiciously like!) the index of the Oxford Book of Aphorisms (they include Bergson, Berlin,

Bruckner, Buber, Cassirer, Darwin, Descartes, Diderot, Eliot,
T. S. and George, Erasmus, Hitler, Hobbes, Huxley, Henry James,
Jesus, Keats, Kipling, La Rochefoucauld, Leibniz, C. S. Lewis,
Mao Tse-Tung, Marx, Milton, Montaigne, Nietzsche, Newman, Plato,
Popper, Ramakrishna, Rousseau, Russell, Schiller, Schopenhauer,
Shakespeare, Spencer, Stendhal, 'The Times', Voltaire and Oscar
Wilde) he is damned dull. Happily the content repays the effort:
it is worth finding out that B. F. Skinner is a more complex and
a more important figure than he is usually given credit for.

7   A NEUROTHEOLOGY OF INTEGRITY

'... But who *are* the grown-ups?'
'Don't ask me,' she answered 'That's a question for a
neurotheologian.'
'Meaning what?' he asked.
'Meaning precisely what it says. Somebody who thinks
about people in terms, simultaneously, of the Clear Light
of the Void and the vegetative nervous system. The grown-
ups are a mixture of Mind and physiology.'

Aldous Huxley: 'Island'

Now we are in a position to pull together all the arguments, considerations and ideas that we have been collecting into a design
specification for a model of Integrated Man. Having done that we
can try to invent a hypothetical organism that does the job. So
what have we learnt about man's first and second nature so far?
(1)   What Integrated Man does, thinks, feels, imagines, hopes,
perceives - all his performance and experience issue from the
interplay of the stuff that he is made of with the world in which
he lives. There is no room over for any ghostly agent in the
machine. There are deeds but no one who does them; experiences
but no experiencer; thoughts but no thinker. The central task of
the model is to explain how we live without control, where the
illusion of the doer comes from, and what effect it has on the
efficiency of the system.
(2)   The illusion stems from the confusion that we make between
prediction and control. Integrated Man can certainly predict. It
is intrinsic to his nature that he should be able to gauge what
states of the world follow each other, and how various possible
interventions on his part will affect the flow of events. This
anticipation requires no agent: it happens automatically. Integrated Man does not succumb to the alternative idea that prediction implies control and control implies a controller.
(3)   It is important that any model of man's first or original nature should also contain within it the seeds of the second. Man's
nature is integral, but it must be capable of apparent disintegration. A model such as Skinner's, as we saw, goes some way
towards unravelling the organismic side of human nature, but has
no way within itself for accounting for the origin or characteristics
of the way we think we are. The picture that Dissociated Man has
of himself cannot just be discounted as 'unreal' for it undoubtedly
exists in all our minds and manifests itself in our confusions and
neuroses. It is a reality in its own right, and therefore needs an
account.
139

(4)   Part of the effort to account for disintegrated man in integrated terms must be to explain our ways of escaping from the conflict between our warring bits and pieces: our defences. Is it possible to use the model to provide interpretations of the mechanism and functions of, for example, repression, projection and rationalization? A more difficult question, and one that I cannot begin to answer here, is why particular people choose particular defensive styles: what makes one man a compulsive intellectualizer, another a schizophrenic and saddles a third with a job as a light-house keeper?

(5)   Any model of Integrated Man must have some recognition of both conscious and unconscious processes. While Dissociated Man identifies himself exclusively with conscious fragments of his process, Integrated Man operates on the principle that this consciousness is the misleading tip of a much greater iceberg of tacit operations which can be trusted to work well if not interfered with. We take the view here that conscious thoughts are transient, discrete, serial products of the continuous, tacit, holistic processing that underlies them. The extent to which an experience can enter conscious awareness is determined by learnt features of the processes by which that experience is registered.

(6)   Man is an intrinsically active part of an intrinsically active world. Many approaches to human motivation have inherited from the animal work of the 1930s and 1940s the idea that we are basically inactive, only being goaded into action by a temporary loss of equilibrium. The prototypical man on this view is Andy Capp, more vegetable than animal, and supine unless disturbed by one of the few calls of nature that he recognizes. This is wrong. Man is fundamentally ert, not inert.

(7)   The model of man must be predominantly a process one, not a structural one. Man is active and changing: the language of structure is passive and persisting. We may talk of structures, but only, as Whyte said, if we can see them as 'limiting cases of process', or perhaps for some purposes as transiently stable products of process. Thus such mental objects as thoughts, images, memories and percepts are to be explained as secondary aspects of the primary processes of thinking, imagining, remembering and perceiving. We need to explain why certain stages in these processes issue in the conscious states that we call thoughts etc., and what the functional significance of these products is within the total processing sequences. We do not need to propose two kinds of knowledge, as are implicit in, for example, most models of memory, where there are 'stores' that 'contain' memories on the one hand and processes and programs that are used for encoding, retrieving and transforming those passive objects on the other. In our nervous system there is a single form of knowledge whose activation results from time to time in certain conscious states.

(8)   It perhaps is one of the basic axioms of Integrated Man that he cannot be divided into compartments. Just as 'organism' and 'environment' are approximate descriptions of aspects of a whole, so are 'reason' and 'emotion'. At an organismic level each is never

to be found without the other. It is only in theory, in our theories about ourselves, that they appear to be separable and antagonistic. The nervous system does not discriminate: it sums all the influences on it at any moment, from the special senses, from the stomach, the heart, the joints, the limbs, into a total pattern that determines what actions, thoughts and feelings will result.

In their eagerness to chop things up psychologists have divided man into cognition, affect, motivation and behaviour, and then divided each of these. Cognition, for example, has been shattered into pattern recognition, attention, short-term memory, long-term memory, problem-solving, language comprehension, concept formation, imagery.... and each of these in turn is ground down still further. Integrated Man has all these facets, naturally, but to understand them we must first have an accurate picture of the whole gem that they are facets of.

(9)   The goal of receiving and processing energy from the outside world is to act effectively in that world and on it. The consensus in the contemporary psychology of human beings is that man's goal in his transactions with the environment is to 'understand' it, or 'construct a meaningful representation' of it. This limited conception has tended to leave man in the 1970s, like Tolman's rats in the 1930s, 'lost in thought'. To put the point another way, what we are after is not the meaning of events in some disembodied, timeless sense, but their significance to us, right now, in terms of who we are and what we need. Thus information processing cannot be divorced from what we are able to do with it, and what we want to do with it. This 'goal', it should be added, is not something consciously conceived and intended. It is intrinsic to all living organisms.

(10)   It follows that our model of man must be sensitive to context. Objects and events derive their significance in part from the other objects and events that attend them. The figure depends on the ground. This being so, all our knowledge and skills must be represented in the nervous system not in vacuo, but together with some indication of when their use is appropriate. These indications of *when* act as codes through which certain states of the world can 'call' the knowledge that is capable of transforming them into other states.

(11)   If knowledge is associated with its antecedent context, it is equally true that it must be associated with a description of its likely consequences. Man's needs fluctuate, and he must be able to select actions that are appropriate not only to the external circumstances, but aspects of the internal such as, to take the simplest cases, hunger, thirst and pain. Knowledge must be stored with some idea of what will follow from its use.

(12)   As well as being sensitive to likely consequences, man must also register actual consequences - otherwise his knowledge of what, when, where and how to act cannot get better. It is intrinsically changing to incorporate new knowledge, skills and expectancies. It must contain a mechanism for inductive learning.

(13)   Inductive learning provides the organism with concepts or

expectancies, each of which is the distillation of a central tendency from a number of different experiences. It follows that these
concepts are not well-defined, but are 'fuzzy', with the central
core of significance surrounded by a range of features that are
more or less strongly associated with it. Many current approaches
to concepts and their internal representation start from the
assumption that they can be treated as atomic: that is as fixed in
form and invariant across situations. The present view denies
this. It is necessary to Integrated Man, as I shall explain later
that his knowledge is indeterminate and shifting.

(14)   He must also be capable of being taught: that is of learning
through symbolic instruction from other people as well as from
direct experience of his own. This question is a crucial one for
explaining the genesis of disintegration, for I have proposed that
it is through instruction - though often instruction of a rather
devious kind - that the child learns to feel at odds with himself.
Dissociation is not a biological inevitability, but it is a social one;
and society's instrument is language.

(15)   Through language we acquire beliefs and ideas that are not
connected with our own experience. How we can register two different, possibly incompatible, pieces of knowledge about the same
area of experience needs explication. Kelly's concept of 'permeability' of constructs, and Rogers's of 'openness to experience' point
the way, but they need interpreting within the biological framework that we are trying to set up. We must account for variability
in openness to experience, between an individual's different areas
of experience at any point in his life, between one point in his
life and another, and between individual learning. The model
needs to give an account of how this occurs, and why some learning experiences but not others achieve it.

(16)   The learning of language itself, as well as its role in the
direction and dissolution of behaviour, has to be incorporated.
What does language consist of; how do vocabulary and grammar
combine to capture an intention; what effects does the very pos-
session of a symbolic language have on the organismic reality to
which it is attached; and how does language, both by its structure
and its content, serve to delimit and distort consciousness; all
these are questions which can and should be touched on in our
description of Integrated Man. And, too, although language is
cast in the role of villain for much of the piece, it is also an ever-
present component of all kinds of therapeutic aid, whether it be
behaviour modification or the apparent nonsense of a Zen master
or the gnomic parables of Jesus. How does it work in these
contexts?

(17)   We have remarked on the fact that language, in conferring
the ability to describe what is the case, also introduces the possibility of communicating what is not. It gives us the powers of
fantasy, imagination and lying. A model of man must explain how
it is that language is parasitic on experience, yet is autonomous
from it in being able to falsify it.

(18)   This freedom of language, and also up to a point of our non-

verbal concepts, from what is already known is central to our
ability to produce novel solutions to problems, to be creative. But
the creativity it allows is limited to recombinations of the known.
Many of the most creative acts, whether intellectual, artistic or
personal, are those that seem to transcend and re-order the basic
assumptions of thought itself. We should be able to say something
about where these insights come from and how they are evaluated.
Under what circumstances can thought exceed its own bounds?
(19)   Finally there is one constraint on a model of man from a
different direction: from below, as it were, instead of from above.
It is that any proposals we make about a 'conceptual nervous system' must be compatible with what is known about the actual
human central nervous system. While the details of this knowledge,
such as, for example, the precise neural mechanisms of learning,
are continually under debate, there is a consensus about how to
talk about the organization and activity of nervous tissue, and it
will help our discussion if this is taken into account.
   In fact the best place to look for detailed ideas about how people
represent their world and attribute significance to bits of it is
within the tradition that uses as a metaphor the language of
neurophysiology. One of the founders of this tradition, D. O.
Hebb, wrote in 1949 his seminal book 'The Organization of
Behaviour', and in it we find a philosophical statement of intent
hearteningly close to the present one. His discussion, he says,
'represents my attempt to be rid once and for all of the little man
inside the skull who *approves* of some sensory events relayed to
him by the nervous system, disapproves of others and guides
behaviour accordingly ... By some such approach as the one suggested, it may become possible to understand the directedness
and order in behavior, and the variability of motivation, as produced by neural functioning alone.' With Skinner, Hebb wants to
be able to provide a mechanical explanation of the control of action
– but unlike Skinner, he is not prepared to do this by buying a
simple-minded environmentalism. Indeed he starts his book with a
demonstration of the insufficiency of the idea that behaviour is
controlled, in any direct way, by sensory events. He informally
introduced the phenomena of 'set, attention, attitudes, expectancy, hypothesis, intention, vector, need, perseveration, and
preoccupation', and concludes that they possess a single common
element. 'That element is the recognition that responses are determined by something else besides the immediately preceding
sensory stimulation. It does not deny the importance of the immediate stimulus; it does deny that sensory stimulation is everything
in behavior.' His view, which I shall take up, is that stimuli from
both the internal and external environments impinge on a complex
neural system that is itself in a constant state of activity, thus
modifying the state of the total system, but not necessarily in a
straightforward way.
   The general picture we are looking at is of a vastly complicated,
interconnected set of channels or pathways, and within this maze
a certain amount of activity or energy that flows about from place

to place. We might visualize it as a tangle of wire with an electric current flowing through it, or of bits of pipe joined together so that a quantity of water can pass along any one of a large number of different routes. This passage from Peter Currell Brown's book 'Smallcreep's Day' gives a feel for the intricate and seemingly haphazard nature of the system.

there were pipes, such pipes as I've never seen in my life. They covered the walls, travelling in every possible direction, weaving and criss-crossing in dazzling patterns. They were of every conceivable size and pattern and colour. There were heavy pipes with big fat joins every few feet like giant bamboo, gregarious pipes marching across the walls in gangs, brisk, business-like, shortest-distance-between-two-points pipes, big rusty iron pipes with wide bolted flanges along them like rows of top hats. There were pipes which nipped off suddenly to right or left to speak to others for a moment before continuing on their original courses, and pipes which branched and branched and branched again for the sheer joy of multiplication, and forgot where they were going and got lost... You could tell the old ones, which were straight because they were there first, whereas the new pipes bustled irritably about all the others, or wandered leisurely about adjusting themselves as they went. There were green pipes, blue pipes, red pipes, pipes once painted white, even a square pipe and one that changed colour three times and then stopped halfway across a wall. And all were dripping and steaming with condensation, and some leaking with long stalactites hanging from them.

Notice that, rudimentary though this metaphor for the mind of man is, it already contains some of the qualities that we are looking for. First there is no executive, no Fat Controller, that stands outside the system and directs or corrects its operation. No HQ; no Executive Committee. We are not in the computer world of separate components, each with its own specialized function to perform on 'information' that is retrieved from one pigeon-hole and delivered, processed and packaged, to another. What we are concerned with is the way the activity flows from one point to another, what effects – perceptual or behavioural – are activated as the energy pattern moves about, and what characteristics of the network of paths influence how the pattern changes. Particularly we shall need to be concerned with the way in which energy arriving from the 'outside world' through the specialized surfaces of the skin we call eyes, ears, nose and tongue, and from other receptors within the body, interacts with the pre-existing distribution of energy in the system.

One of the problems with models that derive their inspiration from the digital computer is that it is very easy for the ghost of the deciding self to sneak back into the picture. Take the model, called ACT, that John Anderson has worked out in great detail in his book 'Language, Memory and Thought'. Perhaps the most basic

assumption in ACT is that there is a 'passive' memory, that contains 'facts' - a 'knowing that' memory - and an 'active' memory,
called the production system, that is the functional, 'know-how'
bit. These two systems have quite different structural, as well as
functional attributes.

The declarative part is similar in appearance to Hebb's 'conceptual nervous system', being a network of interconnected ideas and
links, of which a small and changing part is transiently active.
But, in contrast to Hebb, the way the pattern of connections and
of activation changes is under the control not of properties intrinsic to the network, but of a separate component, the procedural
part. This latter consists of a lot of operations, each of which is
designed to recognize a special pattern of activity in the passive
bit, and, when it does, to work on that pattern so as to alter it
into another pattern.

This question, of whether there are two distinguishable forms
of knowledge represented in the human mind, is an important one.
Most current models of memory - or of the 'representation of knowledge' as it is coming to be called - agree with Anderson in sep-
arating them. This is because most computer memories can be
divided into a program-store (the procedural part) and a data-
base (the declarative part). And it is true also that much human
knowledge can be divided, following Ryle in 'The Concept of Mind'
into knowing-that (I know that too much beer makes me sleepy)
and knowing-how (I know how to undress and put myself to bed).
But the crucial problem is whether these are basic psychological
categories - are they represented differently in the brain - or are
they judgments that we can make about the knowledge we possess,
but which are not themselves represented in terms of the micro-
structure of the nervous system? Anderson and many others
assume the former: Skinner, Hebb - and I - are putting our money
on the latter. There are after all many kinds of judgment we can
make about what we know, but which very few people would want
to say were present as basic distinctions in representational format. I can distinguish between words longer and shorter than six
letters, between events that happened before and after last Tues-
day, and between facts about chemistry and facts about French
(though I could if I thought about it come up with difficult cases
for each). Yet I would not want to say that each of these distinguished between forms of registration in the nervous system. So
with respect to knowing-how and knowing-that, I would rather
say they represented judgments about how the knowledge was
acquired (knowing-that is usually taught, or received through
language; knowing-how is usually learned inductively, through
experience and practice), or about how it is expressed (in words
or in action), not about how it is stored.

Aside from the fact that there is no physiological evidence to
suggest a distinction such as Anderson's the central nervous
system is, as we have already established, ideally suited to com-
bining both the structural (how it is connected up) and functional
(how it affects behaviour) aspects of knowledge. If two assemblies

of pipes, each representing a concept, are associated, and if each has connections that eventually lead to the writing or speaking of certain words - then they represent a piece of knowledge that I can declare, such as 'Birds can fly', or 'Cardiff is in Wales'. But they can equally be seen as bits of functional information about how to react to birds, or find my way to Cardiff. Thus from the point of view of a model of man's mind I see no need to give this distinction a special status. There are researchers in cognitive psychology who agree. Allan Newell, for example, says: 'The wrong way to conceive of it is with the production system (the procedural component) as the active net-interpreter, and with the semantic net as an associative data structure. The right way is that the production system is the associative structure itself.' (The fact that Anderson quotes this statement without comment suggests that he is himself a little uneasy with the choice he has made.)

As I have said, part of the problem here is that much of the language and attitudes of models like ACT stem from computer stimulation research, in which the program-store/data-base distinction has only very recently been called into question. If part of your knowledge is represented as 'operations', it is very easy to assume that another part is 'operated on'. It is much less easy to see that the operations are operating on each other, in an endlessly parasitic fashion. But it is possible to preserve the logic while avoiding the trap if you cast your model not in electronic, but in physiological, terms. From a structural point of view, a 'conceptual nervous system' can be visualized as very like a (declarative) network. Yet functionally the routeing of activity through the network is determined by the nature of the network itself.

The upshot of this is that we do not want to say that Anderson's associative network and production system exist side by side in the head. Nor do we want to select one or the other as the 'right' way to represent knowledge. What is useful is to see that these are two complementary ways of viewing all the knowledge the central nervous system contains, but looked at from different perspectives. We can ask two types of question about the basic 'information' that the system 'contains': how is it organized (or, equivalently, how can we visualize it); and what is it for (what does it do)? There are structural and functional aspects of the same system: we do not have to chop it in two and say 'this is the structural bit' and 'this is the functional bit', any more than I have to postulate two kinds of knife, one that is long and thin with a sharp blade, and another that is for cutting things. The problem is that people are unhappy, in psychology at least, with the idea of using two different languages to ask two different questions about the same thing. Once you change language (from 'structural language' to 'processing language', say) it is very easy to think that you are actually talking about something different. This tendency is a source of endless confusion and useless questions.

Let us now go back and look at this mish-mash of channels rather more closely. Where, first, does the activity come from? Some, as we have seen, arrives from the various terminals that the network has in the body, initiated from the outside by patterns of light, sound and so on, and from within by other patterns that we call motivational or emotional states. But there is another source that complicates the story still further. Remember that gestalt-influenced authors such as Whyte and later Koestler, proposed that any living system is subject to two antagonistic sets of organizing tendencies. There are the internal tendencies of its own structure, that are, literally, self-destructive: when isolated from the demands and influences of its natural environment an organism dies, and the processes of dying correspond to the assertion of inherent trends of development in the organism that are no longer checked and controlled by the environment of which the living organism is an integral component. And there are the influences from the wider field on the organism. The process of adaptive development of an organism to an environment is the process whereby the internal, self-organizing tendencies are hooked up to, subordinated to, constrained, modified and overlaid by, the tendencies of the larger system.

In terms of the activity of a nervous system, we can, therefore discriminate an intrinsic pattern of organization and activity, that is a characteristic of that mass of tissue in isolation, from the pattern that emerges in interaction with the external world. This presupposes, of course, that the nervous system is intrinsically active, a fact proposed by Lord Adrian in the 1930s, and now generally accepted. 'There are cell mechanisms in the brain which are set so that a periodic discharge is bound to take place. The moment at which it occurs can be greatly altered by afferent influences, but it cannot be postponed indefinitely' (quoted by Hebb). If stimulation is continuous, the nervous system will be seen to react in terms of its learned modifications - as if it were tuned to its environment. When stimulation stops, the intrinsic patterns of organization and firing can reassert themselves. Hebb in fact makes one important specific suggestion as to how these two types of organization differ: 'Without the constant sensory disturbances resulting from the motor activity of the waking animal the growth (of neural sub-systems) would make for *local* integration, and hypersynchrony; with them the integration is in anatomically diffuse systems and reduces local synchronization.' In other words, when subject to stimulation from the outside, the activity in the nervous system links together sensory, motor and intervening ('association') parts of the brain, that may be anatomically quite separate. When not subject to environmental control, cells that are close together tend to recruit each other, and local patterns of coherence are observed.

Thus a person's reaction to an event will depend not just on what the event is, but on the existing state of activation, the selective readiness, of his mind, and on the sum total of influences, intrinsic and extrinsic, to which it is momentarily subject. We might illustrate the intricacy of the process with another metaphor. Imagine a swimming pool, recently vacated and therefore choppy, viewed from above on a sunny day. The sun casts an intricate, constantly changing pattern on the bottom of the pool. When someone jumps in – when a new stimulus arrives – the pattern is affected, but it is impossible to identify what particular changes are due to the new stimulus because it is superimposed on a complex network of pre-existing activity. Its repercussions are rapidly dispersed over the entire pool. The instantaneous pattern of activity in the network is not actually random in the way that the dancing filigree of light in the swimming pool appears to be. But it is a useful counterbalance to the easy assumption that the receipt of a stimulus is like turning on a light bulb in a dark room.

And where does all this energy issue after it has been swirled about? Obviously it moves from point to point within the central portions of the system, action here recruiting further action there, in a never-ending cycle. But every so often effects are produced that are either actions or experiences. When activity is routed into the motor terminals of the system muscles twitch, limbs move, the key is struck or the word uttered. When other states occur we experience a thought, a feeling, a mood, an attitude, or an image that we attribute to the present (a percept), the past (a memory) or the future (a fantasy). Note that even what we see is a product of our mind's activity; an output, not an input. Our perceptions are creations that reflect sometimes well, sometimes badly, the impulses that light calls forth from the back of the eyeball.

We need now to introduce three further assumptions. I will simply pull them, like rabbits, out of the hat for the moment and will justify them later by demonstrating their usefulness, rather than trying to argue for their necessity. The first is that the total amount of energy in the system is constant. There is a pool that can be distributed in different ways but cannot be increased or decreased. Because new energy is constantly arriving from stimulation of the senses, what this constraint means in practical terms is that we have to have a mechanism for turning bits of the system off as well as turning them on. Whenever so much excitation is added into the network, an equal amount must be taken away by being inhibited or dampened. Happily real nervous systems possess this mechanism: it is called 'lateral inhibition'. Equally happily we do not need to worry about the details here.

The second assumption says that the energy pool that the network contains can vary not only in its location within the system but also in its concentration. It can at times be bunched up to form a high energy 'knot', while at others it can be distributed over a much wider area as a lower energy 'smear'. The third assumption is where things start to get interesting. This one says that degree of conscious awareness corresponds to degree of concentration or focusing of activity. To be intensely aware of a flower, say, is to have much of the pool of energy concentrated in just those parts of the system that correspond to the shape, colour and perfume of that flower.

These hypotheses expand our image of the system at work. Now we can see the pool of energy flowing like a speeded-up amoeba through the tracks of the network. As it flows it not only changes position, but it is forever convulsing into a small intense spot and relacing into a diffuse glow, convulsing and relaxing. We might imagine the light thrown by a torch whose focus can be varied quickly over a wide range. The torch, having a fixed capacity, like our model, can only give a small bright beam or a wide dim one. It cannot be both broad and bright at once. The experience of this internal flux is the stream of consciousness: a succession of thoughts and percepts, each emerging from the tacit ground of awareness to become the momentary focus of attention and then falling back to be replaced by another and another and another. When the figures of consciousness are generally sharp and clear we are 'alert'; when they are for a period hazy and incomplete we are 'drowsy', 'preoccupied' or 'absent-minded'.

As the pulse and flow arises from an integration of all the current influences on the system, so action and awareness represent a synthesis of the external and the internal, the possibilities that my world affords and the needs and goals that currently have priority for me. My experience is not of 'me' or 'the world' but of 'me-in-the-world' and 'the-world-in-me'. Thus our system has the integrity that we have demanded of it.

We might note one immediate implication of these proposals. A greater part of the network can be active at once if none of the components is conscious, for conscious awareness uses up more of the limited pool of activity than does tacit awareness. This state of 'mind unconscious of itself' (in Japanese, *mushin no shin*) is recognized in Zen. 'When *mushin* is attained, the mind moves from one object to another, flowing like a stream of water, filling every possible corner. For this reason the mind fulfils every function required of it. But when the flowing is stopped at one point, all the other points will get nothing of it, and the result will be a general stiffness and obduracy' (D. T. Suzuki: 'Zen and Japanese Culture'). If the total activity can be allowed to flow tacitly through the system, the organism can perceive more fully the gestalt of sensations to which he is subject, and react more

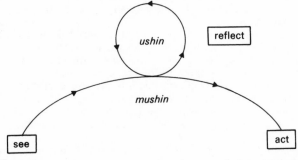

Figure 7

cleanly and subtly. This is following the lower arc in Figure 7.
But with mind conscious of itself (*ushin no shin*) activity gets
'captured' by consciousness, and is wasted. Thinking and doing
compete for the limited resources of energy in the nervous system, which is why self-consciousness leads to clumsiness.

Of course, focused conscious awareness is not necessarily a bad
thing. It has its own functions and appointments. But it becomes
a habit, and prevents us from flowing between focused and dif-
fused attention in a way that is most adaptive. Focused attention,
like the spot-light, casts a very bright and narrow beam. In a
pitch-black cave this beam is not what we need, for it gives us
tiny serial glimpses of the walls that are hard to fit together into
a general impression of the contours of the cave. What is wanted
is an old hurricane lamp that can shed a weak but even glow over
the whole area. If then we find something that looks as if it might
be interesting we can approach and investigate it with the spot-
light. But with the spotlight alone we would have been lucky to
find it in the first place. We must be able to widen or narrow the
beam of our awareness to suit our ends.

It is largely our preoccupation with language as the medium of
thought that gets us stuck in an over-focused mode of awareness,
for it presents the world to us as if it were dissectable into well-
defined and constant chunks, and it strings these chunks together
in serial order, like beads on a string. While it is potentially easier
for non-verbal awareness to oscillate between the global apprehension of a pattern and concentrated investigation of its details,
language, by presenting us with a scenario piecemeal, requires
that our attention flow from item to item in a narrow, high-energy
beam. It is not surprising, therefore, that the Western mind
especially is filled with the incessant nattering of the internal
commentator, weaving its sophisticated stories of profit and loss
on the basis of sporadic samples of experience. The verbal pursuit
of 'why' has managed to displace the felt sense of 'what' with
alarming success.

In the non-linguistic domain the form and function of the mind
is much more fuzzy. Hebb again provides a useful starting point
for visualizing how our 'knowledge by acquaintance', to use Russell's term, is represented. He calls the basic building-block of
the network a 'cell assembly'. Here is his rather technical intro-
ductory statement.

> Any frequently repeated, particular stimulation will lead to
> the slow development of a 'cell-assembly', a diffuse structure
> comprising cells in the cortex and diencephalon (and also,
> perhaps, in the basal ganglia of the cerebrum), capable of
> acting briefly as a closed system, delivering facilitation to
> other such systems and usually having a specific motor
> facilitation... Each assembly action may be aroused by a
> preceding assembly, by a sensory event, or - normally - by
> both.

Cell assemblies are sets of cells distributed throughout the brain
(the anatomical details don't matter) that form a system, in the

sense that activation of part of the set tends to produce activity in the rest. The assemblies are linked together so that the activation of one serves to facilitate or cause the activation of others.

Here we have the central notion of activity moving between interlinked areas of the system, but now we have to go beyond the metaphor of the pipes and see the channels that are followed as being without solid walls. For our experiential concepts are not well-defined, constant things, but are central tendencies of meaning that vary from time to time and place to place. Hebb again:

A concept is not unitary. Its content may vary from one time to another except for a central core whose activity may dominate in arousing the system as a whole. To this dominant core, in man, a verbal tag can be attached; but the tag is not essential. The concept can function without it ... The conceptual activity that can be aroused with a limited stimulation must have its organized core, but it may also have a fringe content or meaning that varies with the circumstances of arousal... What will happen is not determinate, but depends upon the excitability of each sub-system at the moment, and on the facilitation from other concurrent sensory and central activities.

Language, we might say, is like flags planted on windswept sand-dunes: the form and location of the flags are largely determined by convention, and may not correspond to natural hills and valleys. Or they may have corresponded once but the wind of experience has so changed the face of the territory that the flags don't make sense any more and their logic becomes dislocated from the shifting logic of the dunes.

Thus the concepts we possess can be represented as ill-defined collections of features and associations, some of which are central and tightly bound into the package, and others of which are more loosely connected, so that they may or may not be actively associated with the concept, depending on whether they have been 'primed' by the context. And each of these fuzzy collections or circuits is linked in its turn with others to which it may give access.

It may be helpful to provide another metaphorical picture, this time of the way in which what we might call the *experiential plane* (knowledge by acquaintance) of the network differs from and interacts with the *verbal plane* that contains our 'knowledge by description'. The experiential plane is represented as fuzzy and fluid – the shifting sandscape – while the verbal plane is sharper and more static. It looks like an aerial view not of the Sahara but of Greater London, with all the permissible routes clearly visible. Between the two planes there are channels up and down which activity can flow, but the correspondence between the two is by no means exact (see Figure 8). In some areas what we can say may reflect the reality of the organism quite well: in others the disparity between 'me-as-I-think-I-am' and 'me-as-I-am' – the dissociation of Dissociated Man – may be extensive. The points and tracks of verbal thought may bear almost no relation to the

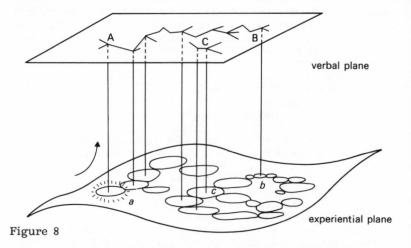

Figure 8

flux of feelings in experience. Thus from time to time conscious
awareness is located in an energy knot in the lower plane - at *a*,
say - but then spurts up immediately into the verbal label at A,
and via there into a string of judgments, memories and associations
that sweep the energy off through the channels of the upper plane
to a distant point B. Meanwhile only enough energy has been left
below to keep tabs in a rather sketchy and usually tacit way on
what is actually going on. If you do not recognize the ubiquitous
and compulsive nature of this leap-frogging through life, try to
be continuously conscious for a minute of the hands of your watch,
and see what your mind does. We have noted already that the
earlier stages of meditation are often unsettling because they
reveal just how polluted a stream consciousness really is.

We need to clear up one other technical detail here. As Figure
8 shows the network is full of branches and forks. If 'I' do not
decide what path to follow, how is the routeing of energy determined? One obvious factor is how much activity it takes to get
each of the exit channels excited. Imagine an activated circuit *l*
(see Figure 9) that has two possible exits, *m* and *n*. All other
things being equal, if *m* is a closer associate of *l*'s than *n* is, then
it will take a smaller build-up of energy in *l* for *m* to be recruited
than *n*. Thus one determinant of the direction of flow is the relative 'resistances' of competing circuits to become active, and this
depends on the history of co-activation of the two circuits, especially on the frequency and success with which they have recruited
each other.

Figure 9

But this is far from the whole story, for we have to remember that activity always impinges on a system whose different parts are already differentially activated. Hebb again provides us with an analysis.

> In a single system, and with a constant set of connections between neurons in the system, the direction in which an entering excitation will be conducted may be completely dependent on the timing of other excitations. Connections may be necessary but may not be decisive in themselves; in a complex system, especially, time factors must always influence the direction of conduction.

If a source of excitation meets a junction from which a number of possible exits exist, then which exit is selected will depend in large measure on the extent to which the exit routes have been primed by other activity in the system. In general each circuit can receive excitation from a number of sources, and can pass it on to one of a number of outputs, each of which can also be excited by other circuits. The nervous system functions as an interlocked set of decision points, each of which sums the influences from a range of inputs, and selects a single channel of output. So the flow of activity in the system depends on the overall temporal and spatial pattern of activity already existing in the system.

So much for the hardware. Now let us put this curious machine to work.

8   LIVING THE SELF-LESS LIFE:
Perception

One's real life is often the life one does not lead.

Oscar Wilde

These concluding chapters are a guided tour through many aspects
of integral psychology to show the real origin and significance of
our thoughts and actions. We concentrate in the main on the more
intellectual and behavioural features of our activity, having
covered the areas of emotional and spiritual development already
in Part I. We start by looking at some aspects of perception.

Perception is usually taken to mean the processes whereby stimulation of the sensory receptors of an organism are turned into a
representation in conscious awareness of the origins and significance of that stimulation: how we convert seeing into seeing *as*.
Within our system the percept that one 'gets' is influenced by
many other factors than the crude pattern of stimulation itself.
The stimulation acts not as building blocks that are laboriously
cemented together to form the perceptual edifice, but as clues, or
triggers, that are used to diagnose the state of the world and what
its current significance is. Perception is not something that happens 'first' and that sets the scene for subsequent action, thought
or problem-solving: the process of perception is already subject
to many of the possible influences of past experience, current
competence, and current need. The goal of perception, as we have
noted before, is not just to find out what's out there, but to know
what to do about what's out there in the light of what's going on
in here.

Thus what guides perception is the need to anticipate: to be
able to predict (in some sense: not necessarily consciously) what
events in the world are likely to follow a given event (man as
observer); and in what way his behavioural intervention in the
flow of events will influence them, i.e. what will be the consequences of action (man as participant).

We anticipate by analogizing. Man's goal is to act in the world in
a way that is appropriate both to the external situation that obtains and to his current needs, and effective in satisfying those
needs. He does this by finding an analogy between the present
situation and generalized descriptions and records of (a) what he
did, and (b) what happened. Thus he can select that action which,
in the past, has tended to produce the consequence that he currently wants. 'Ah ha!' we say, 'This situation is one of those.
And I know what to do with those. I fry them/shoot them/paint
them/make love to them.' (Only on rare occasions does this thought

154

sequence happen in consciousness: it should be seen more as an
anthropomorphic attempt to describe the unconscious way that a
person interacts with his world.) Perceiving is never an end in
itself. It is always guided by current goals, needs and intentions.
In general what the mind does, or tries to do, is select an action
that has a high probability of leading to the satisfaction of the
most important goal. This does not mean doing the most urgent
thing: it means doing that urgent thing that the situation seems
capable of satisfying. Man tries to choose, man's mind is designed
to select, the best compromise between what he wants to do and
what he can do. (Dissociated Man feels himself at odds with this
principle: he often wastes energy worrying and complaining about
the fact that he can't do what he wants.)

What implications does our system have for the way we perceive?
It is a basic attribute of circuits that they tend towards stereo-
typy. Imagine the set of features that form the circuit in Figure
10.1A. The features at the centre of the circle are the core ones

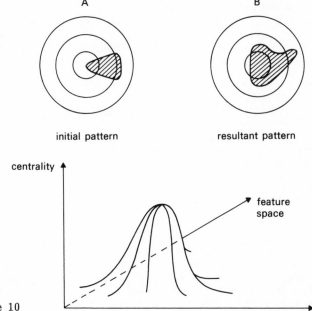

Figure 10

and those towards the outside are the more loosely associated,
optional ones. We might take Figure 10.1A as a bird's-eye view of
the mountain shown in Figure 10.2, where the core features of the
circuit are those at the summit and the optional features are down
on the foothills. The core features have very high mutual excitability; the optional ones are less tightly 'bound' to this particular
circuit.

Now, suppose that the set of features identified in Figure 10.1A

is stimulated, say by the appearance of an object in the visual
field. This particular object may be an unusual exemplar of the
concept that this circuit represents, so it stimulates only some of
the core features and many optional ones. The high degree of
mutual excitability of the core features, however, may mean that
some of the core features not presented are recruited, which
draws activity away from the optional features - leaving a resultant pattern, the pattern that you 'see', more like Figure 10.1B.
It is an intrinsic characterⁱstic of the system that it tends to reg-
ularize and conventionalize the stimulation it receives. So it follows that this tendency is as true of Integrated Man as it is of
Dissociated Man: Integrated Man's perception may be rather more
veridical, as he has no neurotic needs to suppress or distort his
experience, but his perception and memory are still fallible in the
same way. Sometimes, as we saw in Chapter 6, people write about
Integrated Man as if his conscious experience were completely
pre-conceptual, undistorted by any categorization processes,
whether discovered inductively or received via instruction. This
would make the enlightened master's experience a return to
amorphous sensation, William James's 'booming, buzzing confusion'
of childhood, which might be very pretty, but would certainly be
completely useless, lacking any significance to the perceiver. No,
Integrated Man's perceptions are modified by his network, but
they are not modified more than his own past experience warrants,
and they are constantly tentative. He has no egotistical investment in their being 'right'.

The fact that perception involves a summation of pre-existing
and afferent activity is very economical. It means that very little
pick-up of sensory information is necessary to recognize something that one has an expectation of meeting. But by the same
token two other, not so desirable, consequences follow. First, if
something rather similar to what is expected turns up, it is easy
to make a mistake and misclassify it as the thing that 'should'
have happened. Second, once a percept is formed, once the recognition judgment is made, right or wrong, the flow of activity
sets off to explore the consequences of this identification and
further processing of the stimulation stops. At the best this
means that one's percepts are often very sketchy, lacking in the
full recognition of detail that might have led, if one had not gone
off half-cocked, to the choice of a more appropriate reaction. At
worst it means that one doesn't bother to check one's perceptions
at all, and may never recognize a mistake. This leads to the
vicious circle that one sees in defensive or un-self-confident
people. A rash and inaccurate judgment has to be defended,
because the person cannot allow himself to be wrong and the subsequent anxiety leads to even more pre-emptive and silly judgments. It is people with the smallest conceptual hoops who insist
most strongly that the world has to jump through them. Conversely
if one can hold back for a while and let a felt sense of the meaning of one's experience form, rather than rushing in and imposing
a meaning on it, often on the basis of the most minimal amount of

processing, then the action that results will almost certainly be
more effective. Much of the time we operate like a doctor who takes
one look at a patient, sees some spots, and writes out a prescription for measles without more ado.

Our learnt and maladaptive inability to cope even temporarily
with the conscious feeling of not knowing is largely to blame. First
the conscious construction that we put on events is heavily biased
by our culturally absorbed beliefs about the way things ought to
be, so that much of the construction reflects not the organismic
reality of experience but the projection of our, mostly unconscious,
desires, defences and fantasies. Second, as the focused spot-
light of conscious awareness requires more of the limited pool of
activity to sustain it, the breadth of detail that can be active
tacitly is reduced. The flight into a conscious story (often literally a verbal analysis) produces at one stroke both an impover-
ishment and a distortion. Instead of allowing a series of conscious
figures to emerge from the tacit ground, be attended to and dealt
with, and then recede again, we insist on hopping from figure to
figure to figure, and rapidly lose touch with the ground of context, need, and new stimulation. 'Ground' is a good word, for the
figure should be grounded; unless the instantaneous nature of
the ground is allowed to determine its own pulses into consciousness, consciousness becomes ungrounded, disconnected from the
ground of experience.

And there is worse yet. Because conscious awareness is subject
to its own logic of serial, rational, often verbal analysis, that has
no correspondence in the holistic experience of the organism;
and because certain specific aspects of this holistic experience
(usually emotional ones) are blocked, the channels of consciousness inevitably lead one's perceptions further and further away
from their starting points. Instead of strolling through life, we
zoom through it on a rocket-powered pogo-stick, touching 'ground'
every couple of hundred yards, and missing everything in between.

So far I have talked as if perception were simply the detection
of single objects, or at most collections of objects. But it is rarely
if ever like that. The job is to act effectively and this means taking into account the significance of a total scenario, for the meanings of its elements derive from the meaning one ascribes to the
situation they are elements of. My decision that the path across
the field is a short-cut will have different outcomes depending on
whether (a) I notice the large animal in a far corner, and (b) I
see it as a cow or a bull. Perception involves analysis, but the
process is not completed without a synthesis. In fact analysis and
synthesis do not occur in sequence, first identifying the bits and
then fitting them together, but almost simultaneously. The first
glimpse of a scene - the first eye fixation, if we restrict our
attention to visual perception for the moment - activates some circuits and primes others. The precise pattern of activation and
priming, is, as always, influenced by context and current internal
priorities. Because of the limited capacity of the system, only a
part of the information in the scene can be registered in this first

fixation. Then a second fixation occurs the field of which partly
overlaps with the first. The stimulation from this second batch is
now overlaid on the existing pattern, so that the percept that
results incorporates the interpretation of the first fixation. And
so on. In this way the separate fixations, and the objects and
events they contain, are built into a picture of the total scene as
the analysis proceeds. The net result of this is that as we move
about, elements of our perception will form, become central, and
dissolve again in a smooth and continuous manner – exactly as
they do in fact behave. We can add in other senses as well: for
example, hearing integrates percepts over time in just the same
way as I have described eye fixations integrating over space.

ATTENDING

For Dissociated Man there is a clear distinction between attention
being 'grabbed' and being 'paid'. Grabbing attention is something
the environment does: paying attention is something I do. In our
system these are not different in kind, but only in the consciousness, immediacy and complexity of the events that precede the
shift in attention. When attention is grabbed, by a squeal of
brakes, say, or a bright flash, the centre of activation in the
network suddenly shifts from whatever had been going on to the
new experience. This 'break-through' occurs when the stimulation
is either very intense (and so activates the relevant circuit, whatever else is going on in the network) or of some special biological
or learnt significance – which has permanently low 'thresholds'
of firing. The inhibitory mechanisms that we mentioned briefly
ensure that these new events compete with the pre-existing pattern of activation for the limited resources of activity, and so the
grabbing of attention by one area means its loss by the other.
   The process of 'paying' attention is not so immediate: it depends
on the existence within the network of a pattern of priming that
is not entirely known to consciousness. The consciousness with
which 'I' identifies itself does not know how the pattern of activation will move across the net, (a) because it doesn't know exactly
how the energy is distributed and (b) because it cannot predict
perfectly the events in the outside world. To fill this gap of
insecurity, 'I' decides to attribute to itself the cause of the
changes in attention that are happening or are about to happen.
The tacit apprehension of a change in circumstances may issue
almost simultaneously in an automatic shift of attention, and in the
conscious 'decision' to shift attention. Unaware of the tacit antecedents of the shift, 'I' attributes it to itself.
   One particular aspect of the context that triggers selection of
certain kinds of events is instruction. 'Now I want you all to
listen very carefully' may, if it is successful, set the network so
that it gives priority to activation that arises from a particular
location in the outside world – the teacher. 'Pay attention to the
words you hear on the right-hand head-phone and ignore those

on the left' does the same thing. There is absolutely no need to
postulate any intervening stage between comprehension of the
instruction and carrying it out. There is no 'I' who listens to it
and says 'No, I don't feel like it', or 'I say, that's a good idea'.
That 'decision' is made in the process of comprehending the message, because the way it is comprehended, and the pattern of
excitation that results, already reflect the priorities present in
the network.

The effectiveness of an instruction depends on the actual connections in the network, as well as on its transient state. 'Point
out all the animals you can see in this picture' is quite easy, while
'Point out all the objects whose names contain any sequence of
three consonants' is not, however much one might want to do it.
The organization of the network is such that activation of 'animal'
can prime all animals, whereas we do not ordinarily classify words
by length of consonant-sequence, and the channels just do not
exist for the priming to flow. The only way to do this latter task
is by spelling out the names of the objects to yourself.

CONCENTRATION

As soon as attention is deliberately concentrated in a certain
degree, one begins to select from the material before one:
one point will be fixed in the mind with particular clearness
and some other consequently dis-regarded, and in this selection one's expectations and one's inclinations will be followed.
This is just what must not be done, however...
                                Sigmund Freud: 'Collected Works'
Activity within the network can vary in its location, as we saw in
the last section, but it can also vary in its concentration – the
extent to which it is focused in one small area or alternatively
spread out diffusely over the whole net. This section is about
concentration in the other sense, where 'I' thinks that it ought to
be focusing its attention consistently and exclusively on some task
or topic, while the wayward 'me' insists on being distracted by
vague desires, usually for sex and food. Concentrating is a classic example of Dissociated Man in action, and quite different from
the natural and integrated sense of being absorbed, or even 'lost',
in a book or a film or a walk by the sea. Indeed language gives
the lie to Dissociated Man in saying 'I was lost in my contemplation
of the sea' or whatever, for the divisive and argumentative 'I' is
lost in such a whole-hearted commitment to a present experience.

Deliberate concentration is ridiculous for it presumes that my
consciousness knows better than my whole organism and it con-
fuses nerves with muscles. What possible good can be done by
furrowing my brows, gritting my teeth, and fixing my eyes grimly
on a meaningless page? It does no good at all, and more than that,
it makes matters worse than they were; for one thing all this
furrowing and gritting requires activity of motor areas of the net
to maintain it, which means there's less left for the task in hand,

and for another the increase in internal conflict increases anxiety, and the effect of being anxious is again to interfere with the natural flow of activation through the network. Very often what happens is a kind of tunnel vision, where attention becomes rigidly fixed on one or two features of a situation and prevents the formation of an accurate gestalt. This is what happens in 'trying too hard', and in the 'can't see for looking' phenomenon, where one fails to see a sought object (car keys, cigarettes) that is right in front of one's nose. The beam of the spot-light of attention has become so focused that the tacit, 'peripheral vision' cannot work.

There is in psychology a folk-law called the Yerkes-Dodson Function that says that for any task an intermediate level of arousal is best: too relaxed or too excited and performance, especially any kind of creativity, suffers. This follows from our system if for 'arousal' we read 'focusing of attention'. There is no way of increasing or decreasing the total level of activation: all that changes is how it is distributed. If the net is primed very diffusely, then it will be difficult for salient aspects to emerge and be distinguished from irrelevant details, while if the activation is focused tightly before one starts, the situation is pre-empted, and many relevant points, which lie outside this a priori pool of light will be missed altogether. A relaxed but alert receptivity is what is required.

SUBLIMINAL PERCEPTION

Within experimental psychology subliminal perception is treated as something rather suspect and esoteric. Within the integrated network it is an integral and essential component of day-to-day perception. Conscious percepts are always just the decorated symptoms of a whole mass of subliminal (i.e. tacit) activations. It is axiomatic that all our thoughts and actions are shaped and coloured by influences that do not themselves reach consciousness. I can walk down a street responding magnificently to other pedestrians, piles of dog-shit, kerbs, parked cars and the onset of rain while my conscious awareness has been filled with the planning of supper.

Formal demonstrations are really unnecessary but here is one. A person is given stereo headphones and asked to listen to the right-hand channel that, at one point, contains a grammatically ambiguous sentence like 'They are whispering leaves'. Just before, on the left-hand channel, are played either sentences like 'They are shouting helloes' or like 'They are drooping branches'. Although these sentences are not consciously heard by the subject, nor can he recall them, his interpretation of the ambiguous, attended, sentence is reliably influenced. Subliminal perception not only occurs but shapes conscious perception (as our proposals say it must).

INSIGHT

Usually perception proceeds smoothly, each new glimpse of the
world being capable of fitting into and building up 'the story so
far'. There are some occasions, though, when this does not
happen and where either judgment has to be temporarily suspended, pending the arrival of more data that will allow the previous bits to fall into place, or where a picture that has been
built up suddenly has to be turned on its head as a result of new
evidence.

The delayed cohesion effect can be illustrated by an example
from language comprehension - a topic we take up in detail in the
chapter on learning. Reading the sentence

'The notes were sour because the seams split'

leaves one with a slight feeling of puzzlement. What does it mean?
What is it about? You know all the words but somehow the sentence
doesn't gel. If you now go on to read

'So he took his bagpipes to the menders'

resolution takes place. Activation of one's prior knowledge about
bagpipes enables one to select meanings for 'notes', 'seams', and
particularly for 'sour' that make sense in the context. But it is
not really 'one' who selects: the resolution follows automatically,
because the priming of certain features by 'bagpipes' allows a
feature set to become activated for 'sour' that integrates with the
rest of the sentence, where before this did not happen.

JOKES

An Englishman visiting Ireland went into a bar in Dublin and sat
down next to an Irishman. After a minute or two the Irishman
turned to him and said: 'That's a mighty strange dog you've got
there, sir. What is it?' The Englishman replied: 'It's a long-nosed,
long-tailed, short-legged terrier.' After a couple of minutes' silence the Irishman said: 'Does it fight?' 'Yes,' said the Englishman,
'it fights'. 'Bejasus,' said the Irishman, 'It sure is an awful-lookin''
thing. What did you say it was?' 'A long-nosed, long-tailed, short-
legged terrier.' 'Oh. Well, I've got a wolf-hound outside... I'll
bet you five pounds, my dog against yours.' 'O.K.,' said the
Englishman, 'Bring it in.' So the Irishman went out and came back
in with an enormous vicious-looking Irish wolf-hound. The two
animals went for each other and soon it was finished with the wolf-
hound scattered in little pieces all over the bar. 'Christ!' said the
Irishman as he handed over the fiver, 'What kind if a thing *is*
that?' 'I told you,' replied the Englishman calmly, 'It's a long-
nosed, long-tailed, short-legged terrier... but over in England
some people call them alligators.'

Jokes are a good example of insightful integration following suspension and/or reversal. They rely on setting a scene where the
listener's tacit expectancies lead him up the garden path, so that
when the last piece of the jigsaw is given, the punch-line is

delivered, suddenly the whole picture jumps into focus and is found to be quite different from the rather fuzzy image you were trying to build up. The word 'alligator' gives a coherence to the story similar to the previous example 'bagpipes', but here the suspense and the expectations are greater, and the story snaps shut with a chuckle.

The role of one's tacit expectancies in trying to make sense out of a deliberately tantalizing situation accounts for the artistry of telling a good joke. It is said that this is a matter of timing, which it is, but on what does the timing depend? Principally, the magic ingredient of timing is a response by the raconteur to the state of the listener's comprehension. He, the story-teller, must time his delivery so that the punch-line is delivered to an audience which is in a crucial state of expectation, frustration, and partial comprehension. He must be ahead of them, but not too far ahead, or the final piece won't have an almost completed jigsaw puzzle to reorganize.

The importance of timing is similar to that found in psycho-therapy, where it is not the quality of an insight on the therapist's part that counts so much as when and how it is delivered. The client has to 'get' the insight, rather than understand it, in the same way as a joke has to be 'got'. There is an immediacy of impact and an emotional involvement in getting a joke that is not present in ordinary understanding. That is why if a joke does not work at once, it cannot be explained.

Some jokes - witticisms, puns and the like - operate within the logic of the verbal plane: although the substance of the joke is the substance of intellectual understanding, the process of satisfactorily reconciling an unlikely juxtaposition of ideas has an explosive effect on the whole organism. The temporary suspension of understanding, or its sudden interruption, creates a problem, and its eventual solution brings about a release of tension, or an opening of the stuck gate to produce a flood of the dammed activity. Other jokes have their effect because they make connections within the experiential plane. The most poignant jokes, and the most effective comedians, are those that present us to ourselves; they show our defensiveness, pomposity, frailty and stupidity in such a way that we can allow ourselves to acknowledge, just for a moment, the reflection. Getting this sort of joke is, as some people have suggested, a little satori experience, for suddenly Organismic Reality and Conscious Reality coincide and for an instant we become Integrated Man. But 'people cannot bear too much [organismic] reality': we cannot afford to recognize our pretentions and falsity for too long, and the superimposition soon breaks down again.

The power of jokes and humorous anecdotes to slough off their verbal skin and penetrate into the organism explains their usefulness to spiritual teachers. You can explain something to someone till you are blue in the face, but the more logical you are, the more likely your discourse is to remain at the superficial level of rational understanding. Psychology libraries are as sepulchral as

any others: they are not alive with the titters of students recog-
nizing themselves in the pages of the 'British Journal of Social
and Clinical Psychology'. Yet a joke may make exactly the same
point as a research paper in a much more potent way. The Sufis
in particular have made a practice of using jokes to teach. Their
recurrent hero, Mulla Nasrudin, is at first sight absurd, and at
second sight us. For example, Nasrudin was walking home one
day carrying a bag of liver in one hand and in the other a recipe
for liver pie. Suddenly a raven swooped down and snatched the
liver. 'You fool', shouted the Mulla triumphantly, 'You may have
the liver, but it won't do you much good without the recipe.' Our
intuitive sense of the absurdity is more instructive than a detailed
exposition of the 'moral'.

AESTHETICS

> When feelings are too fully expressed, no room is left for
> the unknown, and from this unknown start the Japanese
> arts.
> > D. T. Suzuki: 'Zen and Japanese Culture'

> Music, states of happiness, mythology, faces belaboured
> by time, certain twilights and certain places try to tell us
> something, or have said something we should have missed,
> or are about to say something: this imminence of a reve-
> lation which does not occur is, perhaps, the aesthetic
> phenomenon.
> > Jorge Luis Borges: 'Labyrinths'

Avoidance, or perhaps transcendence, of intellectual understanding is characteristic of that type of perception we call
aesthetic. But unlike humour, the aesthetic experience does not
rely on snap recognition, but more, as Borges says, on an experience that blocks the formation of a rational interpretation, and,
by prolonging the pre-conceptual moment, enables one to become
aware of other levels of experiencing. There is certainly a tradition in art that seems to work this way, though it is more apparent in the painting, poetry and music of cultures such as the
Japanese than in the flashy and egotistical overkill of the post-
Renaissance West. The subtle simplicity of a haiku, such as
Basho's

> A black crow
> Has settled himself
> On a leafless tree,
> Fall of an autumn day

or his classic

> Breaking the silence
> Of an ancient pond,
> A frog jumps in -
> Pa - chink!

sinks through the layers of reason until it touches the whole person at an inchoate and tacit level, like the sound of the frog penetrating the forest, or like a small pebble dropped carefully into the pond. In contrast the cleverness and show of much of Western art is like a plank slapped on the surface of the pond, that makes a commotion but will not sink.

Maybe this is unfair. While the misty suggestiveness of a Turner, or a Zen ink landscape certainly by-passes the traps of understanding, the psychological thrust of the best of the West is designed to show the mind its limitations, and their artefactual nature, by using words to say what cannot be said. By juxtaposing the bestial and the sexual on the one hand with the spiritual on the other, Yeats's 'Magi', for example, forces us to reconsider the assumption in our minds and in our language that these two ideas are at odds, opposite ends of a solid pole. Yeats tries to turn the pole into a hose-pipe, and show that the ends can be brought together if we will only allow it. e. e. cummings makes a similar point about poetry, in poetry, in this extract from 'A Poet's Advice to Students':

> A poet is somebody who feels, and who expresses his
>   feeling through words.
> This may sound easy. It isn't.
> A lot of people think or believe or know they feel - but
>   that's thinking or believing or knowing, not feeling.
>   And poetry is feeling -
> not knowing or believing or thinking.
>   . . .
> Whenever you think or you believe or you know, you're
>   a lot of other people:
> but the moment you feel you're nobody-but-yourself.
>   . . .
> As for expressing nobody-but-yourself in words, that
>   means working just
> a little harder than anyone who isn't a poet can possibly
>   imagine. why?
> Because nothing is quite as easy as using words just like
>   somebody else.
> We all of us do exactly this nearly all of the time - and
>   whenever
> we do it, we're not poets.

In the world of the intellect, I am solid, persistent and detached, capable of reviewing and affecting objects that are themselves solid, persistent and detached. In the world of the organism, all is change and connection, and beauty is immanent in the apprehension of the coming and going of things to which I am related. And room is made for this when the busy-work of normal reason is stymied by the elusive Quality (as Pirsig calls it in 'Zen and the Art of Motorcycle Maintenance') of art.

The mechanism is similar to, but more profound than, the temporary suspension of closure that we talked of before. It is not too fanciful, I think, to sense a kinship between our simple example

The notes were sour because the seams split

and Eliot's

> Garlic and sapphires in the mud
> Clot the bedded axle-tree.
> The trilling wire in the blood
> Sings below inveterate scars
> Appeasing long forgotten wars.

Both stop us in our tracks. But the difference is that with Eliot, in the sudden hush a different process gets a chance to speak. Words stilled by words, yet the ideas awoken by the words can be half-heard playing, and weaving patterns of their own and on their own, like children across a valley on a clear, crisp morning.

Actually this creative process of fitting words together happens all the time, but 'it' happens so quickly, and even if it doesn't 'we' are in a hurry and force the process to a hasty end, so that it cannot be observed. We need the security of thinking that we know what's going on, even if our picture does violence to the facts; if it is true that the aesthetic experience comes from a letting-go, a willingness to let things change and be inscrutable, it comes as no surprise that the commonplaces of our lives lack beauty.

9   LIVING THE SELF-LESS LIFE:
States of mind

Some of our conscious experience is linked to and reflects current
sensory stimulation: this is the area of perception that we have
just considered. Other states of mind are not so linked. These
are the states we call thinking, remembering, imagining, planning,
deciding and dreaming. Some of these have a sensory quality, but
are based only very indirectly, if at all, on information coming in
through the special senses. It is these we investigate here.

THINKING

> Thought is a flow of activation across a passive memory
> surface, not an active stringing together of items from a
> memory store.
> Edward de Bono: 'The Mechanism of Mind'

It is vital in the present context to distinguish thought-as-process
from thought-as-product. They are confused in ordinary language,
because we assume that the conscious flow of 'thoughts', the
stream of internal dialogue, is in some way instrumental in the
processes of deciding, solving problems and selecting actions. If
I see myself as an agent, and if I am identified with my thoughts,
then I must see my thoughts as instruments of control and direction. Integrated Man, however, has broken this identification
and can watch his thoughts arising and passing, as he can watch
his perceptions and his actions, without conferring on them any
such special status. 'Inside and out, there is simply the stream
flowing along of itself.' He can see thoughts as transient fragments of print-out from processing that is autonomous and unob-
servable. This is not to say that the occasions when thoughts
arise do not reflect particular states or phases of this processing;
only that the appropriate word is 'reflect' and not 'control' or
'produce'.

The appearance of conscious thoughts often reflects a blockage
in the tacit processing. When all is flowing smoothly, no conscious
product intervenes between perception and action. Only when no
ready-made response exists - when the situation poses a 'problem'
- does conscious deliberation appear. So it is quite true that the
activity of problem-solving and the conscious experience of 'thinking' tend to occur together, but they occur as separate responses
to the blockage of the tacit flow of activity. The flow is stopped at
some point in the network, and activity therefore accumulates (as
it flows in to the nexus but cannot flow out) until it eventually

escapes into the verbal plane. Activation now has a way of moving – by following the channels of conscious thought that have become available. But this movement represents an avoidance of the problem, not its solution, for the original impasse at the tacit level remains. Hence not only the futility but the positive interference of 'thinking' with the autonomous activity of problem-solving. As we shall see in the section on Creativity, novel solutions tend to emerge from an acceptance of the block, and the ability to stick with it, not from the zealous application of the intellect.

Sometimes problems solve themselves at the tacit level despite the leaking of activity into conscious thought, and these sporadic occurrences tend to reinforce our belief in deliberation. The psychology of learning knows well what it calls the 'partial reinforcement effect', where habits that have been found to be only intermittently successful prove particularly hard to break. The fact that thinking sometimes seems to work causes us to furrow our brows and think harder and harder. The logic, that small effort leads to occasional success, is sound within its own terms: but it is the logic of running faster to get nearer the horizon, or of the dog who died of a heart attack trying to reach his tail. It is interesting to note that prolonged awareness of the state of any other part or function of the body is a sign of pathology; perhaps one's continuous preoccupation with conscious thought is likewise pathological.

It is difficult even to be aware that we spend so much time in thoughts, for we do not watch them, we become them. Only rarely in the normal way do we stand outside the stream of consciousness and look at it – as, for example, when we try to reconstruct a chain of associations. Once that distance is achieved, the nature and function of thought can be seen more clearly too. The function is often to reconstruct an imperfect past ('I should have been firmer with him', 'I wish they hadn't left so early') or to attempt to outwit an inherently uncertain future. In the next three sections we will discuss the mind's projections into the future under three headings – intention, imagination and planning.

INTENTION

The mind's sense of the prevalence of one set of influences over another set: an effect whose cause is the imminence, immediate or remote, of the performance of the act intended by the person incurring the intention. (When figured out and accurately apprehended, this will be found one of the most penetrating and far-reaching definitions in the whole dictionary.)

Ambrose Bierce: 'The Devil's Dictionary'

Bierce is right: his gnomic definition is penetrating and far-reaching. When we have the sense that 'I' intends to do something we construe it as showing that 'I' – the same I that witnesses the

intention – is going to initiate an act, in the near or distant future. It is this construction that is very largely responsible for
the apparent agency of 'I'. It seems to be capable of apprehending certain circumstances or needs, of deciding what must be done
and of then transforming this internal intention into an overt
action or program of action. The crucial thing is that because we
are aware of the imminence of the act before the act itself occurs,
we think that the awareness is somehow instrumental in producing
the act. This logical fallacy, called post hoc ergo propter hoc, is
well known, but it is not so well understood that it contributes
centrally to our common sense of self.

Ambrose Bierce is pointing us towards an alternative construction of the same simple fact – that we sometimes have an accurate
awareness of what we are about to do – based not on 'control' but
'prediction'. The function of the mind network is, as we have
seen, to anticipate future states of the world, the organism, and
the modification of those states by interaction between world and
organism. Some of those anticipations enter awareness, some do
not. Thus while activity is flowing through the network towards
the selection or construction of some behavioural sequence, it is
possible for part of the activity, if blocked, to shoot up into
consciousness, and for the activated Conscious Reality to produce
a prediction of the eventual outcome of the tacit operations of the
Organismic Reality. And because this guess (for that is all it is)
depends on past habits and past experience which may not be
validated by the 'future' that intervenes between the intention
and the action, it often turns out to be wrong. Confronted with
the inadequacy of the Fat Controller view of the ego we either
suppress awareness of the intention ('I never said I wanted to go
to university'), deny its seriousness ('You didn't think I meant it,
did you?') or – and this must take some sort of prize for bare-
faced cheek – we say 'I changed my mind', as if the failure of the
prediction were itself further evidence in favour of the autonomy
and wisdom of the ego. It is in fact an extraordinary testament to
the intrinsic ingenuity of the mind that it can select and distort
its experience with such subtlety that it protects its mistaken
theory about itself against almost continual invalidation.

As with many other states of mind, it is informative to ask when
the sense of intending occurs, for it does not attend the vast
majority of things I do. I do not intend to sip my coffee, blow my
nose, gaze out of the window, turn over the record. They happen
without deliberation. I only sense an intention when the execution
of an action is delayed. This may be because the odds are finely
balanced between two courses of action: the preponderance of one
set of considerations over the other is not very great. Or because
the execution of a clearly indicated act is blocked by other considerations that are not clearly available to conscious awareness
('I intend to give up smoking, to go to church more often, to be
less selfish...'). These New Year Resolution kinds of intention
are notoriously useless. Or the delay may occur because the
intention is not to do something directly, but to achieve something

(a first-class degree, a good marriage, a win at chess) for which there is no obvious behavioural route. If the passage between antecedent and achievement of a desired consequence is blocked, or does not yet exist, or cannot readily be found, activity begins to concentrate at a point in the network and may reach the level required for consciousness of the impasse. Once this happens, channels of conscious, verbal reason may become active, and we experience ourselves as 'thinking', 'deciding' or 'intending'. These conscious products may relate quite closely, or not at all, to the resolution of the impasse, and the resultant actions that actually occur.

We should mention briefly here a class of actions that are sometimes called intentional. These are looking, listening, sniffing, grasping and tasting, which are contrasted with seeing, hearing, smelling, touching and ingesting. (Some of these words, for example 'touching', are ambiguous with respect to intentionality, but language is not at issue here.) What is the essential difference? It is that the former, looking, listening and the like, are learnt actions that are designed to increase the intensity of a weak sensation, or to seek a cross-modal corollary of a sensation. The perception of the weak stimulus, which may be subliminal, provides evidence for the presence of an object or the desirability of a consequence, that is not strong enough to act on its own, but does activate expectancies about certain sorts or sources of corroboration. A half-heard noise from upstairs might have signalled an awake and distressed infant. One's experience says that if a baby is upset and crying it will keep on crying, so the television is turned down or the conversation stopped to create the circumstances in which corroboration can be obtained. Thus these 'intentional' actions which deliberately and selectively seek or heighten certain kinds of stimulation arise from the mechanisms of mutual recruitment or inhibition within the network that are by now familiar. Partial, possibly tacit, activation of a concept leads to a priming of other features of the concept, so that, if present, they require less perceptual activation for recognition to occur. And, because total activity is limited, other potentially competing activities (e.g. shuffling the cards) or sensations (watching the television) are inhibited. We do not need an 'I' who is doing the looking and listening. They represent learnt strategies for improving the effectiveness of one's actions by ensuring that one's apprehension of the current situation is as full, and therefore as veridical, as possible. The homunculus is again unnecessary.

IMAGINATION

> as imagination bodies forth
> The form of things unknown, the poet's pen
> Turns them to shapes, and gives to airy nothing
> A local habitation and a name.
>
> Shakespeare: 'A Midsummer Night's Dream'

Imagination involves the conscious awareness of combinations of ideas or objects that have not, as yet, been experienced. These may appear as creative juxtapositions of 'pure' concepts, unassociated with particular locations in space and/or time, or they may take the form of fantasy events, which may be hypothetically located in one's own future, or not. While both may initially be sensed only in a vague, prototypical way, the former tend to issue in verbal products and the latter in pictorial or imaginal form. We shall pursue the latter in this section, and the former under Creativity.

Imagination and memory are closer to each other than might have been supposed, both being, on the one hand 'imaginary', bearing only a loose relationship to reality as experienced, and on the other grounded in and constrained by that experience. Imagination seems more obviously creative, however, and this creativity needs some explanation as to how and when it occurs.

The experiential concepts that the network represents as fuzzy collections of features are distilled from a range of particular events, some of these features being central, others peripheral, to the meaning of the concept as it might be expressed. We have seen that the particular subset of these features that fires in response to a perceptual event depends jointly on the incoming activation and on the existing distribution of priming activation within the total circuit. We have also seen that circuits can be recruited not only by direct sensory stimulation but by a flow of activity within the network itself – a train of thought, perhaps. These channels of thought tend to run between the verbal labels, the flags that are planted at the summit of the conceptual mountains, not directly between the experiential features themselves. So, to put these two types of priming together – the holistic and the partial – the form in which a concept is experienced as a result of lateral verbal excitation within the network depends on the selective distribution of activity within its feature set that exists at the time of the activation. Thus it follows that concepts can be experienced in imagination in ways they have never been experienced before. And the same applies to combinations of concepts, too. Fantastic objects (unicorns) and scenarios (dreams) can arise because the network contains rules and relationships which are individually derived from experience but which, once incorporated functionally within the network, permit further combinations that may not have occurred or may never occur in the world itself. A cookery book, for example, is an implicit specification of ingredients and rules for their combination that allow many other dishes to be prepared than those that are actually spelt out. Of course, the more sophisticated and accurate this rule system is, the less deviation from what is possible in the world it permits: which may be why children's fantasy worlds are much richer than adults'. Though we should note that much of the limitation on adult imagination comes not from the organismic structure but the socially apprehended lets and hindrances that overlay it. One of these prohibitions refers to the process of imagining itself, labelling it as non-serious, non-productive, self-indulgent, 'childish' and the like.

How do 'images' - which is what we call the transient non-verbal
products of the process of imagining - come to have their quasi-
sensory quality? What happens when a concept is aroused associatively is essentially the same thing as when it follows a sensory
event. A circuit of features fires. But there is a difference in
emphasis and degree. When an object is present, the sensory
processing activates many features in the network that correspond
to the perceptual details of the object. Many of these will not be
essential to the categorization of the object: they are accessories
to the fact. But none the less when the conceptual circuit fires,
it will contain many of these incidental attributes. When the same
circuit is fired associatively, these accessories have not been
activated in the process of recognition, so the set of sensory
'extras' that serve to flesh out the bones of the concept will be
missing. Some sensory features will be fired, from above, as it
were, rather than from below, if they are core features of the
concept or if they have been primed sufficiently by the context.
Thus the experience of imagery has the familiar ghost-like quality,
possessing some of the aspects of a seen object and lacking others.

PLANNING

Our friend Bierce might have glossed this as 'Plan v. To prepare
in fantasy a course of action to be implemented in circumstances
that will not occur.' It is imagination for a purpose, and involves
projecting not just states of affairs, but the form and effect of
various alternative interventions. The activity presupposes that
such alternatives are and will be possible, a presupposition that
is inherently untestable, and only tenable because the imagined
future must be stereotypical and so incomplete. I imagine a party
where both Fiona and Jackie will be present, and try to plan my
reactions and advances to each. But I only have the freedom to
do so because I cannot know that Fiona will have fallen in love
with John, that Jackie's mother will have died, and that her desperate and brittle gaiety will repel me, and that Anita, unattached
and lovelier than ever, will invite me home. If I go armed with
plans, contingency plans and counter-plans, my mind 'made up',
I will be less open to opportunity, more resistant and inflexible in
the face of things I hadn't bargained for, and fall between the
stools of expectation and fact. If I were as free to abandon my
plans as I felt to construct them, nothing much would be lost. But
I have an investment in their being right, because I have to think
myself an effective planner. So I am caught in inhibition and deliberation, frozen by my plan. The 'Tao Te Ching' says 'Bend and
be straight: yield and ye shall overcome'. And less cryptically,

> When a man is to take the world over and shape it
> I see that he must be obliged to do it.
> For the world is a divine vessel:
> It cannot be shaped;

Nor can it be insisted upon.
He who shapes it damages it;
He who insists upon it loses it.
Therefore the Sage does not shape it,
He does not damage it;
He does not insist upon it,
So he does not lose it.

The lunacies of conscious attempts to plan are best seen at the corporate level: tower blocks, DDT, Los Alamos all started out with good intentions and ended up paving the road to Hell. It is no wonder that it was J. Robert Oppenheimer, midwife to the birth of the atomic bomb at Los Alamos in the early 1940s, who ended his life saying that the only thing to do to stop the world going to Hell is nothing. If we stop the supply of paving stones, the road will soon get overgrown and impassable.

I have a friend who is being paid £8,000 a year to estimate the manpower needs of the National Coal Board in the year 2000. It is amazing how busy you can keep yourself with a little guesswork and a lot of computer time. £8,000 a year seems a lot to bet on the fact that all your assumptions (demand, supply, work-habits, social stability, competitive fuels, permeability of the atmosphere to infra-red radiation ... the list is literally endless) will still be valid in twenty-two years' time.

At the individual level planning is not inherently a bad thing: it becomes so when it slips over from being an anticipation of possible futures to an insistence that only some of these (the ones I want, or can at least plan how to cope with) may occur. For then perception becomes cloudy and selective and action unspontaneous. Planning is also counter-productive when it becomes compulsive, as it does for many people, especially as they become older and more vulnerable - not just psychologically but biologically - to future fluctuations from the familiar. Being preoccupied with fantasies of impending threat ('worrying' we call it in its less extreme forms) is unpleasant in itself, for it generates exactly those feelings of anxiety, incompetence, inadequacy or whatever, that it is designed to forestall. And the possible pleasures of the present, large or small, go unnoticed and untasted, for one's mind is elsewhere.

On the other hand there are three positive features of planning that sometimes show through. First, if one's plan of action is held tentatively, and in a loosely articulated fashion, then it may provide a source of bricks, each of whose viability has at least been partially checked, out of which an appropriate, tailor-made action can be built. Second, if one's anticipation of a difficult or dangerous future turns out to be substantially accurate, one may be less thrown by it, less ready to flee from the unknown-ness and insecurity of it, and more able therefore to remain in the present and by registering it fully, act effectively. And finally, if we are able, we can use our awareness of the inadequacy of our plans to good effect.

We must surrender our hopes and expectations and march
directly into disappointment... Disappointment is a good
sign of basic intelligence. It cannot be compared to anything else: it is so sharp, precise, obvious and direct. If
we can open, then we suddenly begin to see that our
expectations are irrelevant compared with the reality of
the situations we are facing. This automatically brings a
feeling of disappointment.
Chogyam Trungpa: 'Cutting Through Spiritual Materialism'

CREATIVITY

To arrive at the simplest truth, as Newton knew and practised, requires *years* of *contemplation*. Not activity. Not
reasoning. Not calculating. Not busy behaviour of any kind.
Not reading. Not talking. Not making an effort. Not thinking. Simply *bearing in mind* what it is one needs to know.
And yet those with the courage to tread this path to real
discovery are not only offered practically no guidance on
how to do so, they are actively discouraged and have to
set about it in secret, pretending meanwhile to be diligently
engaged in the frantic diversions, and to conform with the
deadening personal opinions, which are being continually
thrust upon them.
                    G. Spencer Brown: 'The Laws of Form'
In the section on Imagination we discussed a commonplace but
limited form of creativity: the production of a novel experience
out of a train of thought. The direction of the process was from the
intellectual to the experiential. By creativity in this section I am
meaning a process that is in some ways the reverse. It is a bub-
bling-up from tacit processes into conscious awareness. The
bubbles are often misty and symbolic to start with, only later
being converted in the clear but linear print-out of Conscious
Reality. Einstein, for example, in commenting on his own creative
process said: 'The words of the language as they are written or
spoken do not seem to play any role in my mechanism of thought.
The physical entities which seem to serve as elements in thought
are certain signs and more or less clear images ... In a stage
where words intervene at all, they are, in my case, purely aud-
itive, but they interfere only in a secondary stage.' Like images
they have an imprecision and an experiential quality, but far from
conforming to the patterns of conscious reason, they may be, when
unpacked and interpreted, of a most radical nature. To imagine a
world containing unicorns is no problem and no threat. To imagine
one where space and time form a single dimension, where they are
seen as mental constructs, not as absolute properties of reality,
where 'space by itself, and time by itself, are doomed to fade
away into mere shadows, and only a kind of union of the two will
preserve an independent reality' (the words used by Minkowski,
introducing the idea in 1908) is difficult and dangerous. One's

construct system either refuses to entertain it at an experiential level at all, or else one feels the very foundations of one's Newtonian common sense begin to tremble. Integrated Man, incidentally, knows Einstein's Special Theory of Relativity in his bones: for him 'as a fact of pure experience, there is no space without time, no time without space; they are interpenetrating' (D. T. Suzuki).

The centre of the creative experience, Poincaré's 'moment of illumination', is the apprehension in conscious awareness of formulations that are as yet beyond its own logic. The attempt of thought to transcend itself has ground to a halt and in the silence that follows - sometimes immediately, more often after a delay - an answer to our problem 'comes to us'. Thinking establishes a framework within which what would count as an answer is defined as clearly as possible. It constructs a net for catching solutions. But it cannot conjure up the fish, for the solution, the truly creative solution, inheres not in a new product of thought but a new way of thinking. And the dogged application of the old way is precisely what stands in the way of the new, for it prejudges what is relevant and prevents a familiar collection of perceptions merging into a different gestalt. The solutions come from within - they are literally 'insights', glimpses inwards - and the amazing thing is not that they do come, but that we so distrust the wisdom of the organism that we have grown almost deaf to its whispers.

Scientific and artistic creativity both rely on the same ability: to prepare, and then shut up, let go, be passive, receptive, without judgment while the workings of the tacit mind are trusted to deliver the goods. One must be without intention, even without the intention to be receptive. But they differ in how they choose to express the sense of truth, the intuition, that results. A work of art is a prosthetic device for extending one's powers of intuition. It is not an attempt to explain an experience, but to provoke it, for the artist sees the mistiness of his intimations not as a nuisance, a fog to be dispelled, but as, in some way which is itself incommunicable, essential to the experience. The scientist and the philosopher, however, are playing a narrower game; they are committed to explaining and describing rather than alluding and provoking, and that commitment leads them into an intricate but somehow leaden dance with language that has no end: a mazurka arranged for tubas. The more profound the issue the more inadequate language becomes, for every language is saturated with the assumptions that are being questioned. Being a philosopher - one with a deep appreciation of the limit of language, but a philosopher none the less - Wittgenstein was forced at last to say 'Whereof we cannot speak, thereof we must be silent'. But had he widened his vision, he could have seen, and said, that whereof we cannot speak, thereof we must tell jokes, paint pictures, compose music, invent parables, and dance.

It can be seen that creativity, of whatever sort, large or small, is diagnostic of integrity, for it requires a coming together of

Organismic and Conscious Realities and a cessation of the ego's abortive attempts to extort intelligence from itself. At the moment of creative insight, as at the moment of getting a joke, the internal divisions are temporarily reunited. Small wonder that creative people, whether artists, scientists, psychotherapists or whatever, are so often drawn further and further into the world of the mystical.

INTUITION

> Who can wait quietly while the mud settles?
> Who can remain still until the moment of action?
> Observers of the Tao do not seek fulfillment.
> Not seeking fulfillment they are not swayed
>   by the desire for change.
> Empty yourself of everything.
> Let the mind rest at peace.
> The ten thousand things rise and fall
> While the Self watches their return.
> They grow and flourish and then return to the source.
> Returning to the source is stillness,
>   which is the way of nature.
>
> 'Tao Te Ching'

In-tuition means letting your insides teach you. It involves a relaxing of conscious programs and logic and thus allowing yourself to hear and to heed the tacit working of the mind in a more direct, less muddy way than usual. It is the everyday equivalent of the 'act of creation' that we have just discussed, but operating more in the personal and interpersonal spheres than the artistic or scientific. Our intuitions - about other people, or about the sources of our own distress, for example - are not always accurate, and the more dissociated a person is the more contaminated will his intuitions be. The more of the iceberg of one's personality one has had to submerge, the more misleading will be the tip. But if we do pay attention to them they are often surprisingly acute, in the same way that the immediate response of an animal or a child to a stranger may prefigure an adult realization that takes months to bubble up through their much more viscous minds. It is actually a good bet to trust one's intuitions, for they are a product of the whole organism, not just a small part. Eugene Gendlin, author of 'experiential psychotherapy', which we discussed in Part I, states this philosophy very simply. 'The body is wiser than all our concepts, for it totals them all and much more. It totals all the circumstances we sense. We get this totalling if we let a felt sense form in inward space.'

What one discovers through one's intuitions may be wise or foolish: as one begins to relearn the sensitivity to oneself that Gendlin is talking of, one will find that the water remains muddy from the recent stomping about of the intellect, and one's glimpses to

the bottom sometimes partial and mistaken. But the more we let
things settle, the clearer our in-sight becomes. And anyway, the
only way to find out whether an idea is right or wrong may be to
accept it on trust and pursue it to its limits. In either case,
whether right or wrong, the outcome for the person will be wisdom if he persists (with awareness) in his folly.

DECIDING

To succumb to the preponderance of one set of influences over
another set.

> A leaf was riven from a tree;
> 'I mean to fall to earth', said he.
> The west wind, rising, made him veer;
> 'Eastwards,' he said, 'I now shall steer.'
> The east wind rose with greater force:
> Said he: 'Twere nice to change my course.'
> With equal power they contend:
> He said: 'My judgment I suspend.'
> Down died the winds. The leaf, elate
> Cried: 'I've decided to fall straight.'
> 'First thoughts are best?' That's not the moral:
> Just choose your own and we'll not quarrel.
> Howe'er your choice may chance to fall
> You'll have no hand in it at all.
>   Ambrose Bierce: 'The Devil's Dictionary'

Men think themselves free because they are conscious of
their volitions and desires and are oblivious to the causes
which dispose them to desire and to will.
                              Spinoza: 'Ethica, II'

It is in making decisions that the reflective and proactive
powers of the self seem to reveal themselves most clearly. Through
'weighing up the pros and cons', or through arguing things out
with ourselves or with others, and coming to a reasoned choice
about what to do, we have a sense of our selves at their most
potent and autonomous. Yet here too that sense is mistaken. All
our conscious experience of selecting and assessing evidence is
of the same status as other conscious experience: that is to say it
reflects tacit processing, may at times predict it, but never controls it. In fact we can maintain the idea of a separate, controlling
island of intellect only by ignoring the tacit sea that surrounds it.
If we ask of a decision, for example, why we chose just those
arguments to consider, why we accepted the validity of some data
at face value but not others, why we stopped gathering information when we did, why we consulted these authorities but not
those, why we chose to implement the decision in the manner and
at the time when we did, we begin to wade into the waters of the
irrational and the tacit. Decision-making in fact has nothing to do

with the internal chatter, the sole function of which seems to be to keep us entertained while the real decision-making processes do their work.

How, then, do decisions happen?

Tucked away deep in the most arid regions of experimental psychology is a model of 'choice reaction time' performance called the Random Walk model. It applies in its simplest form to the case of trying to decide which of two similar stimuli has been shown to you - they might be lights of slightly different brightnesses, or circles of slightly different size, for example. The model proposes the analogy of walking down the middle of a street, at a constant speed which represents the passing of time (see Figure 11). On one side of you is a pavement labelled A1, which corresponds to one of the two stimuli, and on the other side is the label A2, the other stimulus. Stepping on to either of these pavements represents a decision in favour of the relevant stimulus. As you walk along, you collect various bits of information which seem to point to either A1 or A2, and each one of these pushes you towards one pavement or the other. So you stroll on, picking up evidence as you go, and wandering backwards and forwards across the road until you eventually hit one side or the other.

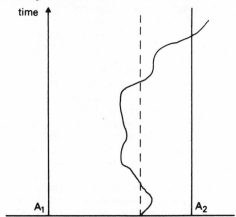

Figure 11

Now how long it takes to arrive at a decision depends on three things: whereabouts in the road you start, how similar A1 and A2 are, and how wide the road is. If you are biased towards A2, and A2 happens, you will reach the A2 pavement quite soon. For if you have some reason to believe to start with that A2 is more likely to happen than A1, say, then it makes sense to edge over towards the A2 pavement a bit before you set off. If A1 and A2 are very similar then you will wander on for some time before enough information for one alternative over the other accumulates. And if the costs of making a wrong decision are high, then the boundaries will be set far apart, so that the chances of crossing one 'by mistake' will be very low.

This is a prototype of all decision-making. There may be more than two alternatives - like which restaurant to go to - and the factors involved may be very complex - like whether to get married - but the mechanism involved is exactly as I have described.

And what of the 'Self'? Where have the conscious deliberations of the rational intellect gone? On this model they have disappeared (or at least they have lost any special status) from the decision-making process itself; but has the ego really gone, or has it just gone to ground? There seem to be three possible stages in the process where it might still be at work. Who (or what) selects the information to be considered; who sets the width of the street; and who decides on whereabouts in the street you start?

Fortunately we can show that all of these 'decisions' can be explained just as automatically as the decision-making process itself. To do so it will be helpful to link together the Random Walk model with the network model with which we have been working. Recall that each circuit is characterized at any moment by the levels of its 'threshold' - its resistance to excitation - and of its activity. The activity varies, and may be at any level, either above or below the threshold, depending on the overall state of the network. Thus, if the preceding context is such that a particular outcome is likely to occur, the activity level of the relevant circuits may be almost up to threshold - even before the eliciting stimulus has actually appeared. So if the context 'primes' A2 rather than A1, the amount of extra activity needed to fire A2 will be smaller than that needed to fire A1: there will be a bias in the system towards the perception of A2. Which side of the street you start on can be altered quite automatically.

Now recall that we supposed that the mind stores not only the occasion and consequence of action, but its significance. It is not much use knowing what will happen if you do not know whether it matters or not. Where one is choosing between two possible courses of action, therefore, it is possible to compute the relative desirability of the two outcomes, and the cost of error. (I am just assuming here that such computation is possible. David Marr has described neurophysiological mechanisms that could do the job.) The cost of error is reflected by a raising of the thresholds of both the outcomes, so that premature decisions can be forestalled. This is the mechanism by which the width of the road is set, and it is accomplished by learned routines within the system, not by the interventions of an intelligent supervisor.

The third way in which the self might operate is in the selection of evidence. But this can also be accomplished by the automatic raising and lowering of activity levels and thresholds in parts of the net, based on learned contingencies of context and consequence. In the chapter on Perception we discussed mechanisms which can do this.

RECOLLECTING

When an experience is incorporated into an organism's process,
so that it changes the way it reacts on later occasions, we talk of
learning. When it changes the way we perceive, we call that perceptual learning. But in addition to these alterations in capacity,
we also seem to be able to re-experience some of these earlier
events in a more direct way, and this is the province of remembering or recollecting. The latter term, though less fashionable,
is preferable, for remembering refers both to processes of registering new experience ('I am trying to remember these French
verbs for a test tomorrow'), and to those of recall - of bringing
previously registered events back into conscious awareness ('I
thought I'd learnt them but I couldn't remember a single one').

Our common-sense theory of recollection is simply that we register events in the way that a film or tape-recording does, and
then play them back later; but this is false. It implies that records of experience exist in the head, quiescent and unchanging,
until reactivated, when a near literal copy of the original event
pops into consciousness. And it involves some active agent or controller, outside the memory system, who does the selecting and
activating. Both of these are ideas that, for reasons discussed
previously, we need to be rid of. Just as in perception we had to
go beyond the distinction between the percept and the perceiver,
so the ego has much invested in a distinction between the remem-
berer and the remembered. We must explain how recollecting
occurs without recourse to an 'I' who 'has' memories.

As well as reinforcing the notions of separateness and agency,
memory gives us our sense of permanence and continuity. I can
look around my room and feel defined, and reassured by its contents, 'my possessions'. I am separate from them, I own them, yet
derive my identity, my sense of a core of 'me' that has persisted
through the collection of my clothes, my junk and my treasures,
from them. They 'fix' me, like a butterfly in a board, and though
they prevent much movement, they tell me who 'I' am, and to that
I cling. Just so with memories. With so many treasures stuffed
into one room, it is no surprise that I cannot concentrate on the
view out of the window. It is very easy to go shooting off down
the channels of a past that may never have happened and miss
the present that is happening right now. 'Having memories' is
often another defence mechanism, like rationalization, that sidesteps a threatening awareness by substituting something safer.

Towards the end of his career, a British Airways pilot, a Captain Thompson, used to fly a small passenger 'plane round the
Scottish islands, which had no partition between cabin and flight
deck. Thompson would board with the other passengers, wearing
plus-fours, a tweed jacket and carrying a deer-stalker, and take
a seat at the back. 'He and his fellow passengers would get
increasingly irritated at the non-arrival of the pilot. Thompson
declared that he had read a book about flying, and thought he
could manage to get the thing up and probably down. Indeed, if

the damn pilot didn't turn up in three minutes, he'd try it. Time up, he then strode to the pilot's seat. He took off, flying in a deliberately eccentric manner, while musing aloud about which chapter had said what about landing' (Brian Moynahan: 'Airport International'). We spend a lot of our time trying to remember what the book said as the mountains loom up.

True to our emphasis on process-as-primary, we can start by viewing recollection not as the reinstatement of past records but as a current activity. Recollection is a state of consciousness that is attached to a sense of the past, just as imagination is associated with the future, but both of them only have existence in the present, and they reflect the current knowledge and priorities of the network that produces them, as well as the set of features that were interconnected by a past experience. 'Having a memory', like all other actions and experiences, occurs in the context of a complex pattern of stimulations and needs that may recruit a 'memory' circuit, but at the same time reduce or embellish it considerably. As a recently spotted piece of graffiti says, 'Nostalgia isn't what it was'.

As well as distortions of 'memory' by the overall transient state of the network which subserves the experiences, there is another major distortion. Memory circuits are not created and then filed away somewhere like entries in a diary. A memory circuit is a weak linking together of conceptual circuits (some of them fixing the circuit as a whole in a certain spatio-temporal location in the individual's autobiography) that are continuously being activated in different contexts, and gradually being modified as a result. Thus the feature-sets that comprise 'a memory' are themselves shifting and changing with intervening experience.

This fact, incidentally, explains why the experiences of early childhood cannot be recalled. It is not that they have been erased from the network, or even simply overwritten, but that the conceptual terms in which they were registered have changed so much that it is almost impossible to reactivate enough of the original to recruit the whole. It may also explain why those childhood memories that we can recapture are such a mixed bag of the trivial and the significant. Although significance plays a part in establishing the strength of the original event, its recollection depends as much on the amount of intervening experience with, and modification of, the constituent conceptual circuits, and on the overall present pattern of activation - much of which may, just by chance, be priming parts of the old episodic circuit.

There are at least three ways in which the past seems to surface in the present. The first is recognition, where one identifies a particular individual or scenario not just as being of a certain sort, but as being someone, something or somewhere of which one has had personal experience before. This may be signalled in conscious awareness either by a feeling of familiarity, or by association with particular past episodes, or, most usually, both of these.

As well as reinforcing one's own sense of permanence, the

recognition of particular individuals leads one to treat them as permanent and unchanging as well. Indeed the latter supports the former, for if one views other people as persisting unchanged through time, then one has, by analogy, to apply the same view reflexively. As we saw when discussing perception, the network identifies an object as being 'an X' and then tends to turn it into a stereotype by ignoring its individual features. The same process happens with individuals, so that changes in an individual's behaviour from one occasion to the next may be rationalized, excused, or even just ignored. Often this works, because individuals collude with each other in appearing to be predictable. But when we caricature other people, when our approximate descriptions become imprisoning prescriptions, then we are setting the scene for a way of life, a way of construing that is fundamentally misconstrued. You cannot step down into the same river twice, and, even more significantly, you cannot meet the same person twice. It is said that once a man, speechless with anger, spat in Buddha's face. A day later, after a sleepless night and full of remorse, he returned to beg forgiveness. But Buddha replied, 'Look at the Ganges. In twenty-four hours how much water has flowed past here? That much life has passed in me, that much life has passed in you. You are not the same man who spat, and I am not the same man who was spat upon. So what is there to forgive? And who can forgive whom?' We store up memories of encounters with people who don't exist any more. We make theories about corpses and fit our friends with strait-jackets, because if you can do nothing I can predict what you will do. And the prime instrument of this violence is memory.

Recognition is the first of the three ways of feeling that one is re-experiencing the past. The second is recall. While in recognition this awareness results from retrieving context from content (an object is seen, and its place in one's autobiography retrieved), what is called recall works in the reverse direction. 'What were you doing last Thursday?' gives a context and asks for the re-activation of circuits that have 'last Thursday' as a constituent part. Sometimes this happens automatically, without any thoughts intervening between question and answer. At other times the clues given may be inadequate on their own to recruit any appropriate circuit, and in this case they can be used indirectly to try to increase the activation, and often lead to apparent chains of reasoning. 'Now wait a minute ... Thursdays are my day off so I was probably at home ...' If indeed I was at home, this 'hypothesis' reflects the routeing of activity into the conceptual circuits to do with my flat, and this extra activity may now be sufficient to trigger off the sequence of episodes I want.

In this type of deductive recall, it is tempting to think that there is an 'I' which is using its intelligence to support and direct the recollection. But it is not necessary. If the target episode is slow to fire, the flow of activity is blocked, and activity accumulates in some of the component concepts of that episode. Before the episode can fire as a whole, other conceptual circuits that are not themselves part of the episode, but that are conceptually related to the already activated circuits, will fire. In some cases these will set off channels of thought that are irrelevant to the original question. One's mind will wander. But in others they may function by by-passing the original block, and entering the episodic circuit again at a different point, helping to recruit it.

In both recall and recognition the present and the past co-exist in awareness. One has simultaneously a sense of oneself 'now' re-experiencing something that happened 'then'. In some forms of recollection, however, the sense of 'now' is lost and one's experience is not just of bringing a past event to mind but of re-living it. This can happen in nightmares, for example, where an actual terrifying or disgusting event returns to haunt someone night after night. It also happens quite deliberately in certain types of therapy, like Janov's Primal Therapy, where intensely emotional and evocative situations are used to precipitate people backwards into their early childhood experiences. When successful, clients become totally immersed in their childhood history: in a sense they are not just recalling events (as might happen in psycho-analysis, for example), they become small children.

But these total regressions are no more literal re-creations of the past than are recall or recognition. Part of the theory behind cathartic therapies of this sort is that the person can resolve early crises by allowing himself to experience for the first time the feelings of frustration, loneliness, fear or fury that were latent in the original. In terms of the model, this is represented as the reactivation of old processes that have been overlaid, but not destroyed, by subsequent layers of personality and competence.

DREAMS

> In all of us, even in good men, there is a lawless wild beast nature which peers out in sleep.
>
> Plato: 'Republic, Book IX'

> It is on the whole probable that we continually dream, but consciousness makes while waking such a noise that we do not hear it.
>
> C. G. Jung: 'Seminar on Children's Dreams'

Our model's guiding principle is to build up, on the basis of its experiences, circuits that represent expectancies about ante-cedents, behaviours and consequences. It has no selective intelligence in this process in that it links all features of situations, actions and results together, gradually refining these specifications as it accumulates further, similar experiences. In child-hood, as we have seen, we learn that certain states of awareness, and the actions that go with them, are unacceptable, in the sense of leading to adverse consequences (punishment or at least disapproval) from significant other people. But the network, being

what it is, registers that the associations between its feelings
and punishment are conditional on the presence of two general
factors: the existence of stimulation from the outside world, and
the execution of real action - irrespective of what that stimulation
and those actions are. When we are asleep, on the other hand,
these two features are missing (or at least very much reduced),
and the learnt correlations between 'bad' feelings and unpleasant
consequences no longer applies. If it is true, therefore, that
dreams are free of the 'censor' of the waking intelligence, and
can thus express in consciousness some 'wish-fulfilment', this is
explicable as a result of basic discriminative learning, and the
liberated nature of dreams follows directly from the discriminative
nature of the mind. The fears of rejection, the learnt avoidance
of taboo areas of experience like sexuality, anger and fear itself,
and the consequent distortions of conscious awareness are conditional on such waking factors as the presence of other people,
the production of movement and speech, and even perhaps on
incidental features like daylight and everyday sounds. On this
analysis one reason why people are afraid in the dark or on their
own is not that they are afraid of the dark, or of being alone
(although these may be fear-arousing for some) but that the normal processes of suppression and avoidance only work, or work
most strongly, in the daylight and in company. The conditions in
which one sleeps do not necessarily produce fear, but they may
permit it. The terror in a nightmare is real enough, but if one
wakes up, it is compounded by the waking consciousness catching
the Organismic Reality out in the open, like a badger in a car's
head-lamps. 'I' catches a glimpse of the naked 'me' and is further
frightened by the power and uninhibited expression of this un-
welcome stranger. It is like going down for a drink of squash in
the middle of the night and finding a 'terrorist' (which is literally
what the organism is to the ego) ransacking the kitchen.

So much for the emotional significance of dreams: but why is
the actual content so odd? While I suspect it will always be impossible to 'explain' dreams completely, some speculations are possible.
Normally our behaviour results from the interaction of four
sources: the form of the associative network itself, activity arriving from outside, activity arriving from inside, and the intrinsic
activity of the network. During the day this latter factor (that
we discussed when talking about Hebb's theory) is probably over-
ridden by the afferent activity. But during sleep, things change.
Stimulation from outside is reduced severely. Stimulation from
internal receptors is also very much reduced because the body
isn't moving. The affective and motivational neuroendocrine system is also quiescent - unless aroused by a dream. The upshot is
that the pattern of activation within the network is now controlled
very much by the intrinsic structural and functional features of
the network itself. Couple this with the likelihood described above
that the normal demands of waking consciousness for consistency,
a 'logical' flow of ideas, and the avoidance of irrelevant or silly
associations, are also relaxed, and it is not surprising that what
comes up is a bit different.

Freud's analysis of dreams was largely right: they are the royal
road to the unconscious. All I have done here is to sketch how
dreams arise from the nature of the mind, without the help or
hindrance of a homunculus, who wearing one hat constructs
ingenious symbols for dangerous ideas, and under another, labelled 'Censor', tries to stop them sneaking through into conscious
awareness.

We can see how symbols are created 'automatically' with the help
of Figure 12. Suppose a dream begins to form around the satisfaction of a taboo desire - incest, say. Dangerous circuits become
tacitly active, but the 'threshold' for conscious awareness is high.
As activity continues to arrive at the circuit it cannot reach the

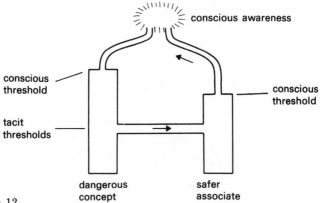

Figure 12

level of concentration required for conscious awareness and instead leaks away as lateral excitation of association circuits. Some
of these, while sharing features with the original taboo idea, are
safer and have low conscious thresholds: so what pops into consciousness is not the desire to make love to one's mother but the
wish to please her in some quasi-sexual fashion, by buying her
perfume, for example: or one may even get a clang association,
one of Freud's beloved visual puns, where one 'screws' up a
photograph of her into a little 'ball'.

HALLUCINATIONS

All our perceptions are hallucinations, for what we see is a projection of our expectations and beliefs. But clearly some perceptions are more hallucinatory than others. Like dreams, what
one calls hallucinations result from a decoupling of the flow of
activity in the network from new stimulation, so that the flow
follows the internal habits and desires of the organism, and the
mildly hallucinatory 'real world' is replaced by a full-blown fantasy. Hannah Green's autobiography 'I Never Promised You a Rose

Garden' that I quoted from earlier, charts the development and dissolution of a schizophrenic fantasy world, as rich and complex as the 'real' one, the one the rest of us agree to inhabit, and, at the height of her psychosis, in all respects more real and compelling. The hallucinations of madness represent a final escape from the pain of insecurity and failure into a world that may not be benign but is at least consistent.

Depriving people of sensation while they remain awake can lead after some time to an assertion of intrinsic tendencies and consequent hallucinations. John Lilly's 'The Centre of the Cyclone' describes how vivid and bizarre these images can be if sensory stimulation is reduced to an absolute minimum.

10 LIVING THE SELF-LESS LIFE:
Passions and actions

MOTIVATION

'Are you actually interested in psychic phenomena?'
'Psychic phenomena ... Yes. Hunger.'
(Interview with Alfred Hitchcock)

The motor individual is driven from two sources, the world
around it and its own lesser world within. It can be re-
garded as a system which in virtue of its arrangement does
a number of things, and is so constructed that the world
outside touches triggers for their doing... Its own internal
condition has a say as to which of those things, within
limits, it will do, and how it will do them.
C. Sherrington: 'Man on his Nature'

There are two questions that have arisen in connection with motivation, one of them misguided, and needing not solution but
dissolution, and the other deserving of a serious answer. The
first is 'why are organisms active?' - that is, why do we behave
at all? To take this question at face value leads one towards the
postulation of the internal source of petrol that can be accumulated and dissipated in action, that we criticized earlier. To say
that something is alive is to say that it is active. No further
explanation is necessary or possible.

The second question is 'why is this organism active in this way
rather than that?' - what collection of influences are determining
the particular form of its current activity? And for an answer to
this we can look at the model again. It shows us that it is too
simple to say that any behaviour is activated by the presence of
its associated antecedents and a desire for its consequences.
Because of the structure of the network, and the fact that the
amount of activation it can sustain at any moment is limited, different routes are in competition with each other. What one does
reflects not just one's desires and possibilities but an ordering of
priorities between different desires or needs. The wrong way to
construe motivation is to see us as intermittently prodded into
action by the activation of a need, upon the satisfaction of which
we slump into inactivity again. A better way is to see us as continuously engaged in satisfying the need nearest the top of the
pile that seems capable of being satisfied. As soon as it is satisfied, or the situation changes significantly, so that the first
activity is disallowed and others permitted, then a new action,
directed towards the attainment of a different end, starts up.

Everything we do, even sleep, is an activity, and directed towards some achievement - even though we may not be conscious
of what that achievement is.

What we do reflects the summation of activation from any or all
of our four different sources - the external world, via the sensory
systems, the internal world of the body, lateral excitation from
within the network itself and intrinsic activity. Thus even a
simple action like eating, for example, can be primed by a drop
in the blood sugar level, by the sight of food, by a train of
thought or by a combination in differing measure of all three.
Eating is by no means, therefore, the simple activity that psychologists have sometimes assumed it to be. We may eat when
hungry - i.e. when the body needs sustenance - but we may not:
it depends upon the other priorities. If I wish to finish a good
book I can suspend my hunger. An anorexic girl and an Indian
samana have higher and more complex priorities than food, and
can do without to a degree that most of us find incredible. On the
other hand there is what has been called the 'salted-nut' phenomenon, where a particular appetite is suddenly aroused by the
appearance (often the smell) of just those dainties that can satisfy
it. The salted nut effect is a close relation of the 'impulse buy',
and explains why most supermarkets have racks of sweets by the
side of the checkout queues.

Not only eating but the experience of hunger itself is regulated
by learnt cultural and social effects. We tend to feel hungry at
meal-times, and to eat at those times consistent amounts, regardless of the level of physiological hunger. Interestingly enough,
this is an everyday example of man's dissociation. A biological
signal ('I'm full') comes into competition with a social convention
('Eat up your nice greens, darling') and loses. The way out of
the conflict, here as elsewhere, is for a child to suppress his
awareness of his own physiology and thus he learns to lose touch
with the fine tuning of his own organism. Which is why Western
people tend to be overweight. Eating is controlled almost exclusively by the presence of food, and ceases to be controlled by
internal signals of satiation. (Animals do not become obese unless
you deprive them of exercise or crucial portions of their brain.)

NEEDS AND DESIRES

as intellectual development takes place, as we grow up, the
sense-domain is invaded by the intellect and the naiveté of
sense-experience is lost. When we smile, it is not just
smiling: something more is added. We do not eat as we did
in our infancy; eating is mixed with intellection. And as we
all realize this invasion by the intellect, or the mixing with
intellect, simple biological deeds are contaminated by ego-
centric interest. This means that there is now an intruder
into the unconscious which can no longer directly or
im-mediately move into the field of consciousness, and all

deeds that have been relegated to biologically instinctual
functions now assume the role of consciously and intellectually directed acts. This transformation is known as
the loss of 'innocence' or the acquirement of 'knowledge'
in the usage of the Biblical myth.
                D. T. Suzuki: 'Zen Buddhism and Psychoanalysis'
I have used the words need and desire interchangeably till now,
but they need to be contrasted. Desires differ from needs in
being mediate rather than immediate, insatiable rather than sat-
iable, and fantastic rather than realistic. Although these three
contrasts are closely interconnected, it may help to look at them
in turn, each with the help of a quotation. The first characteristic of a desire, mediacy, is what Suzuki means by 'invasion by
the intellect', and is illustrated by the discussion of hunger which
closed the last section. A simple biological act becomes clouded
and contaminated by extrinsic considerations picked up from social
models - greed, self-consciousness, the desires to please or impress or insult. I have an image of the mistress of the house forever interfering with the cook, criticizing, making suggestions,
tasting and questioning, until the latter resigns in exasperation,
saying 'If you're so damn clever, do it yourself.' And of course
the lady cannot cope on her own, being able to worry about what
the neighbours may think, but not to boil potatoes.
    In fact Dissociated Man has precious few pure needs left.
Actions which are performed with an enviable singleness of purpose in the animal kingdom - finding a home, copulating, rearing
the young, finding and eating food, even defecating and urinating
- are often confused and difficult in mankind.
    As well as being invaded by the mind in their execution, desires
are often incapable of satisfaction, because they exist in the future: we desire something that may happen tomorrow but that
tomorrow never comes.

> Needs can be fulfilled, but desires cannot be.
> Desire is a need gone mad.
> Needs are simple, they come from nature;
> Desires are very complex, they don't come from nature.
> They are created by the mind.
> Needs are moment to moment,
>   they are created out of life itself.
> Desires are not moment to moment,
>   they are always for the future.
> They are not created by life itself,
>   they are projected by the mind.
>   Bhagwan Shree Rajneesh: 'When the Shoe Fits'

Desires are like the horizon. You can see something in the distance and you can wish to obtain it, but however far you walk you
can never reach the horizon. The distance between a man and his
desire remains the same, because they are illusions, projections.
It looks as if just one more promotion, one more book published,

one more lover, one more million will bring the happiness and
peace of mind you want. But when you get there, there is another
record to be broken, another sacrifice to be made, always another.
The ideas of happiness, security, success, fulfilment that underlie all this hurry and sweat are just as intangible, as misunderstood, as the horizon is.

The goal is always changing and expanding because it is not the
'real' goal. We have a mistaken theory that security is to be found
in some achievement, but anything that can be achieved gives at
best only a transient or a partial satisfaction. Despite many inval-
idations of this fallacious modus operandi, we cling to it, finding
it preferable to the alternative - acceptance of the wisdom of insecurity.

There are two ways of looking at the insatiability of desire. One
we have met already is that of the dog chasing its tail round and
round in circles. Not realizing that it owns the tail, it chases
after it, only to find it travelling away from him - infuriatingly -
at exactly the same speed as he travels towards it. His logic is
clear: 'Obviously I'm not trying hard enough. I must run faster
and faster. Then I will catch it.' This elementary misconception
leads to a cycle of frustration, effort and increasing desire that
is real enough, for all its delusory basis. The second way is to
see that very often we frustrate our own desires, hankering with
half our mind and withholding with the other. Sexual desire is
perhaps the most common example these days. Adolescents (of all
ages) construct elaborate fantasies in Conscious Reality, largely
at the instigation and with the aid of the sexual exhibitions and
prohibitions with which society surrounds him. These unnatural
parasites invade, confuse and subvert the natural host of developing sexuality, holding out great promise with one hand and
building insuperable barriers with the other. Hence the boy
whose head is full of sex, but who cannot manage even social
intercourse, let alone sexual, when the opportunity presents itself. He does not need a woman to frustrate him: he is his own
prick-teaser. We will return to the mechanism of desire in a
moment.

Because desires exist in our projections, they form and deform
what we see. Here is Hermann Hesse in an essay written in 1917
called Concerning the Soul:

The eye of desire dirties and distorts. Only when we desire
nothing, only when our gaze becomes pure contemplation,
does the soul of things (which is beauty) open itself to us...
The man whom I look at with dread or hope, with greed,
designs or demands, is not a man but a cloudy mirror of my
own desire. Whether I am aware of it or not, I regard him
in the light of questions that limit and falsify...

At the moment when desire ceases and contemplation, pure
seeing and self-surrender begins, everything changes. Man
ceases to be useful or dangerous, genial or rude, interesting or boring, strong or weak. He becomes nature, he
becomes beautiful and remarkable as does everything that is
an object of clear contemplation.

Desire is one name – fear is the other – for what takes man out of the present. If I meet you in the hope that I can get something from you, or the fear that you might do something nasty to me, or the regret that I have not declared something to you in the past, I am not here with the full reality of you now. We meet, whether we know it or not, as business men, commercial travellers: head hunters or bargain hunters. We may be able to come to an agreement, or we may not, but we cannot allow ourselves to be complete and uninhibited, or the compact may be broken, and we will not get what we want.

This is perhaps why our meetings with nature, or our brief encounters with unlikely people, children or animals are often marked by Hesse's quality of pure contemplation and are deeply satisfying and healing in themselves: because there is nothing to be got. As I watch seagulls circling by a cliff, or lambs playing on a tree stump (clichés, but for good reason) I have no thought of what I can do with them or for them; my plans of profit or loss, my efforts to impress or appease become irrelevant, ridiculous, and I can just be there, for as long as it takes. Unless of course, I have with me that instrument of rape and symbol of acquisitiveness, the camera.

Desires are like the 'salted-nut phenomenon' gone mad: they are wants without needs. Learnt channels exist which tend to trap and hold activity within certain areas of the network. Thus one does not meet the world fresh, or transiently primed for certain experiences by the internal or external context, but permanently set, as Hesse says, to 'dirty and distort' the reality seen. Needs arise, are attended to and satisfied and sink down again, but desires are always with us. We are biased to see things in certain ways and perform in certain ways because we think we want to see and perform thus. Activity may be flowing in one area of the network when it hits a desire, which is like a trapdoor leading to an underground pipe-line that suddenly whips the activity off to somewhere else. The trigger may be an event, an odd word in a train of thought, a memory, or whatever, but once it is pulled you are precipitated back into your preoccupations, obsessions and frustrations. Conscious fantasy takes over, activity having been captured by the channels of thought, and one is off into what one is going to do tomorrow, or ought to have done yesterday, while the organismic reality of right now is forgotten and deprived of much of the pool of activity it needs to function efficiently and adaptably. If you need to take a different bus one morning, you are most likely to get on to the usual one, absent-mindedly, if you have had an argument before leaving home, or are going to a very important meeting – events that will tend to preoccupy you with past or future, and divert your attention from the special demands of the present.

If activity keeps going to certain parts of the network, how come its business is never concluded, and it keeps returning? Firstly, the appropriate behaviour may be inhibited. Here is a desirable consequence – having sex. Here is an antecedent –

someone who is either Robert Redford or his spitting image. But
where is the behaviour? Blocked by a learnt fear, so that before
it can be energized the activity spills over into an alternative,
'displacement' activity and she feels sick, spots a friend who she
absolutely must have a word with, or starts a violent argument
about sexism and the evils of viewing other people as sex objects.
Thus one reason why desires remain is that we sabotage our own
efforts to satisfy them.

Alternatively, as we have already seen, we may obtain what we
think is the right consequence, only to find the satisfaction mysteriously missing, always popping up out of any hole but the one
you happen to be looking down, like cartoon rabbits. The right
channel exists, and can be traversed, but it is based not in
organismic need but in the shadowy world of belief and promise.
There is no feedback loop from the attainment of the desirable
consequence to turn off the desire. Seeking physical contact may
reflect a need for comfort and security, but people often construe
it as sexually motivated: they rush about having unsatisfactory
affairs when all they really want is to be held. The impulse to
make love may reflect the voice of society, telling you 'what comes
next', rather than an organismic urge.

In short, desires are maladaptive because they override one's
fluctuating needs, and make one insensitive to the shifting balance of natural priorities. They connect parts of the network that
ought not (in a particular situation) to be associated, and they
drain off and capture activity, thus reducing the sensitivity of
the network to the promptings of the needful and the possible.

MOTIVES

> The true and primary motives of the greater part of my
> actions are not so clear to me as I have for a long time
> imagined. (Rousseau)

> Chemists at least can use analysis; patients suffering
> from a malady whose cause is unknown can at least call in
> a doctor; criminal cases are more or less cleared up by the
> examining magistrate. But for the disconcerting actions of
> our fellow men, we rarely discover the motive. (Proust)

Motives are the stories we tell ourselves about the causes and
purposes of actions - our own and other people's. The motive for
attributing motives is to try to render intelligible actions whose
point is not immediately obvious. The trouble with this is that the
mechanism trying to do the understanding is the rational conscious mind, while the mechanism that acts is the whole organism.
The act comes out of the experiential plane while the 'motive'
comes out of the verbal plane. Attributing motives is an effort by
the part to understand the whole - an exercise which is consequently of limited value. The intellect selects aspects of the antecedent situation, the behaviour, and its consequences, moulds

them into its own logic, and then attempts to string them together
to make a plausible tale. The plausibility of the story is rarely
checked back against reality: it is held up to the window of pre-
cedent and projection with which the intellect thoughtfully provides itself for this purpose. In fact motives are inferences, the
validity of which can never be checked, for their touchstone is
the largely unconscious experiential plane. Sometimes people own
up to the fact that their motives are inferred. 'I'm sorry I was
ratty last night – I must have been tired.' Most often, however,
we present statements of motivation as if they were statements of
fact: 'he only does it to annoy because he knows it teases', which
is a nice example because the duchess's hypothesis about the
baby's action involves attributing to the baby a hypothesis about
his own action – wheels within wheels.

We can never know another person's motives, nor can we know
our own if we go at it with the sledgehammer of the intellect. The
effort is as futile and as frustrating as trying to catch fish by
jumping on them. We can, however, begin to discover the contexts
and desires that attend our actions if we take a rather different
tack and allow the answers to come to us through intuition, by
opening ourselves and shutting up, rather than by stomping
about in great big waders.

Finding reasons is misguided, but unfortunately it has a purpose, and that is, as so often, the avoidance of an unpleasant
present. It may be unpleasant because it seems meaningless,
chaotic, and one can insulate oneself from feeling the insecurity
by conducting an enquiry into its origins. Or there may be a
stirring of feelings – aggressive, sexual, frightful – that one has
learnt to avoid. The search for reasons is an attempt to distance
oneself from these threats to one's image and control. We are, as
Jung once said, like a householder who hears a noise in the cellar
and immediately rushes up to the attic to search for the intruder.
It remains, strangely enough, a favourite defence, particularly of
people who pride themselves on their rationality, despite the
experience which everyone must have had of the futility of inces-
santly asking 'Why?' The question why is a violin on which we
fiddle whilst our vitals burn.

The most common situation in which we use this device is when
having rows. Someone says something which strikes home, an
unpalatable truth that we would rather not acknowledge, and
against which defences must be raised. 'You're only saying that
because I pointed out that you haven't washed up once this week';
'Just because you were too frightened to say you wouldn't go on
holiday with your mother, there's no need to take it out on me'.
And so on. Whatever the truth of the counter-claim, its main
effect is to divert attention – yours and hers – from the previous
thrust. Whole conversations, whole marriages are built on extra-
ordinarily subtle variations and elaborations of this game.

It is significant that we only talk of motives in situations of
apparent choice. If we watch a demonstrator being frog-marched
by a couple of big policemen into a Black Maria, we don't ask what

his motives are for entering the van. To ask 'why?' in such a
context sounds silly: 'he had no choice', we would be inclined to
reply. The attribution of motives presupposes the attribution of
choice, in the sense of being 'free' to choose one course of action
rather than another. Dissociated Man can talk of motives because
he sees himself as an agent – but even Dissociated Man must
restrict his talk to the fields of his apparent agency, as we have
seen. Integrated Man, however, cannot fall into the trap, because
he knows himself to be an organic part of a larger whole, and can
see that the sense of agency arises from a failure to appreciate
and live in harmony with this tacit mutuality. We might overhear
Ribosome saying to Mitochondrion 'Why are you synthesizing all
that ATP?' and Mitochondrion replying 'Well, I had some time on
my hands, and I remembered Endoplasmic Reticulum telling me he
thought it was going to be a hard winter, so I thought...' The
conversation is absurd because Mitochondrion is not autonomous –
and neither are we.

SKILL

> You are said to have mastered the art [of swordsmanship]
> when the technique works through your body and limbs
> as if independent of your conscious mind... When the mind
> itself is lost so that even devils cannot trace its where-
> abouts you can for the first time make full use of the
> technique acquired.
>   D. T. Suzuki: 'Zen and Japanese Culture'

Here we shall be concerned with the execution of well-practised,
highly automated skills or sets of skills, such as are required
for the competent participation in physical sports. We leave the
issues of spontaneity and self-consciousness to later sections in
this chapter.

Sports can be contrasted along many dimensions, but two of
major significance are the time allowed to prepare an action and
the variety of actions that may be required. In sports like archery,
or the more homely equivalent darts, there is much time and little
variety. One is not required to react quickly to changing circumstances. The archer must strive again and again for the perfect
execution of a simple, seemingly unvarying action. (I assume the
day is calm, the target of fixed size and distance, and so on.) It
is one of the most elemental of all sports, and perhaps for this
reason it is often used as a vehicle for spiritual training. One of
the most popular of pop-Zen books in the West is Eugen Herrigel's
'Zen in the Art of Archery'. Darts, snooker and billiards, and
golf, though allowing some variation, all appeal in large measure
for a similar reason: the challenge of operating at the limits of
precision is if anything more important, more compelling than that
of beating an opponent. Thus one good shot can more than com-
pensate for an otherwise disastrous match. What is required in
these sports, as Tony Jacklin described from his own experience

in an interview in the 'Sunday Times' a few years back, is precision of two sorts. First one has to construct a model, or a program, in one's mind, of the 'ideal' shot. The sportsman may not
develop a complete visual image, but in addressing the ball, or
holding the bow at full stretch before releasing it, a sense is
forming of what the right action would feel like. The existence of
this mental model is attested to by the (usually) accurate feeling
of whether the shot is good or not immediately after, or even
during, the action, and well before one has the objective corroboration of a bull's eye or a hole-in-one. The second stage is of
course the execution of the act itself: the running of the program
that one has just constructed. For success, both stages must be
right: the program must be appropriate, and its implementation
must be error-free.

These stages require closer scrutiny, for the central problem
to be explained about skilled action is its creativity. Even in
archery the drawing and releasing of the bow is not in fact a
unitary, invariant 'response' to the 'stimulus' of the target. No
two shots are the same because with each the archer becomes a
little more practised, a little more fatigued, or bored or interested,
or relaxed or tense, or attentive or distracted. Within his organism the neuromuscular effort needed to draw the bow varies, and
the amount of free activity in his nervous system with which he
can construct and activate the requisite motor program also varies.
In these sports consistently high performance is difficult to
achieve because the construction of the right model is highly sus-
ceptible to the general state of the sportsman. In others, such as
team games like football or rugby, this factor combines with the
difficulty of making split-second decisions about how to act in the
face of rapidly changing and distracting external circumstances.

Skilled actions are creative in the same way, and for the same
reasons, as perception is creative. The network stores motor
'schemas' - behavioural circuits - that are generalized and ill-
defined clusters of elements of behaviour that have become more
or less loosely associated together as the result of common use.
Two or more of these circuits may be called by the stimulus situation, but their simultaneous activation, itself overlaid on a
selective pattern of priming within the total network, means that
the particular feature set that results will be derived from, but
not reduceable to, the individual behavioural circuits. In addition
to these background influences, experience will have laid certain
specific channels of excitation and inhibition between active or
potentially active sets of features which will effectively permit
some simultaneous combinations and exclude others. It is this process, of a total circuit of active units being discovered that as
nearly as possible meets the demands of the situation, while not
containing any mutually exclusive sub-circuits, that, in some
situations, takes time: and this is the process of constructing a
model of the intended action. No 'self' is needed. Here again the
time is taken not by an intelligent executive but by the special
need to find the best possible compromise between all the current
demands and constraints.

   The interaction between general and specific influences on
action can be illustrated by the problem of hitting a particular
'double' on a dart-board. There is little reason to suppose that
any double is intrinsically easier or harder than any other: certainly darts players differ widely in their 'favourite' double, some
choosing the top of the board, others the bottom, some the left
and some the right. Yet it is undoubtedly true that, for all except
the very best and the very worst players, each individual differs
consistently in his preference for certain doubles and his success
at hitting them. There seem to be specific expectations about one's
ability to hit a given double, originally based on a history of success or failure that may well have been fortuitous, but now operating as a self-fulfilling prophecy. A feeling that one double is
difficult, however irrational, becomes true because it activates
extraneous, pessimistic associations and these decrease the possible precision of a concurrently active motor model. It is for this
reason that one often performs better at these kinds of sports
when one is 'just practising' than when playing for real. The
latter situation calls all kinds of tensions, both physical and
psychological, that are not called by the former. 'Trying too hard',
'stage-fright' and the like all involve this characteristic of the
arousal of specific bad feelings that subvert effective action. They
also involve the non-specific effect, that we met before when talking about 'not being able to see for looking', of a too narrow
focusing of activity within the net so that the percept or the
mental model becomes a crude caricature rather than a subtle
portrait of what is desired. Because of this constriction, actions
not only become cruder but they may be highly energized, and
implemented in a way that is too vigorous and/or repetitive.
Anxiety about success makes action tight and clumsy: watch a
child trying to carry a full cup of tea under threat of punishment
if he spills it. Or, indeed, Virginia Wade.
   The importance of being able to construct a model becomes clear
in the very early stages of learning a new movement in, for example, gymnastics or diving. Once one has performed a sequence
in a very approximate way (i.e. not landed on your head, or done
a belly-flop) the process of refining the action may take time and
coaching, but is relatively straight-forward. But the first time,
one simply doesn't know what to do: one's body feels as if it has
suddenly lost all its intelligence, and refuses to obey instructions.
(Trying to dive backwards off a two-metre spring-board will, if
you have never done it before, generate this experience quite
well.) The action itself is simple, but its difficulty demonstrates
the extent to which our behavioural creativity is firmly based in
and limited by well-learned precedents. Once a situation calls a
behaviour, the motor program can be modified by other aspects
of the context: it can be sculpted to meet the current needs and
circumstances. But if the situation fails to call an action, it is
impossible to 'work it out' - you just have to hold your nose, jump
and hope that trial-and-error deals with you mercifully.
   Other sports impose an additional condition: motor models must

be constructed and executed fast as well as accurately. A bats-
man, for example, has just half a second from the moment when
the ball leaves a fast bowler's hand to the moment when he has to
strike it: half a second in which he has to compute the line,
flight, pitch and turn of the ball, for those fine details of the
situation to call and construct an appropriate stroke, and for the
execution to be well under way. For minor variations in the ball
bowled, the action produced may vary from a leg glance, to a
thumping drive over extra cover, to a flexing of the knees to
allow a bouncer to go whistling overhead. Yet he has a pause
between strokes in which to settle and clear his mind (more accurately, of course, for the mind to settle and clear itself) that the
tennis player has less often, the boxer less often still, and the
rugby forward may not have for many minutes on end. It is
interesting to note that every sport is intermittent in some way,
either by virtue of its explicit structure as in cricket or tennis,
or by the 'rules' that provide less regular but still quite frequent
breaks such as throw-ins, free kicks, set scrums and penalties.
These allow some physical recuperation, true, but the present
analysis suggests that they also have an important psychological
function. Concentration has to be maintained through these breaks,
but in a 'mindless' way that allows activity to disperse from one
focal train of motor thought, and so allow a new, perhaps better,
figure to emerge from this state of tacit receptivity when the next
phase of the game starts.

The state of mindlessness, and its sisters effortlessness and
purposelessness, are crucial to the inspired performance of motor
skills, whether making a break of 100 points in snooker or playing
a Beethoven violin sonata. It is in these moments when, as Suzuki
says, 'the technique works through your body and limbs as if
independent of your conscious mind.' The skill runs itself so
sweetly that all you can do is stand aside and watch your own
performance with gratitude and admiration. Two things are necessary for this stage to be reached. First one needs vast experience and virtuosity, so that the network of expectations and
actions is so subtly differentiated that any possible event (within
the rules of the game) can call an appropriate response without
pause. But this virtuosity can be empty, as it is for example with
the pre-pubescent rubber bullets that pass for the world's best
women gymnasts at the moment, or with Oscar Peterson or Fritz
Kreisler; an emptiness that is strikingly obvious in contrast with
the maturity, grace and serenity of a Turescheva, an Ashkenazy
or a Menuhin. What the virtuoso lacks is the second necessity, a
lack of purpose. If any shred of intention or planning remains –
especially the intention to play well – there is desire in the sense
we discussed earlier, and this deforms the memory network and
introduces tensions between different parts. Consciousness becomes set and rigid, activity is annexed, clouds of concern and
distraction appear in the empty sky, movements become just a
little stiff, and integrity, and its outward face, serenity, are lost.
For all except an enlightened man this wholeness is fragile and we
are easily pushed back off-centre, or out of balance.

SELF-CONSCIOUSNESS AND EFFORT

> The kind of clumsiness which is due to the fact that focal
> awareness is directed to the subsidiary elements of an
> action is commonly known as self-consciousness.
>   Michael Polanyi: 'Personal Knowledge'

Even the most energetic of actions can be performed without a
subjective or objective appearance of effort. In states of great
fright or great rage, for example, people can do things, without
thinking, of which they would normally have thought themselves
incapable. Such moments are moments of unity when body and
mind put aside their bickerings and act, for once, in concert.
The converse, more familiar, feeling is of even small necessities –
going to the launderette, answering letters, paying bills - being
somehow heavy: they can become quite literally 'a drag', like an
anchor that prevents us running fully before the breezes of other
opportunities and wishes. We have left undone those things we
ought to have done, and done those things we ought not to have
done, and are therefore sinners, guilty, and 'there is no health
in us'. All this bad karma is unfinished business in the sense that
it leaves behind a trail of oppression that tinges new acts, even
the felicitous, with self-consciousness and a loss of lightness and
spontaneity. The unified organism, Integrated Man, does not have
to try to do things: he does them or he doesn't, and if he does
they may be satisfactory or not. But he knows that to try to get
up earlier is as much a misunderstanding as it would be for a
healthy, unrestrained adult to try to walk across a room. The
idea of 'trying' in the sense of mental effort is a bad metaphor
from the muscular to the neuronal. I can certainly try to lift up
a weight, and by this I mean I am engaging in a contest with an
external force (gravity) whose outcome I cannot predict. The
sense of trying is a sense of muscular strain. But to try psychologically is a mistake, for the contesting forces are figments of my
imagination, aspects of myself that I can separate and oppose only
in theory. My attempts to side with one against the other are like
siding with the front wheel of a bicycle against the back. It is
this mistaken metaphor that leads to the idiotic learnt confusions
between muscular and neural effort, like knitting one's brows in
order to think better, or gritting one's teeth in the attempt to
'control oneself', that we mentioned before.
    Self-consciousness is associated with mental effort, and has two
aspects. First, it is an awareness of actual or impending inadequacy, as is anxiety, but the awareness seems to split sharply
into two components: an acting part and a judging part. The
latter is the key to self-consciousness, because it distinguishes it
from self-awareness. I can be aware of my actions, thoughts and
feelings as I am aware of my perceptions. The tree outside my
window is not a 'good tree' or a 'bad tree' - I have no standard
for it, and no need for it to be other than it is. Indeed it *is*, it
just is. It is possible to be acutely aware of oneself, but with the
same tolerance, though that is an art that many people have not

yet learnt. Dissociated Man knows a simple logic: awareness means blockage (we have seen that focal, conscious awareness develops when the flow of activity in the network is inhibited), blockage means inadequacy, inadequacy means possible incompetence, and incompetence is bad, something I shouldn't show. Thus when one begins to be aware of oneself in a clearer, more in-focus way than previously, the first reactions are ones of threat and defensiveness. Point out to an acquaintance some harmless habit like always folding his handkerchief up after blowing his nose, saying 'I mean ...' at the start of most sentences, or the fact that he always wears brown to the office, and you may well be met with 'Well, what if I do' and a reasoned (or unreasoned) defence to a charge that has never been put. He supplies his own prosecution. It is difficult to delay the judgment long enough for a felt sense of the antecedents and consequences of the habit to emerge and for its function to speak for itself.

A related aspect of self-consciousness is its highly focused and therefore partial, nature. Conscious awareness has become for Dissociated Man like the spotlight that we talked of earlier, selective and linear, rather than diffuse and gestalt-oriented. And because focused awareness absorbs much of the limited supply of neural activity, close attention to a part of one's behaviour leads to a breakdown of the whole. We become like the centipede who found he couldn't move when asked which leg he moved first. Michael Polanyi has devoted much time to the analysis of this problem. He writes

> Whenever we are focusing our attention on a particular object, we are relying for doing so on our awareness of many things to which we are not attending directly at the moment, but which are yet functioning as compelling clues for the way the object of our attention will appear to our senses... if identified and seen in themselves [these clues] would lose their suggestive powers as clues and bereft of this function would tend to be lost among other meaningless details.

VOLUNTARY ACTION

> The authorship of action does not in reality belong to the 'I'. It is a mistake to understand that 'I' do this, 'I' experience this and 'I' know this. All this is basically untrue. The 'I' in its essential nature is uncreated; it belongs to the field of the Absolute. Whereas action, its fruits and the relationship between the doer and his action belong to the relative field ... The attribution of authorship to 'I' is only due to ignorance of the real nature of 'I' and of action.
> Maharishi Mahesh Yogi: 'Commentary on the Bhagavad Gita'

We have already covered most of the issues that are relevant here when discussing intention and motivation. Voluntary action is that

which is preceded by an awareness of what one is going to do,
and is accompanied by awareness as it happens. Those are the
facts: the theory that 'I' is therefore in control is a gratuitous
embellishment.

If we look at how the relationship of 'I' to action is incorporated
in ordinary language, we can see how closely it is bound up with
the feeling of apparent choice about whether to act or not, or to
act in one way rather than another. It is anomalous, for example,
to say 'I am beating my heart'. We are allowed to say 'I am digesting my food', but only in the sense that something is happening
within me, not that 'I' am doing it. In an intermediate class of
cases 'I' appears as the agent not in the sense that it is actively
doing something, but that it apparently chooses not to not do it,
and could intervene to stop it. 'I am growing a beard' combines
the idea that 'I' is an address where something is happening with
the idea that I am choosing not to shave. 'I am breathing' means
breathing is going on in my body, and I could hold my breath
(for a time), if I wanted to. In these examples I-as-address and
I-as-agent get conflated. By the time I get to 'I am tying my shoe-
laces' and 'I am walking the dog' the address meaning is submerged, and the agent has taken over, because the choice, like
the 'I' it spawns, is a conceptual, not an experiential one. To
show that choice is a fact, not just a theory, we would have to
show that we were at one instant capable of choosing A rather
than B, but this would require turning the clock back to relive
that moment again, which we cannot do. So we can never know
that it was actually possible for us to have done otherwise than
we did. Not being aware of all the circumstances past and present,
internal and external, that add together to prime one action
rather than another, we fill the apparent gap with an insubstantial agent whose sole function, as Skinner said, is as a dummy to
prevent further enquiry. He doesn't do anything except field
awkward questions. The longer one allows those questions to
stand, the more insubstantial 'I' becomes. Once we turn the
energy of reason through 180 degrees, and reflect it back at its
source we can see that it is a snowman, not a person, and watch
it melt under its own heat.

STYLE

> Our intonations contain our philosophy of life, what each of
> us is constantly telling himself about things. (Proust)

Two features of action are often overlooked: so far we have considered the substance of an act, its 'verbal' component, but acts are
never produced without the adverbial aspects of time, manner and
place. Where, when and how a behaviour is produced are just as
important in terms of the consequence that results as what it is.
We saw that the way an object is perceived is always dependent on
the context in which it occurs: exactly the same figure-ground
relationship determines the style of an action. Any statement such

as 'He picked up the book' is essentially incomplete. A fuller description must include the elaborations 'quickly', 'angrily', 'with
resignation', 'calmly' or whatever. And the mechanism is similar
to the perceptual one as well. Activation of a specific behaviour
is always overlaid on a pattern of priming which reflects the general state of need and anticipation of the organism. It also reflects
the long-term biases and predispositions that constitute the organism's 'personality'. So the particular way in which an act appears
– its 'intonation', if we may use Proust's word metaphorically –
always says something general about the philosophy of life of its
author, as the act itself tells us specifically about his current
wishes. It is not surprising, therefore, that these intonations,
what George Mead called the 'expressive', as opposed to the
'coping' aspects of behaviour, play a central role in psychotherapy.
They represent information about ourselves that we leak, often
unconsciously, and which a skilful observer can pick up and
reflect back.

MORALITY

> Discipline ceases to be the attempted denial of dissociated
> and distorted components of the person, and becomes edu-
> cation in the appropriate *timing* of these functions.
>> L. L. Whyte: 'The Next Development in Man'

> A dog is not reckoned good because he barks well, and a
> man is not reckoned wise because he speaks skilfully.
>> Chuang Tsu

Traditionally morality has been concerned with what to do and
what not to do, and many attempts have been made to cast rules
of conduct in absolute terms of right and wrong. This attitude
must have been partly responsible for the assumption in psychology, prevalent until very recently, that an animal does or does
not possess certain behaviours, habits, skills, strategies or cap-
acities, and that if it does possess them, their essential characteristics remain fixed with respect to variations in the time,
manner, place and purpose of their manifestation. At the centre
of this book has been a consistent denial of this 'isolationist'
attitude, and a complementary assertion that all our organismic
knowledge is necessarily associated with a sense of purpose and
of occasion. This position in its turn requires of us a morality
that is based on appropriateness, not on universal prohibitions
and prescriptions. The questions, Should one kill, steal, torture,
honour thy father and mother, eat meat, or go to church, are
nonsensical, unanswerable, and they are pernicious because when
we do take them seriously, and opt for an answer, we are setting
up an inevitable clash with the situational fluidity of our natural
morality. 'If you want to make sense, I've learned, you should
never use the word *should* or *ought* until after you've used the
word *if*' is the way John Barth, exemplifying his own precept,

puts it in 'The Floating Opera'. Yet this too falls short, for any
verbal formulation of the contingencies involved will simplify and
fragment them, and lose the conditional subtlety of the gestalten
that the organism senses.

This is the conflict within any taught morality: it may serve to
guide a learner towards certain combinations of experience and
activity whose mutual suitability he can then learn for himself.
Instruction in how and when to act from a more to a less experienced person may cut out much trial and error. In this it is no
bad thing, provided the learner remains open to his own experience. Instruction may also lead the learner to act 'on trust' for a
while, because he will not yet be able to appreciate the wisdom of
doing things this way. Again this is helpful unless his confidence
in his experience is thereby undermined - which is quite possible.
But where the instruction is a prohibition, it cannot become an
experiential reality for the student, because it denies him the very
experience that could validate it. It follows that prohibitions cannot promote learning; in fact they prevent it.

From what we have said it also follows that moral prescriptions
will not promote learning unless they can be converted into experience, just as a medical prescription will not promote health
unless turned into medicine and ingested. 'Thou shalt love the
Lord thy God with all thy heart and with all thy mind and with
all thy strength' is a useless instruction for most of us. We do
not know what it means, nor what to do about it. Jesus is right,
'this is the first and greatest commandment'. But to people who
cannot absorb it its effect is to confuse and disintegrate, to make
them feel vaguely but persistently guilty, in Kafkaesque fashion,
for not following an instruction they don't understand, and to
engender limited and misguided habits, like going to church or
trying to be good that miss the point and prevent, rather than
produce, any spiritual growth. Only if they struggle with this
absurd injunction to the absolute limit with they eventually break
through the cloud into the sunny atmosphere of Integrity.

Instructions are delicate instruments, for they cannot be understood without substantial experience of that to which they refer,
and for someone who has that experience already the instruction
may be redundant. If it is understandable, it is not necessary; if
necessary, not understandable, we might be tempted to conclude.
But this conclusion reckons without tacit knowledge. The instruction may resonate with, or call, something that we know in part, or
approximately, or intuitively, and may help us to become more
aware and more precise. Most learning is not acquisition of new
information or skills en bloc, but the gradual refinement and de-
contextualization of things already known. The effectiveness of
an instruction also depends very much on the relationship, and
particularly on the degree of trust, between the tutor and the
taught.

When used without a sensitivity to style and occasion so-called
moral codes serve only to split the recipient by providing him with
a second centre for evaluating his actions which is not based in

his personal experience and so is often at odds with the first. We should remember, though, that codes such as the Ten Commandments do tend to reflect natural morality: that is, they are rather crude distillations of the ways in which organisms of a certain kind (man), habitually exposed to a social and physical environment of a certain kind, come to behave. Moral injunctions are, initially, rough descriptions of how we behave naturally. But they are often expressed in terms which ignore the contexts and purposes for which the behaviours in question have been developed. The behaviour is ripped from its origin in certain prevalent states of the environment, and imposed on people - especially children. As the context is ignored, it is not admitted as an equal and indissociable partner, with the organism, in the control of action: all the onus is - spuriously - placed on the person, who must therefore supplement his natural morality with an - illusory - sense of 'will'. Moral injunctions do not and cannot specify precisely when and how they are to be applied: violence is done to the subtlety and fluidity of the natural morality from which they arose, by presenting the injunctions as enduring values in their own right, unassociated with spatio-temporal limitations. The basic confusion in received morality is to suppose that because things tend to be so, they must be so; and that they will not continue to be so unless we exert a deliberate effort to keep them so. A further problem is that the creation of a linguistic term also creates its opposite, so any moral code necessarily gives life and possibility to its contradiction. Moral arguments become possible about the reality and relative merits of polar oppositions, and their essential and implicit mutuality, and subordination to purpose and circumstance, becomes obscured.

COMMUNICATING

> This private association of mine [between the smell of elder and a Schubert lied] ... can be communicated certainly, as I have communicated it to you just now. But it cannot be transmitted. I can make you understand my association, but I cannot so affect a single one of you that my private association will become a valid symbol for you in your turn.
>
> Herman Hesse: 'The Glass Bead Game'

Before we leave action, one special type, linguistic communication, needs to be considered. I shall use as an example speech, though the points will apply equally to writing, sign language and other media.

Remember that we represented experiential knowledge as a convoluted surface containing a network of probabilistic associations of great complexity. Verbal knowledge is a simpler plane surface with fewer associations between well-defined entities. Some of these entities, the basic ones, are connected with clusters of features in the experiential plane: others have no direct experiential referent, but are defined via associations within the verbal plane. Thus verbal knowledge is at the same time rooted in experience, and to a great extent autonomous of it. Some of the knowledge in the verbal plane can, by following a chain of associations, be explicated, or at least exemplified, at the organismic experiential level. Much of it cannot, for it contains conventions of logic and syntax that are not encashable, and that permit the representation of propositions that are counter-factual in either content ('Nixon is an honest man') or presupposition ('Einstein has lived in Princeton', by its form, presupposes that Einstein is alive).

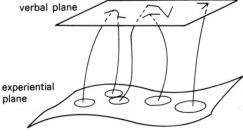

Figure 13

Now the precursor of a spoken utterance may be a pattern of activation in either the verbal or the experiential surface. Much of our communication comes directly from the verbal level and the processes and rules that guide the routeing of patterns of activity into the activation of the muscles of the tongue, lips, larynx and chest in an appropriate sequence are the province of contemporary linguistics and psycholinguistics. Most attempts to find a formal semantics, for example in which the meanings of words and sentences can be derived from a fundamental set of postulated entities and operations (just as geometrical theorems are derived from Euclidean axioms) constitute hypotheses about the verbal plane and its organization, not about the relation between the verbal and the experiential. Likewise recent attempts to discover the structure of so-called 'semantic memory' within psychology have proved highly confusing because the existence of the two planes of knowledge has not been understood. A sentence like 'A mouse is a rodent' can be verified either by tracing a path between two nodes at the verbal level, or by superimposing their two referent circuits at the experiential, or by both simultaneously.

What has received much less attention is the way in which an experiential pattern is converted into a sentence. Here there is the important additional problem of decomposing the total pattern into parts and relationships that correspond to the vocabulary and syntax of the person's language, and this may be quite difficult. It is like taking a meal and trying to infer the ingredients and operations that produced it. If the meal is roast beef and two veg. it is quite easy. If it is a more subtle concoction like boeuf stroganoff the analysis will be more problematic. A further complication arises in speech where one is not just declaiming in vacuo, but trying to communicate the recipe to a listener about whose knowledge the speaker has to make certain assumptions. One will talk differently to a cordon bleu cook and one's teenage daughter. The problem to be solved, then, in trying to communicate an experiential event is principally one of chopping up the total pattern into chunks for which the language has words, and of which the listener can be presumed to have some knowledge himself. To give one simple but topical example, English has no pronoun for a person whose sex is unspecified. If I want to refer to the cook in my previous example, who could be either male or female, I may use the traditional form 'he', or some less elegant variation like 's/he' or 'he or she'. Which I choose depends in part on how I feel about the possible offence that the simple form 'he' may give to some female readers.

The way I dissect a pattern will depend on many factors that contribute to the overall state of the experiential network, in the same way that the gestalt that forms when I hear a sentence depends on the a priori distribution of priming. In fact the two processes of comprehension and production are in many ways mirror images of each other. The main difference is that in production all the relevant details of syntax - word order, function words, inflections - have to be put in, while in comprehension one may not process these details in full if the juxtaposition of content words is sufficient to specify a single gestalt. Thus the syntax is more important in understanding 'The hippie was kissed by the debutante' than in 'The truck was crashed by the mechanic.'

THE FINAL WORD

Part II could go on for ever: the images that it introduced and used come to function more and more as a whirlpool for my own psychological thinking, sucking in any theory or body of research that happens to be floating near by, chewing it up, and throwing out an ever expanding range of ideas about, if not actually explanations for, the way human beings go about the business of being human. But that's not just one, but a lifetime of books' work. All I have been able to do here is show that the mechanism through which we lead our life is self-less and integral, however much our experience tries to persuade us to the contrary. And it is absolutely up to us how we react to the revelation of our own unity, for to be reborn into that world we have to die to almost everything we thought we were. For most people the thought, let alone the prospect, of giving up the idea that H.Q. resides in the ball of meat that sits atop their shoulders is a threat. The more seriously they allow themselves to entertain the possibility of their selflessness, the more real the threat becomes. Yet, the more rational attitude is one not of despair but of joy. The truth about man's original face must be a source of liberation, for it is only our ignorance of it that is responsible for the joy-lessness, and ultimately, as death approaches, the emptiness and vanity of the life we assume we have been leading. To recapture this truth, existentially as well as intellectually, need not change the content of a life one iota. I do not necessarily drop thinking, planning, worrying, regretting, resenting, nor shed forever embarrassment or the peculiar anxiety involved in taking things back to shops. All that happens is that I realize that the dramas are part of the flow, the harmony of life, not resistances or oppositions to it. And I also see that I am not 'all that stuff'. I am not my body, my knowledge, my possessions, my prestige, my feelings. I am in reality the dramatist, the perpetrator of the community of selves that inhabits my awareness. Hitchcock, we might say, was never seen in any of his movies, though an instantly recognizable body, bearing, confusingly, the same name, made small appearances in all of them.

What could be more reassuring than to know that, however hard I play the game, I am 'home' already; or what more enlightening than to see that perfect freedom is the perfect acceptance of necessity - even of the necessity to worry and to scream and to kick against the pricks?

Werner Erhard wrote:

If God told you
exactly what it was you were to do,
you would be happy doing it
no matter what it was.

What you're doing is
what God wants you to do.

Be happy.

BIBLIOGRAPHY

Anderson, J. Ř. 'Language, Memory and Thought', Lawrence Erlbaum: Hillsdale, New Jersey, 1976.
Bannister, D. and Fransella, F. 'Inquiring Man', Penguin: Harmondsworth, 1971.
Barth, J. 'The Floating Opera', Doubleday, New York, 1967.
Basho, 'The Narrow Road to the Deep North', Penguin: Harmondsworth, 1975.
Bierce, A. 'The Devil's Dictionary', Dover: Toronto, 1958.
Borges, J. L. 'Labyrinths', Penguin: Harmondsworth, 1970.
Brown, G. S. 'Laws of Form', Allen & Unwin: London, 1969.
Brown, P. C. 'Smallcreep's Day', Gollancz: London, 1967.
Burrow, T. 'Science and Man's Behaviour', Philosophical Library: New York, 1953.
Capra, F. 'The Tao of Physics', Wildwood House: London, 1975.
Chew, G. Bootstrap: A Scientific Idea? 'Science', Vol. 161, 1968.
Claxton, G. 'Cognitive Psychology: New Directions', Routledge & Kegan Paul: London, 1980.
Cummings, e. e. A Poet's Advice to Students, 'Journal of Humanistic Psychology', Vol. 12, 1972.
de Chardin, T. 'The Phenomenon of Man', Collins: London, 1959.
Dostoyevsky, F. M. 'The Possessed', Macmillan: London, 1948.
Einstein, A. 'Ideas and Opinions', Souvenir Press: London, 1973.
Eliot, T. S. 'Selected Poems', Faber & Faber: London, 1961.
Ellis, A. Rational-Emotive Psychotherapy, in D. Bannister (ed.), 'Issues and Approaches in the Psychological Therapies', Wiley: London, 1975.
Fodor, J. 'The Language of Thought', Harvester Press: Hassocks, Sussex, 1976.
Frayn, M. 'Constructions', Wildwood House: London, 1974.
Freud, S. 'Collected Papers', Vol. 2, Hogarth Press: London, 1974.
Fromm, E. Psychoanalysis and Zen Buddhism, in E. Fromm, D. T. Suzuki and R. De Martino, 'Zen Buddhism and Psychoanalysis', Harper & Row: New York, 1960.
Gendlin, E. T. Client-Centered and Experiential Psychotherapy, in D. Wexler and L. Rice (eds.), 'Innovations in Client-Centered Therapy', Wiley: New York, 1974.
Gibran, K. 'The Prophet', Heinemann: London, 1970.
Goleman, D. 'The Varieties of the Meditative Experience', Rider: London, 1977.
Green, H. 'I Never Promised you a Rose Garden', Gollancz: London, 1964.
Harding, D. 'On Having No Head', The Buddhist Society: London, 1976.
Hebb, D. O. 'The Organization of Behaviour', Wiley: New York, 1949.
Hemingway, E. 'Death in the Afternoon', Penguin: Harmondsworth, 1966.
Herrigel, E. 'Zen in the Art of Archery', Routledge & Kegan Paul: London, 1975.
Hesse, H. 'My Belief', Triad/Panther: St Albans, 1979.
Hesse, H. 'The Glass Bead Game', Penguin: Harmondsworth, 1975.
Holt, J. 'How Children Fail', Penguin: Harmondsworth, 1973.
Hunt, J. McV. Experience and the Development of Motivation, in 'Personality Growth and Learning', Open University, 1971.
Huxley, A. 'The Doors of Perception', Chatto & Windus: London, 1954.
Huxley, A. 'Island', Chatto & Windus: London, 1962.
Illich, I. 'Limits to Medicine', Penguin: Harmondsworth, 1978.
James, W. 'Varieties of Religious Experience', Collins: London, 1960.
Jung, C. G. 'Collected Works', Routledge & Kegan Paul: London, 1953.
Kelly, G. A. 'The Psychology of Personal Constructs', Vol. I, Norton: New York, 1953.
Kierkegaard, S. 'Purity of Heart', Fontana: London, 1961.

Kopp, S. 'If You Meet the Buddha on the Road, Kill Him!', Sheldon Press: London, 1974.

Laing, R. D. 'Self and Others', Penguin: Harmondsworth, 1971.

Lilly, J. C. 'The Centre of the Cyclone', Paladin: St Albans, 1973.

Loewy, A. and Siekevitz, P. 'Cell Structure and Function', 2nd edn, Holt, Rinehart & Winston: New York, 1978.

Maharishi Mahesh Yogi. 'On the Bhagavad Gita', Penguin: Harmondsworth, 1969.

Marr, D. A theory for Cerebral Neo-cortex, 'Proceedings of the Royal Society of London', Series B, 1970, Vol. 176.

McFadden, C. 'The Serial', Pan: London, 1978.

Merton, T. 'The Wisdom of the Desert', New Directions: New York, 1960.

Milne, A. A. 'The House at Pooh Corner', Methuen: London, 1965.

Moynahan, B. 'Airport International', Pan: London, 1978.

Naipaul, V. A. 'The Mimic Men', Penguin: Harmondsworth, 1969.

Neisser, U. 'Cognition and Reality', W. H. Freeman: San Francisco, 1976.

Ornstein, R. 'The Psychology of Consciousness', Penguin: Harmondsworth, 1978.

Otsu, D. R. 'The Ox and His Herdsman', Hokuseido Press: Tokyo, 1969.

Perls, F. 'In and Out of the Garbage Pail', Bantam Books: Toronto, 1972.

Pincus, L. 'Death and the Family', Faber & Faber: London, 1976.

Pirsig, R. 'Zen and the Art of Motorcycle Maintenance', Bodley Head: London, 1974.

Polanyi, M. 'Personal Knowledge', Routledge & Kegan Paul: London, 1973.

Rajneesh, Bhagwan Shree. 'When the Shoe Fits', Rajneesh Foundation: Poona, 1978.

Reps, P. 'Zen Flesh, Zen Bones', Penguin: Harmondsworth, 1975.

Rinehart, L. 'The Dice Man', Panther: St Albans, 1976.

Rogers, C. R. 'On Becoming a Person', Houghton Mifflin: Boston, 1961.

Rosen, R. D. 'Psychobabble', Wildwood House: London, 1978.

Schloegl, I. 'The Zen Way', Sheldon: London, 1977.

Sherrington, C. 'Man on his Nature', Cambridge University Press: Cambridge, 1963.

Simkin, J. Gestalt Psychotherapy, in D. Bannister (ed.), 'Issues and Approaches in the Psychological Therapies', Wiley: London, 1975.

Skinner, B. F. 'Beyond Freedom and Dignity', Jonathan Cape: London, 1972.

Skinner, B. F. 'About Behaviorism', Jonathan Cape: London, 1974.

Smith, M. J. 'When I say No, I Feel Guilty', Bantam Books: New York, 1975.

Suzuki, D. T. Lectures on Zen Buddhism, in E. Fromm, D. T. Suzuki and R. De Martino 'Zen Buddhism and Psychoanalysis', Harper & Row: New York, 1960.

Suzuki, D. T. 'Manual of Zen Buddhism', Rider: London, 1950.

Suzuki, D. T. 'Zen and Japanese Culture', Routledge & Kegan Paul: London, 1959.

Trungpa, C. 'Cutting Through Spiritual Materialism', Shambhala: Berkeley and London, 1973.

Vonnegut, K. 'Mother Night', Jonathan Cape: London, 1968.

Watts, A. W. 'The Book on the Taboo Against Knowing Who You Are', Abacus: London, 1973.

Watts, A. W. 'Does it Matter?', Vintage: New York, 1970.

Watts, A. W. 'Nature, Man and Woman', Abacus: London, 1976.

Watts, A. W. 'Psychotherapy East and West', Penguin: Harmondsworth, 1973.

Watts, A. W. 'This Is It', Vintage: New York, 1973.

Watts, A. W. 'The Wisdom of Insecurity', Rider: London, 1954.

Whyte, L. L. 'The Next Development of Man', Cresset Press: London, 1944.

Winnicott, D. W. 'Playing and Reality', Penguin: Harmondsworth, 1974.

Wittgenstein, L. 'Tractatus Logico-Philosophicus', Routledge & Kegan Paul: London, 1974.

Zola, E. 'L'Oeuvre', Pasquelle: Paris, 1978.

INDEX

209

DATE DUE

DATE DUE			
NOV 0 1 1996			